Trans-Atlantic Engagements

German Educators' Contribution to and Impact on US Architectural Education

Steffen Lehmann

With a Preface by Alexander Eisenschmidt and a Foreword by Peter Bosselmann

ORO Editions
Publishers of Architecture, Art, and Design
Gordon Goff: Publisher

www.oroeditions.com
info@oroeditions.com

Published by ORO Editions.

Author: Steffen Lehmann, Las Vegas/Berlin
Preface: Alexander Eisenschmidt, Chicago
Foreword: Peter Bosselmann, Berkeley
Book Cover Photo and Design: Cida de Aragon, Las Vegas/Sydney
Book Design: Fortino Acosta, Las Vegas
Managing Editors: Gordon Goff and Jake Anderson, San Francisco

10 9 8 7 6 5 4 3 2 1 First Edition

ISBN: 978-1-951541-31-6

Color Separations and Printing: ORO Group Ltd.
Printed in Hong Kong.

ORO Editions makes a continuous effort to minimize the overall carbon footprint of its publications. As part of this
goal, ORO Editions, in association with Global ReLeaf, arranges to plant trees to replace those used in the
manufacturing of the paper produced for its books. Global ReLeaf is an international campaign run by American
Forests, one of the world's oldest nonprofit conservation organizations. Global ReLeaf is American Forests'
education and action program that helps individuals, organizations, agencies, and corporations improve the local
and global environment by planting and caring for trees.

**This study and publication has been endorsed and supported by the Association of Collegiate Schools
of Architecture (ACSA), Washington, D.C.**

Graham
Foundation

This study received support from the Graham Foundation for Advanced Studies in the Fine Arts.

Endorsements

Bold in scope and packed with detail, the writing presents compelling pedagogical engagements as well as an impressive array of profiles and interviews with constant architectural commitment. It forces us to rethink the Bauhaus legacy, including the likes of Lilly Reich and Ernst Neufert who both stayed in the United States briefly, and alters the way we observe architecture not only through exhibitions but also how we manage data. Its educational strategies endeavors to reshape architectural education for future generations in the United States. "Trans-Atlantic Engagements" is a long overdue survey that steers one in new directions, by rekindling and renewing architectural exchanges across the Atlantic Ocean and beyond.

— **Annette Condello**, Ph.D., Author of The Architecture of Luxury, Curtin University, Perth, Australia

Steffen Lehmann's "Trans-Atlantic Engagements" is a critical study and timely pedagogical research of German architects' definitive contribution to educating generations of American architects. Broadly focused on world-renowned figures who came to the US following their escape from the Third Reich, as well as on less acclaimed subsequent and contemporary educators, this inquiry puts in perspective a vital collection of case studies. Himself born and raised in Stuttgart, Germany, having devoted years to academia all over the world, and now being a leading educator in the US, Lehmann's important book presents the in-depth personal quest. Tracing both contrasts and commonalities the author brings to light various teaching models based on increasingly relevant cultural, regional and national identities.

— **Vladimir Belogolovsky**, Curator and Author of Conversations with Architects, New York City

There is a need for more analytical histories of architectural pedagogy to advance the understanding of how to educate the next generation of architects, and the ACSA strongly endorses this book. It investigates the influence of German educators on US architecture schools and on architectural pedagogy over the last eighty years, featuring profiles and interviews with current professors; it explores how two pivotal German architects and educators—Walter Gropius and Ludwig Mies van der Rohe influenced contemporary educational strategies and shaped their relevance. The book makes a significant contribution to the understanding of architectural education in the US and its historical cross-fertilisation with innovative German educational concepts at large.

— **Michael J. Monti**, Ph.D., Executive Director, ACSA, Washington, D.C.

Critical aspects of the original Bauhaus curriculum –aimed to balance interdisciplinary learning with a process-driven focus on method, material craft, and industrial production in response to cities, and a society, in crisis– can be easily identified in contemporary approaches to pedagogy in US architecture schools. Yet, these trajectories have seemingly developed into independent strands within architecture education today rather than working in concert. Steffen Lehmann's exploration of the legacy of Bauhaus pedagogies offers a timely reflection on parallels and differences at a time when a new crisis in the form of a global pandemic poses uniquely spatial problems and forces educators to question both how, and what we teach in schools of architecture.

— **Antje Steinmuller**, Chair in Architecture, California College of the Arts, San Francisco

The contribution and impact of German educators in the United States can be directly connected to teachers and students of the Bauhaus, a topic that this book unfolds. What is also relevant and of current interest is the legacy of the Bauhaus-related ideas, which is a self-standing research topic that this book uncovers. Following the recent Bauhaus centennial, this book arrives as a mature and well-cooked treatment of some critical episodes of architectural education, and sheds light on the trans-Atlantic exchange of ideas that had a strong impact on the discipline. The book fills a gap in the history of US architectural education.

— **Andres Lepik**, Ph.D., Chair in Architectural History and Curatorial Practice; Director of the Architecture Museum, Technical University of Munich, Germany

"Trans-Atlantic Engagements" is a fascinating book and a valuable body of work. I am sure that it will become a standard reference whenever considering the history and future trajectory of architecture education in the US, or the time and impact of the Bauhaus philosophies outside of Germany. I found it immensely entertaining and captivating, which cannot be said often when it comes to subject books. The book is well written and it is a joy to read, casting a broad and expansive big picture while still uncovering thought-provoking details.

— **Mark Mueckenheim**, Graduate Director of the School of Architecture, Academy of Art University, and Principal, MCKNHM Architekten, San Francisco

This engaging study of the contributions of German architects, past and present, to architectural education in the United States is relevant to any design related field, not only to architecture. Given the focus of the book on the influence of cultural, regional and national perspectives on teaching philosophies and pedagogical models, it is of interest to any educator committed to the notion that new times require new thinking—and there could not be a more relevant time for Steffen Lehmann's book than ours.

— **Sabine O'Hara**, Ph.D., Distinguished Professor and Ph.D.-Program Director Urban Leadership and Entrepreneurship, College of Agriculture, Urban Sustainability and Environmental Science, University of the District of Columbia, Washington, D.C.

"Trans-Atlantic Engagements" offers a long-awaited critical analysis of the pedagogical influences of German educators within schools of architecture across the United States. As an American architectural practitioner from German descent, I personally find this forward-thinking appraisal both relevant to our time and fascinating in its connection of history with the contemporary. The legacy of the century old Bauhaus and notable protégés, Gropius and Mies van der Rohe are amply understood. Steffen Lehmann eloquently cross-examines the pedagogy of his German/Austrian/Swiss contemporaries and interprets their reach and influence on American architecture today.

— **Dwayne R. Eshenbaugh**, AIA, 2020 President of the AIA Nevada Chapter; Principal, NOVUS Architecture, Las Vegas, Nevada

Other Books by the Author

Contents

Synopsis

Trans-Atlantic Engagements: German Educators' Contribution to and Impact on US Architectural Education takes a critical look at the influence of German educators. It is a long overdue survey and publication that explores the history of pedagogical concepts of German-born and -trained professors of architecture at schools in the United States. The research and book publication are structured in three parts: Part I. Early German Influences, Immigration and Assimilation; Part II. Consolidation of the Modernist Approach in US Architectural Education; Part III. Trans-Atlantic Engagements Today: German Educators Currently at US Schools (including the interviews). It aims to make a significant contribution to the understanding of architectural education in the US and its historical cross-fertilisation with German educational concepts at large, with research outcomes responding directly to current and future educational and societal challenges.

The ideals of the Bauhaus school shaped more than just design and architecture around the world; these guiding principles and pedagogy also transformed design teaching. The project examines the post-Bauhaus influence on these German-born educators today and how the Bauhaus model has evolved over the last fifty years. The Bauhaus aimed to unite all creative arts through direct field and workshop experience; it was a school of art and design which included architecture, and not a school of architecture per se. Gropius resigned in 1928, and it was largely under the directorship of Ludwig Mies van der Rohe from 1930 to 1933 that the Bauhaus developed into a school of architecture with subsidiary art and workshop departments.

There are currently over fifty German-speaking educators (born in Germany, Austria or Switzerland), active in shaping architectural and design education in the US, influencing thousands of students as the next generation of architects in this country. Compared to other professions, succeeding in studies of architecture is known as a long endeavor that requires a strong commitment and dedication from the student. The task for the educators is to turn the studies into a positive experience and fun to become part of a demanding profession. The book features interviews (conversations) with six selected professors and explores if the Bauhaus legacy of Gropius and Mies van der Rohe is still relevant for their educational strategies and design teaching today. The pedagogical experiments of the Bauhaus, imported by Gropius, Mies, Hilberseimer, Albers, Moholy-Nagy and others to the US system, challenged traditional Beaux-Arts thinking and played a crucial role in shaping and consolidating 1950s modern architectural education. Historically, the German architectural training has always been different from the French tradition. These new interdisciplinary and technology-focused modes of teaching architecture and design had long-lasting impact, however, are now again transformed by the contemporary educators currently active in reshaping curricula. The conversations reveal the critical and independent thinking of this group and how they make a meaningful contribution to the discourse of architectural education appropriate to the 21st century.

Authored by an internationally-recognised scholar with personal insight into the topic, the six selected educators interviewed in this volume render visible a broad array of discursive pedagogical strategies that only partially build on the seminal educational model of the Bauhaus; they have transformed it to new contemporary pedagogical models. The study provides insight into the ways in which these German-trained educators influence architectural and design education in the United States to this day.

Acknowledgements

This book is the outcome of many months of work and commitment of numerous people. I would like to express my thank you for the generosity of everyone involved, especially all the experts and colleagues who made this comprehensive study possible. I always knew that there were many of us and that our contribution to architectural education worldwide—not only in the US—is enormous.

Firstly, in our increasingly digital world, I would like to thank my fearless publisher and his very competent team at ORO Editions: Gordon Goff, Federica Ewing, Jake Anderson, and Alejandro Guzman-Avila. Your trust and experience in managing the production of this publication was crucial. You believed in the project from start to finish, and it has been a joy to work with you.

I owe a tremendous debt to the immensely talented colleagues, the German-born professors of architecture teaching in the United States of America. I am grateful for their participation and contribution of significant interviews (that make up such an important part of the book) and insight presented in this book. Your tireless concern, pursuit of design excellence and dedication to the best possible education for the next generation of architects inspires me every day. Getting this project done would have been impossible without the collaboration of these educators; especially a big "thank you" to the six educators profiled in the interview section in Part III: Martin Bechthold, Peter Bosselmann, Ulrike Heine, Barbara Klinkhammer, Mark Mueckenheim and Antje Steinmuller (in alphabetical order). I thank you for your time out of your busy schedules!

My warmest thanks go to two valuable contributors of ideas: to Peter Bosselmann at UC Berkeley and Alexander Eisenschmidt in Chicago, for providing an interesting and critical Foreword and Preface to this book. Especially professors Peter Bosselmann and Mark Mueckenheim provided critical feedback to an early draft of the manuscript which made this a better book.

I worked on this book during the 2020-pandemic, when we had a stay-at-home order, and was all focused on the project that it made my quarantine time fly. This book would not have been possible without the generosity of the University of Nevada Las Vegas. Many colleagues have been supportive and I am grateful for their wise comments; and the conversations we had, which were relevant for the direction of this publication. My committed Ph.D. student Fortino Acosta was instrumental in the design of the book. — You all made this a better book!

I would like to thank the colleagues at the Association of Collegiate Schools of Architecture (ACSA), especially the ACSA's Executive Director, Michael J. Monti, for their support and endorsement. Also thanks to the Goethe-Institut in the US, particularly the Goethe-Institut in Washington, D.C., and in Los Angeles. Without their strong support this study would not have been possible.

My thank you goes also to the Graham Foundation for Advanced Studies in the Fine Arts, Chicago, for their support of this study. And a big thank you to the AIA Las Vegas, Randy Lavigne, and the following Las Vegas-based companies for their great support: Marnell Corporation, Tom Schoeman, LG Architects and KGA Architecture.

Many thanks go to Cida de Aragon for her support, encouragement and understanding over the last thirty years; and the beautiful book cover photo of Route 66 and book cover design.

My friendship with many other colleagues and scholars provided me thoughtful guidance and is a daily inspiration. I thank you all for your encouragement and relentless curiosity during the preparation of this book: Fortino Acosta, Heiko Achilles, Pal Ahluwalia, Iman Ansari, Erieta Attali, Martin Bechthold, Eike Becker, Vladimir Belogolovsky, Kai-Uwe Bergmann, Leonard and George Bergman, Paola Boarin, Peter Bosselmann, Peter Brandon, Keith Brewis, Andrea Brizzi, Andreas Bruemmel, Niccolo Casas, Cesar Ceballos, Bill Chapman, Javier Castanon, Edwin Chan, Akhtar Chauhan, Rafaella Colombo, Annette Condello, Peter Cook, Edoardo Croci, Mario Cucinella, Mahesh Daas, Luca D'Acci, Cida de Aragon, Cees de Bont, Neil Denari, Antonino Di Raimo, Paolo Di Nardo, Khoa Do, Markus Dochantschi, Harry Edelman, Hisham Elkadi, Sura El-Maiyah, Dwayne Eshenbaugh, George Ferguson, Galya Gerina, Georg Gewers, Edward Glaeser, Tigran Haas, Catherine Harper, John Hartley, Peter Head, Ulrike Heine, Peter Herrle, Richard Horden, Simi Hoque, Donald Houston, Alvin Huang, Kurt Hunker, Claus-Peter Hutter, Yasuhiro Imai, Arata Isozaki, Helmut Jahn, Dieter Janssen, Mike Jenks, Mitchell Joachim, Charles O. Job, Ahmed Z. Kahn, K.K. Philip Kang, Irma Karjalainen, Louis Kavouras, Kisa Kawakami, Lance Kirk, Thomas Kiwitt, John Klai, Barbara Klinkhammer, Joerg Knieling, Branko Kolarevic, Franz Krenn, Ralph Krohmer, Norbert Lechner, Margit and Werner Lehmann, Andres Lepik, Pekka Leviakangas, Nina and Daniel Libeskind, Bob and Vicki Liljestrand, Dirk Lohan, Bart Lootsma, Piotr Lorens, Winy Maas, Adrian McGregor, Dale Medearis, Peter Murray, Antonello Marotta, Alessandro Melis, Walter Menteth, Michael J. Monti, Mark Mueckenheim, Gjoko Muratovski, Ethan Nelson, Boonlay Ong, Sabine O'Hara, Dominic Papa, Mita Patel, Emily Penn, Dario Pedrabissi, Igor Peraza Curiel, Ralph Dlugosz, Rodrigo Perez d'Arce, Antoine Predock, Samia Rab Kirchner, Karim Rashid, Carlo Ratti, Victor A. Regnier, Charles Renfro, Saffa Riffat, Tom Rivard, Paco Francisco J. Rodriguez-Suarez, Stefan Rossner, Paola Ruotolo, David J. Sailor, Norma Saldivar, Matheos Santamouris, Saskia Sassen, Tom and Susan Schoeman, Ehsan Sharifi, Brigitte Shim and Howard Sutcliffe, Charlotte Skene Caitling, Dean Sakamoto, Peter Cachola Schmal, Bleyer Schneider, Malcolm Smith, Werner Sobek, Thomas Spiegelhalter, Antje Steinmuller, Monika Szopinska-Mularz, David Turnbull, Ed Vance, Thomas Vonier, Frank Werner, Jenny Wu and Atiq U. Zaman. — You are all incredible!

I would also like to thank all photographers, architects and archives for making images and information available. Every effort has been made to trace the copyright holders, and we apologise for any unintentional omission; the publisher would be pleased to insert the appropriate acknowledgement in any subsequent edition.

Lastly, as a full professor of architecture for the last two decades, I am fortunate to be working on three continents, including as Director of the UNLV School of Architecture in Las Vegas (USA) and Head of the School of Architecture in Perth (Australia). Hence, this book is partially autobiographical and relevant to my own work as German-born and -trained educator and architectural researcher. I am grateful to have been able to work with over a thousand inspirational, talented and hard-working students of architecture and design at various schools in the US, Australia, Germany, UK, Singapore, China, India and the UK over the last decades. The history and influence of German-trained educators in the United States is obviously of particular relevance to me.

Much remains to be done. My hope is that we will work together to turn the study into a future exhibition and symposium on the topic.

Euch allen: gutes Gelingen!

— Steffen Lehmann, September 2020

Preface

Alexander Eisenschmidt

> *America, you've got it better*
> *Than our old continent. Exult!*
> *You have no decaying castles*
> *And no basalt.*
> *Your heart is not troubled,*
> *In lively pursuits,*
> *By useless old remembrance*
> *And empty disputes.*

> — Johann Wolfgang von Goethe, "To the United States," 1827

German infatuation with the US is unparalleled. Rarely was a culture more mystified and captivated by another. And, Goethe's poem is an indication of the long history of that fixation. Of course, Goethe was not speaking of the brutal realities of America, or what he (mis)understood to be the "New World." What he saw as a virgin land was far from uninhabited and his notes pay no attention to the massacre of First Nations or the slave trade. Instead, he conjured up an ideal continent, a parallel terrain, an analogous land through which he could critique the conservatism of Europe—a continent largely responsible for the atrocities taking place across the Atlantic. That idealisation of the US is present in countless examples before and since Goethe's notes. Likely, every child who grew up during late-19th and across 20th century Germany(s) has heard of the adventures of Winnetou and Old Shatterhand in the "Old West." The fictional characters by the best-selling author, Karl May, portrayed a tantalising fantasy of a possible reconciliation between an intruding and existing culture and had little in common with the actualities and traumas of colonisation. To say the least, German fascination with the US is not just complex but part of a rarely acknowledged complicit writing of history.

During the rapid and unparalleled growth of US cities during the 19th century, the country continued to enthrall Germans. This time, less for its uncharted history but because of the urban and architectural intensities that places such as Chicago, New York, Boston, Philadelphia, Detroit, San Francisco, and later Los Angeles embodied. It was fueled by travel reports and immigrant accounts during the largest exodus of Germans to the US between the Revolution of 1848 and World War II. The sociologists and political economists Max Weber, Werner Sombart, and Ferdinand Tönnies, for example, traveled to Chicago en route to the Congress of Arts and Science in St. Louis in 1904 and returned to Germany with the most vivid accounts of cities that they interpreted as the fullest expression of modern reality.[1] For them, the US was the *Großstadtland,* the land of the metropolis, a country with cities that were incomparable to the urban situations they knew from home. And yet, observing the unruliness and force of American metropolitan urbanity became for these figures a way to look into the future, a future that for cultural figures such as Walter Rathenau and Karl Scheffler had already arrived in Berlin, "the first Americanised city in Germany."[2]

In fact, "Americanism" became a widely debated topic, both to articulate an American aesthetic and the act of urban transformation according to it.[3] Most viewed it with a mixture of horror and fascination, an agony about the potential overrunning of German culture and an excitement about the potentials for what these foreign forces might hold.[4] While the former entered the ever-stronger nationalist tendencies of *Heimatstil* that escalated in the 1930s, the latter formulated a cosmopolitan outlook that eventually became the foundation for a metropolitan architecture. Karl Scheffler's publication of 1910, *Berlin – ein Stadtschicksal* (Berlin – Destiny of a City), makes one of the more complex and penetrating arguments in this regard. While rhetorically criticising Berlin's Americanism as the "capital of all modern ugliness," he also linked it to a metropolitan urbanisation that was free from the shackles of history and, therefore, able to produce a new type of architecture.[5] With the lack of a coherent history, of traditional culture, and of urban form, Scheffler saw an urban and cultural *Spielraum* (room to maneuver and play) for new spatial, material, and programmatic experimentation emerging in Berlin.[6] Americanism, and particularly the conflation of Berlin and Chicago, became in Scheffler's work a kind of trans-Atlantic encounter that enabled a forecasting and visualisation of an accelerated urbanity and an architecture deeply connected to the metropolis.

Building on these ideas, Scheffler's subsequent writing on *Die Architektur der Großstadt* (1913, The Architecture of the Metropolis), prompted Ludwig Hilberseimer to search for a *Großstadtarchitektur* (Metropolitan Architecture) by relying heavily on built examples from the US and eventually publishing his findings in 1927.[7] By that time, Hilberseimer was able to source from a vast amount of German publications on North American architecture. While Scheffler's study only obliquely addressed American cities, more didactic reports and visual accounts of buildings in the US were circulating since the end of the 19th century, facilitating a trans-Atlantic engagement as German architects increasingly longed for a deeper understanding of American building culture. *Neubauten in Nordamerika*, by Paul Graef (1899); *Das amerikanische Haus*, by Rudolf Vogel (1910); *Amerikanische Parkanlage*, by Werner Hegemann (1911); "*Die Entwicklung moderner Industriebaukunst*," by Walter Gropius (1913); *Amerikanische Architektur und Stadtbaukunst*, also by Hegemann (1925); *Städtebau und Wohnungswesen* in the *Vereinigten Staaten*, by Walter Curt Behrendt (1926); *Amerika, Bilderbuch eines Architekten*, by Erich Mendelsohn (1926); *Wie Baut Amerika?*, by Richard Neutra (1927); *Städtebauliche Probleme in amerikanischen Städten und ihre Rückwirkung auf den deutschen Städtebau*, by Martin Wagner (1929) are only a few examples in the large catalog of German publications that focused on American architecture and urbanism.[8] Early on, several publications would study the contributions of the so-called Chicago School and introduce architects such as Henry Hobson Richardson and Louis H. Sullivan to a European audience; later, more visual analyses of hotels, industrial plants, and tall office buildings would dominate the heroic narratives of American building culture.

Special attention should be given to the urban theorist Werner Hegemann. His fluid engagements with the US did not just provide an account of buildings beyond the often-cited works but also structured a discourse that connected architecture to the newly emerging discipline of planning and influenced the ways in which urban design programmes would be established in the US. His first of many encounters with North America came in the summer of 1897, when the sixteen-year-old Hegemann spontaneously bought a bargain ticket to board a ship to New York, where he wandered the streets of Manhattan for a few days before returning home. He traveled again in 1904 to study at the University of Pennsylvania and would return to Philadelphia after the completion of his dissertation in 1908. It was here where his career as an urbanist began. Reporting on the American condition for different magazines in Germany, Hegemann effectively crafted a more nuanced image of the US that goes beyond a laissez-faire model of economic pressures on architecture and urbanism. After being part of the curatorial team for the ambitious *Boston 1915* exhibit in 1909, he curated the influential *General City-Building Exhibitions* of Berlin and Düsseldorf in 1910. There, photographs and drawings of US-based projects were foregrounded and received special attention: the parks, parkways, and infrastructures of Boston; the inner-city playgrounds of Chicago; and the *Burnham Plan* for the city, to name a few. The display was unorthodox as all the material from different countries was not organised by location but rather by topic. While Hegemann's display of countless projects and statistics on cities overwhelmed its viewers, the exhibition design also allowed for intentional cross-references, chance encounters, and locational slippages. As such, the exhibition performed a trans-Atlantic oscillation that pointed at an architectural urbanism beyond national identity—an alternative locale for a new kind of urban practice.

While living once more in the US between 1913 and 1921 (visiting more than forty cities, giving lectures, working as a consultant, and establishing his office in partnership with landscape architect Elbert Peets),[9] the American context and especially its university campuses aided Hegemann's concept of the "grouping of buildings." This was an urbanism defined less by planning strategies than by the positioning of architectural typologies. While these ideas emerged through a thorough study of the American urban milieu, they also point to an important difference between German *Städtebau* and American planning. After all, *Städtebau* does not translate as planning in a technocratic fashion but rather as "city building," the design of the city through architecture.[10] It is this sensibility that Hegemann brought to the US and that eventually would support the formation of urban design as distinct from city planning. His influence on the German *Städtebau* discourse cannot be overstated, but his contribution to the American academy might be even more consequential and original. His ideas received much attention and he amassed a large network of followers, one of which was Joseph Hudnut, who met Hegemann in 1917 and became his assistant. As Hudnut recalled in retrospect, working with Hegemann was a life-shaping experience that made him see the city "not as an arrangement of spaces which afford building sites" but rather as "a living and growing organism."[11] It was that kind of teaching that Hudnut implemented once he became dean at Columbia University in 1933 (the same year that Hegemann left Germany) and that he carried with him when he became founding chair of Harvard's Graduate School of Design in 1936 (the year of Hegemann's untimely death). At Columbia, Hegemann was invited to teach urbanism studios and at Harvard, Hudnut reworked the entire curriculum with a common first-year course that taught civic design in the spirit of Hegemann. Architecture's relationship to the city would become even more paramount when Josep Lluís Sert took over the school. While Sert seemed to have joined Harvard at the invitation of Gropius, Sert's book *Can Our Cities Survive?* (1942, with a foreword by Hudnut) and his later Urban Design Conferences, were much more Hegemannian than early CIAM in nature.

The following pages present a comprehensive list of German architects whose works have influenced US education and of whom Hegemann is only one of the many examples. For the immigrants documented in this volume, the US became not just a safe haven from totalitarianism and anti-Semitism, but it was viewed as a country in which a new metropolitan architectural language had emerged and was, therefore, inviting new experimentation. German fascination with

US architecture and urbanism, long before the rise of Nazi Germany, made the country across the Atlantic one of the most compelling locations for architects and urbanists. The present book organises a thorough catalog of these personalities, a directory that goes beyond the heroic figures of modernism. By expanding the cast of characters and stories to reach into the 19th century and towards the present, this book is a welcome contribution, and, even more importantly, acts as an invitation for further research. The final part of the book, with interviews of contemporary German academics who are active in US universities today, sheds light on current motivations for young architects to settle here. These interviews reveal as much about the conditions in US academies as they are a commentary on current German architecture education. It is refreshing to hear that most of those interviewed don't see themselves as "German architects" and don't find the national identification as productive. One senses an intentional distanciation from the homogeneity of Germany and a deliberate alignment, not necessarily with the US but with a multi-dimensional pluralism that goes beyond borders, cultural identity, and homeland. During a time when the US and Germany/Europe increasingly restrict movement,[12] the interviews remind us of the promise, value, and power of not just trans-Atlantic but trans-national and trans-continental movements. And, if the present research tells us anything, it's that there is enormous productivity in the hybridisation and jumbling of an established condition, or to paraphrase Salman Rushdie, mélange is how newness appears "it is the great possibility that mass migration gives the world, …"[13] and we should embrace it.

Notes for the Preface

[1] For more on the trans-Atlantic exchanges between Berlin and Chicago, see "No Failure Too Great," in *Chicagoisms: The City as Catalyst for Architectural Speculation*, eds. Alexander Eisenschmidt and Jonathan Mekinda (Zürich: Scheidegger & Spiess / Park Books, 2013), 150-166.

[2] See Walther Rathenau, "Die schönste Stadt der Welt," *Die Zukunft*, no. 26 (1899) and Karl Scheffler, *Berlin – ein Stadtschicksal* (Berlin: E. Reiss, 1910).

[3] Americanism and Americanisation was debated not just in Germany but across Europe. See Jean-Louis Cohen, *Scenes of the World to Come: European Architecture and the American Challenge*, 1893-1960 (Montreal: Canadian Center for Architecture, 1995).

[4] For more on the US influence on Germany, see Frank Trommler, "The Rise and Fall of Americanism in Germany," in Frank Trommler and Joseph McVeigh, eds., *America and the Germans: An Assessment of a Three-hundred-Year History* (Philadelphia: University of Pennsylvania Press, 1985); Alf Lüdtke, Inge Marßolek, and Adelheid von Saldern, eds., *Amerikanisierung. Traum und Alptraum im Deutschland des 20*. Jahrhunderts (Stuttgart: Franz Steiner Verlag, 1996); Alexander Schmidt, Reise in die Moderne (Berlin: Akademie-Verlag, 1997).

[5] Karl Scheffler, Berlin – *ein Stadtschicksal*, 166.

[6] For more on Scheffler's theories, see the second chapter of *The Good Metropolis: From Urban Formlessness to Metropolitan Architecture* (Berlin: Birkhäuser, 2019).

[7] For more on the history of "metropolitan architecture," see *The Good Metropolis*.

[8] Most of these authors would eventually settle in the US, Neutra moved there in 1923 while others followed ten years later to escape Nazi Germany.

[9] After a lecture tour through the US in 1913, the outbreak of World War I provoked Hegemann's extended stay.

[10] *Städtebau* emerged as a term in the late-19th century and entered the German academy in 1907. The institutionalisation of *Städtebau* was already underway before 1900. The first teaching of *Stadtplanung* (city planning) was done in Stuttgart and Dresden in 1896; early lectures on *Stadtbaukunst* (the art of city building) were delivered by Theodor Goecke, Joseph Brix, and Felix Genzmer in 1903 at the Königliche Technische Hochschule in Berlin-Charlottenburg; and the first recognized academic seminar on *Städtebau* followed in the winter semester of 1907/08.

[11] Joseph Hudnut, Statement on Werner Hegemann, July 29, 1936, GSD Papers, Harvard University Archives: 322.7, sub. I. For more on the influence of Hegemann on Hudnut, see Jill Pearlman, "Joseph Hudnut and the Unlikely Origins of 'Post-modern' Urbanism," *Planning Perspectives 15* (July 2000): 201-239; "Breaking Common Ground: Joseph Hudnut and the Prehistory of Urban Design," in *Josep Jluís Sert: The Architect of Urban Design, 1953-1969*, eds. Eric Mumford and Hashim Sarkis (New Haven: Yale University Press, 2008), 117-129; and Christiane Crasemann Collins, "Camillo Sitte Across the Atlantic: Raymond Unwin, John Nolen, and Werner Hegemann," in *Sitte, Hegemann and the Metropolis: Modern Civic Art and International Exchanges*, eds. Charles C. Bohl and Jean-François Lejeune (London: Routledge, 2009), 175-195.

[12] Think of the Syrian refugee crisis on the doorsteps of Europe or the Latin-American refugee crisis on the Mexican American boarder.

[13] Salman Rushdie, "In Good Faith," in *Imaginary Homelands: Essays and Criticism, 1981-1991* (London: Granta Books, 1991), 394.

Alexander Eisenschmidt, Ph.D., is a designer, theorist, and Associate Professor of Architecture at the University of Illinois at Chicago, where he also directs the *Visionary Cities Project*. His recent book is titled *The Good Metropolis* and his work has been exhibited internationally in venues such as the Venice Architecture Biennale and the Shenzhen Biennale of Urbanism and Architecture.

Foreword

Beyond the Bauhaus: Towards an Interdisciplinary Environmental Design Education

Peter Bosselmann

The influence of German architecture education on American Schools of Architecture is strongly linked to a generation of architects born in the last decade of the 19th century. They were born to parents who had experienced endless wars during their lifetime, fought largely by Prussia over the hegemony of central Europe. Wars only led to other wars, all precursors to the First World War (1914–1918), where this generation served as soldiers. In 1918, now in their late 20s, or early 30s, they witnessed the fall of an autocratic regime and the transformation of Germany into a republic. With it came liberation in the arts and culture.

History gave this generation of architects and designers 15 to 20 years until a totalitarian regime returned which forced them to emigrate, either because they were Jewish, married to a Jew, socialists, otherwise left leaning or forced to leave because their work was considered entarted, a loaded concept, meaning an art foreign to the German identity. Not all of them were German, but Swiss, Austrian, Czech, Hungarian, Dutch or Scandinavian. Also, the modern architecture movement had precedent. Important in this context and influential to the Bauhaus was the Dutch movement de Stijl which started in Leiden in 1917 with the work of the painters Theo van Doesburg, Piet Mondrian and the architects Gerrit Rietveld and Jacobus Oud. Even earlier, a reform movement, likewise with origins in the visual arts was called *Neue Sachlichkeit*. The commonly used English translation, "New Objectivity", is somewhat misleading. More literal is a translation that describes an architecture executed in a matter-of-fact like manner as was evident to Bruno Taut, when he in 1933 praised the 1624 Katsura Villa in Kyoto for its simple, orthogonal design. Even prior to *Neue Sachlichkeit* was the government sponsored association, German *Werkbund* of 1907 to 1937, founded with the intent to develop the Arts and Crafts movement into an industry designed to compete with the United Kingdom and the US. Members of the Werkbund included Walter Gropius (1883–1969), Moholy-Nagy (1885–1946), Mies van der Rohe (1886–1969), Erich Mendelsohn (1887–1953) and many others.

The narrative that follows focuses on immigrants who exercised direct or indirect influence on architecture education in the US, including at UC Berkeley. However, among those mentioned thus far, only Erich Mendelsohn ended up in Berkeley. In Germany, Mendelsohn had joined the "Zehner-ring", a loose professional community of ten designers formed to reunify inseparable components in the creation of a new architecture; they included, among others, Gropius, Mies van der Rohe, Bruno Taut, Mendelsohn and others. However, given their strong personalities, they did not necessarily get along well with each other. In a letter addressed by Mendelsohn to his wife Luise dated August 19, 1923[1] he includes highly critical comments on the work of his colleagues Gropius and Mies van der Rohe, which do not bode well for their need of mutual support as immigrants in the US in the 1940s. Mendelsohn writes about the Bauhaus exhibit of 1923: "The architecture exhibition is a Gropius with Adolf Meyer event. Its international character is only a stage set for a Gropius performance." Mendelsohn praised the talk by the architect J.J.P. Oud on the Dutch contribution to modern architecture. Apparently, Oud showed the work of Hendrik P. Berlage, who Mendelsohn realises might very well have been the first European architect to break with classical eclecticism. Mendelsohn is impressed by Michel de Klerk's *Het Ship*, an urban block of housing in Amsterdam with a post office and primary school that Oud included in his lecture. De Klerk's work was, and still is, noteworthy for its simplicity of the housing units tailored to the needs of a former rural population forced to make a living in the urban economy. Yet at the same time, the detailing is rich in expressing the identity of the block as a community.

With the Bauhaus exhibit of 1923 modern architecture had become an international movement; further broadened by Gropius through his association with the *Congrès International d'Architecture Moderne* (CIAM) in 1928; that year Gropius participated at the first CIAM conference with Le Cobusier, Mart Stam from Holland, Sven Markelius from Sweden and with Sigfried Giedion as first secretary. But the interdisciplinary dimension of the Bauhaus as an educational model remained limited to the collaboration of architects with professionals trained in the visual arts, especially those working with photography, ceramics, textiles, wood, metal and glass (Gropius, 1978).

Historically, and to a large extent still today, architecture education in Germany and in other European countries was offered at technical universities or art academies and was not an integral part of comprehensive universities, where the humanities, social and natural sciences dominate higher education. This point became important when the German educators arrived in the United States, where architectural education was organised differently. In 1937, Joseph Hudnut (1886–1968), dean at Harvard's Graduate School of Design appointed Gropius as chair of the architecture program. The policies of the "New Deal" (1933—1938) required Hudnut to balance Gropius's form-based architecture education with faculty appointments in the social sciences. He appointed G. Holmes Perkins who in his teaching stressed the political dimension of architecture. Even at the Massachusetts Institute of Technology, a polytechnic university, Dean William Wurster appointed Gregöry Kepes, who had worked with Moholy-Nagy in Berlin and London, to teach in the School of Architecture and Planning and paired him with Kevin Lynch. Together they started truly groundbreaking work on how residents perceive their city and what they commit to memory.

Mies van der Rohe might have had an easier role in Chicago. He left Germany in 1937 and was given a position at the Armour Institute, later renamed Illinois Institute of Technology (IIT), where he served as chair of architecture. It is doubtful that Mies experienced the same dual foci on design and also on the social political dimension of architecture. As a private institute, Armour had originally been formed to foster engineering, chemistry, architecture and library sciences. Moholy-Nagy and Ludwig Karl Hilberseimer (1885–1967) joined Mies in Chicago in 1938 to continue the educational model at the New Bauhaus.

Initially, several American-born housing advocates introduced the American public to Germany's modern architecture. Catherine Bauer (1905–1964) studied architecture at Cornell followed by a liberal arts education at Vassar College. From 1926 to 27, she lived in Paris and visited workers' housing by Le Corbusier. She also visited Ernst May in 1926, who was developing affordable housing with improved social and hygienic conditions in Frankfurt. In 1930 she returned together with Lewis Mumford to visit the newly completed Römerstadt, a project in Frankfurt that together with the 1927 Weissenhof Estate in Stuttgart, represented the two most exemplary modern housing developments of the Weimar Republic. Her book "Modern Housing" (Bauer, 1934) draws heavily on her experience in Europe. In her view the European examples she had seen were radically different from the American tenement housing she despised. During the Roosevelt administration Bauer rose to much acclaim as the principle author of the Federal Housing Act that eventually became law in 1937.

Lewis Mumford, historian and architecture critic, wrote for the *New Yorker* magazine. As a member of the Regional Plan Association of America, he together with Catherine Bauer and fellow members Clarence Stein and Henry Wright presented their ideas about modern housing at the Metropolitan Museum of Modern Art in New York on the occasion of the 1932 exhibit on modern architecture (Sachs, 2018). The exhibit, curated by Henry-Russell Hitchcock and Philip Johnson, was a large success. Mumford continued his support for German architects of the modern movement. In 1941, he signed the affidavit for Erich Mendelsohn (already in exile since 1933) when Mendelsohn immigrated to the US coming from Palestine after work there on major projects was interrupted by World War II (James-Chakraboty, 1997). Mumford had met Erich Mendelsohn on his first visit to New York in the winter of 1924, a visit that brought Mendelsohn also to Taliesin in Wisconsin. Wright welcomed Mendelsohn warmly. He had learned about his work from Richard Neutra, who as a former employee of Mendelsohn in Berlin was now working for Frank Lloyd Wright.

In 1933 Mumford, together with Philip Johnson, helped Josef Albers to a teaching post at the newly founded Black Mountain College. Josef and Anni Albers had been at the Bauhaus as students in the 1920s, and became teachers in 1923. Josef Albers taught the "Werk-Kurs", best translated as a course that trained future architects to improve hand-eye coordination while making objects in a workshop. At the same time the painter Paul Klee taught theory of composition. Albers left Germany in 1933. He successfully offered the same foundation course at Black Mountain College in North Carolina until 1949, when Albers moved to Yale. Black Mountain College was a school established on the educational model of John Dewey. Dewey was known for his profound commitment to democracy at all levels of society. He strongly encouraged educators to foster experimental intelligence among their students and stressed the importance of plurality. Indeed, the influence of European immigrants in the 1930s and 40s was strong, so was the support they received from American institutions and individuals. But immigrants seeking employment at American schools of architecture also met with opposition.

Erich Mendelsohn followed an invitation to lecture at Berkeley in 1942. In a letter to his wife on the 17th of April[2] he writes enthusiastically about San Francisco. He is invited for dinner at the home of William Wurster and Catherine Bauer. Wurster and Bauer had married in 1940 and he had opened an architecture practice in Berkeley. In his letter, Mendelsohn praises both: Wurster is "the best fruit of the country" and Catherine a "courageous fighter". The three talks at Berkeley went very well. He is lauded by the director of the architecture school, Warren Perry: "extraordinary lectures". Provost Monroe Deutsch attended and mentions a full professor position that Robert Sproul, the Chancellor, had offered to fill with a modern architect. Deutsch discussed the salary associated with the position, but cautions Mendelsohn that the faculty had to initiate a request. Unknown to Mendelsohn, the request was never made. Dean Perry remained committed to the traditional Ecole des Beaux-Arts education. Serge Chermayeff, Mendelsohn's former partner in London, was also considered for the same position with the same result; an educator too radical for Dean Perry.

Together with Catherine Bauer, Mendelsohn visited Telesis where he met a young interdisciplinary group advocated for a comprehensive approach to the design of the rapidly industrialising San Francisco Bay Area (Sachs, 2018). Mendelsohn was also invited by Walter Haas, who served on a committee to bring the United Nations Headquarters to San Francisco. Already Mendelsohn saw himself in the role of a Berkeley professor; he and his wife settled in San Francisco to open an architecture practice in 1945. After all such efforts, Mendelsohn was only given a temporary teaching appointment at Berkeley, but not as a faculty member (Lowell, 2009, pp. 270, 303). Real innovation to architecture education could not take place until Warren Perry retired, and that would not happen until 1950 when William Wurster was appointed chair of the Department of Architecture.

In 1945, Catherine Bauer and William Wurster moved to Cambridge; Wurster with the intent to enroll in the GSD's graduate program at Harvard, and for her to teach courses on housing. Together they attended Martin Wagner's course, who took a loyal socialist approach to civic design. Wagner had been a leading planner in Berlin, responsible for 70 percent of all new housing finance in the interwar period through the establishment of a not-for-profit community-oriented housing association. But already by 1940, Wagner's relationship with Gropius was strained. Wagner complained of Gropius abandoning the underlying social principles of modernism, and practicing modernism only as a style.[3] While studying at Harvard, Wurster was recruited to serve as Dean of Architecture at MIT. There Wurster followed Hudnot's earlier model to create a combined school of architecture and urban planning. Committed to establishing a research tradition at MIT, Wurster hired Kevin Lynch upon recommendation of Lloyd Rodwin. Lynch was Wurster's first faculty appointment in 1948. Prior to coming to MIT, Lynch had apprenticed at Taliesin with Frank Lloyd Wright, but left opposed to Wright's individualistic social philosophy, which Lynch considered backward looking, with a view of an individualistic society (Banerjee & Southworth, 1990, p. 18).

To give a taste of the continued struggles in the two related disciplines of planning and architecture, a MIT student at the time, later faculty member, Julian Beinart, recalls the dichotomy: "embrace architecture as a 'social art' while clinging to an insistence that it, at the same time, be a fine art" (Sachs, 2018, p. 28).

City planner Jack Kent, after returning from Berlin as a member of the US occupation force, convinced William Wurster to repeat his MIT success back at Berkeley. Kent, a former MIT student, had been a founding member of Telesis, a concept labeled with a neologism. The idea was to respond in an interdisciplinary mode to changes in culture and technology with the aim to integrate functions in cities and the region. Members included architects, planners and landscape architects like Vernon de Mars, Thomas Church, Garret Eckbo, Geraldine Knight Scott and Fran Violich. The promise by the group to work towards a combined school persuaded Wurster and Bauer to return to Berkeley. Wurster became chair of the school of architecture in 1950. His early appointments included Vernon de Mars, Charles Eames, Philip Thiel and Claude Stoller. Stoller had been a student of Josef Albers at Black Mountain College. He most clearly was Berkeley's early direct link to the Bauhaus tradition.

Was Wurster setting up the new college in the Bauhaus mold? The record is mixed because the collective memory of college history has faded. Richard Peters recalls: "Wurster disagreed with the Bauhaus idea that architects should learn to become plumbers and brick layers, and he argued that the single most important thing is that a person have an inquisitive mind (Peters, 2009). In a clear break with the Bauhaus tradition, Wurster hired the historian James Ackerman. History, including architectural history, had no role in the Bauhaus model. At Berkeley, Ackerman was the first in a linage of scholars teaching architecture history that included Norma Evenson, Stephan Tobriner, Dell Upton and Spiro Kostof. Consistent with the Bauhaus tradition, Wurster hired two additional faculty members, Jesse Reichek and James Prestini, both came directly from the New Bauhaus in Chicago where Reichek had been a student, and where Prestini taught with Laszlo Moholy-Nagy and Mies van der Rohe. In remembering James Prestini, four of his colleagues wrote the following tribute:

> Together they (Prestini and Reichek) set up a foundation program for beginning students that became one of the best courses of its kind—perhaps the very finest—in American architectural education, Prestini set forth by precept and example the Bauhaus philosophy with pioneering zeal. "The modern movement for him," his colleague Claude Stoller recalled at a memorial gathering, "was a revolutionary way of getting back to basics: not a new style but a new way of thinking. He tended to tell his students that the thinking was most important; that he would provide them with no solutions, only an approach to problems of design" (Peters, Reichek, Stoller, & Temko, 2011).

In the meantime, Catherine Bauer joined Jack Kent in the Department of City and Regional Planning, an independent department at UC Berkeley since 1948. Landscape Architecture had its root in the Forestry Department since 1914. Catherine Bauer became a driving force in establishing an interdisciplinary college. After much back and forth about its name, in 1959, the new college with four separate departments: architecture, planning, landscape architecture, and decorative arts became a reality as the College of Environmental Design (CED) with Wurster as dean until 1963. It is the inclusion of decorative arts as an independent department in the college that provides clear evidence of Wurster's intent to establish a school in the mold of the Bauhaus. Alums still recall the names of faculty members like Hope Gladding's[4] (history of interior design), Herwin Schaefer (1970), the weaver Ed Rossbach, the aerial photographer William Garnett,[5] and the ceramists James Melchert and Peter Voulkos. These are all former college faculty members that still enjoy name recognition for their contribution to an interdisciplinary design education despite the fact that the design department closed, as early as 1974.

By the 1960s, already under Wurster, college deans were hard pressed to advance those faculty members through the tenure review process who were purely concentrating on design without evidence of scholarly reflection on its context within society. As a research university, the academic senate at Berkeley insisted on a strong publication record that involved research. This led the deans that followed Wurster like Martin Meyerson, William Wheaton and Richard Bender to establish research units in the college, initially under the university-wide graduate division, later under the vice-chancellor for research. Recruitment of faculty with research backgrounds also became a priority. Two of the last appointments initiated by Wurster were the hires of Christopher Alexander and Horst Rittel, both with a background in mathematics. Alexander was working on a form-generating language of components that he called patterns. Rittel had taught at the Hochschule für Gestaltung in the city of Ulm; the school was established in 1953 as a successor to the Bauhaus in West Germany. Avigail Sachs wrote: "Rittel was intrigued by the balance between rational and non-rational elements in the design process. Rather than argue that the two are separate, he was interested in how they came together and to what extent they can and should be made communicable to others" (Sachs, 2018, p. 69). Appointments followed under Dean William L.C. Wheaton, a political scientist and internationally acclaimed housing expert who followed Wurster in 1968; his hires included Roger Montgomery and Donald Appleyard.

At a time of much social turmoil, Berkeley became a draw for students from around the country and the world. Foreign students no longer came because of the European influence on architectural education. That influence clearly waned and a reverse influence set in that transferred knowledge from the US back to Europe. I reached out to former students who had studied in Germany and came to Berkeley. In addition, I talked to Thomas Sieverts about the timing of the tipping point when the reversal set in. Sieverts taught a seminar, "Housing and User Needs" with Willo von Moltke at Harvard in 1970. There is agreement among those I talked to that a selected set of publications started to influence schools of architecture and planning worldwide in the early 1960s: Kevin Lynch, *The Image of the City* (1960), Jane Jacobs, *The Death and Life of Great American Cities* (1961), Ian McHarg, *Design with Nature* (1969), Donald Appleyard, Kevin Lynch and John Meyer, *The View from the Road* (1965), and Christopher Alexander et al, *Houses Generated by Patterns* (1970). This conclusion was further confirmed by what three former students wrote who now hold faculty positions after studying at Berkeley.

- Hans Joachim Neis, Ph.D. Associate Professor at the University of Oregon, Portland, studied under Theodor Adorno in Frankfurt and Thomas Sieverts in Darmstadt (Neis, 2019). He wrote:

  "We in the European student movement failed to create a new architecture and renewed urbanism that could provide fresh opportunities for a better world, not just in the developed world but throughout the world. The European and German architecture student scene at that time was strongly influenced by the confrontation with the father generation, by social concerns, participation, house squatting (in Frankfurt and Darmstadt), but it was mostly socio-political actions or liberating actions, without a true new positive architecture in itself, without a new urban development, perhaps with approaches here and there, but nothing fundamentally new with architecture as the central core. In this context, I went to Berkeley for a year to work on my dissertation. Fortunately, at that time Chris Alexander taught in Berkeley. His teaching aroused the hope of a new urban planning and architecture, as it seemed to me possible in my early student days as a progressive concrete utopia." (Neis, 2019)

- Alexander Schmidt, Ph.D., Professor em. M.Arch, had studied at the Technical University of Stuttgart and wrote: "Berkeley was my first choice - primarily because of the political, social and ecological trends that originated at Berkeley in the years prior to my arrival":

  "I was strongly influenced by the faculty members who taught at Berkeley during my time. The nature of the city and my understanding of city design were formed by Donald Appleyard primarily, but also by Kenneth Craik, Clare Cooper Marcus and Russ Ellis, the latter served as adviser of my master's thesis on participatory design with the focus on the role of the Simulation Laboratory. It was the openness to unrestrained thinking, the discovery of new ways of linking various fields of knowledge and to expand the boundaries of limited professional discourse that made my time at Berkeley meaningful. Though it was only for one year it had a lasting impact. Upon return in the early 1980s, this influence led me to apply, not for a position at a school of architecture or planning, but at universities with engineering and transportation planning faculties. The University of Duisburg-Essen offered me plenty of city specific interdisciplinary research opportunities. I established the university's Joint Center Urban Systems together with engineers, social and cultural scientists, physicians and epidemiologists. The Berkeley influence determined the topics of my research, e.g. the future of villages in the context of their landscapes, urban mobility, the healthy city, urban climate adaptation. I also never abandoned my concern for the quality of life and the beauty of cities." (Schmidt, 2019)

• Ralf Weber, Ph.D., Professor em. at the University of Dresden. Weber came from Dresden in the German Democratic Republic (GDR) to West Germany and studied at the University of Stuttgart. He commented:

"Architecture education in the East was very technical—almost confined to structural engineering. At Dresden I had never heard of Berkeley. Also at Stuttgart, Berkeley's influence was not very prominent. We heard about MIT, Yale and Columbia. However, we had Horst Rittel (1930 —1990) who shared his faculty appointment between Berkeley and the Technical University at Stuttgart. After a number of faculty members gave only a humored appraisal of my plan to study architecture aesthetics, Rittel listened to me for 10 minutes and offered to chair my Ph.D. dissertation. I remember we talked about Berkeley, and he thought that a certain stiffness induced by my East German upbringing could be loosened by a stay in California. Well, there was no holding me back, and anyhow, I wanted to go out into the world, so I applied. It was the best decision I made during those years. I did not study much architecture at Berkeley, although I graduated with a Master of Architecture degree. The most intriguing thing at Berkeley was that one could be a student with a truly interdisciplinary focus. I took courses in art history, psychology and philosophy. Occasionally, I attended classes in social geography and much else. For me it was a dream come true that I could finally be a student in the true sense of the word. Instead of taking in already formatted knowledge, I could select the topics relevant to my curiosity. Of course it was hugely interesting to exist as a Ph.D. student inside the conflict between the worlds of Horst Rittel and Christopher Alexander. Initially, blue-eyed as I was, my expectation had been that both could serve on my Ph.D. committee. To give credit, both jointly supported my application to the doctoral program. What I regret deeply was the death of Donald Appleyard. In all likelihood, I would have moved closer towards city design, because I was drawn to his work right from the start of my stay at Berkeley. After having received my Ph.D. and having taught for several years at Berkeley, I went back to Germany because of its re-unification. The circumstances allowed me to take on a position as Chair of Spatial Design at my old Alma Mater. I never regretted that I landed back in Dresden. The freedom of a German University Professor is simply unmatched.

Sixty years after the foundation of Telesis, Vernon de Mars, one of its founders, established a financial legacy to fund a post-professional degree program to be jointly staffed by faculty from the three departments in the College of Environmental Design. The new program attracts students with professional degrees in architecture, planning and landscape architecture. The focus remained on design through studio instruction. The program is supplemented by a course on History and Theory of Urban Form. A second course, entitled Environmental Design Research Methods continued the Lynch/Appleyard tradition of taking measurements in the real world, and conducting interviews about people's perceptions and cognitions of social and environmental issues (2018). This course has drawn on our own joint research with colleagues in psychology (1986), building sciences (1995), on climate (1989), the design of streets (1997) (1999), and fluvial geomorphology (2019).

"The Bauhaus strives to bring together all creative effort into one whole, to reunify all the disciplines of practical art – sculpture, painting, handicrafts, and crafts – as inseparable components of new architecture."[6] (Gropius, 1919)

One hundred years after Gropius's statement, the disciplines taking responsibility for designing physical space had to adapt and draw from a greater number of knowledge domains. The need for humane design that is equitable, just and affordable requires interdisciplinary approaches. What I hope comes through to the reader of this Foreword is the struggle for a foundation in educating students in the three related fields of architecture, planning and landscape architecture. The goal is to learn how to design the world around us, the environment with all its social, physical and natural processes. The many individuals mentioned here have left a mark in that struggle.

Acknowledgements

The author contacted the following friends and colleagues for comments and sources: Richard Bender, Elizabeth Byrne, Sheila Dicky, Kathrine James-Chakraboty, Ray Lifchez, Waverly Lowell, Maren Moegel, Hajo Neis, Avigail Sachs, Catherine Schiltz, Alexander Schmidt, Tom Sieverts, Heidi Sokolowski, Claude Stoller, Michael Southworth, Marc Treib, and Ralf Weber.

References

Arens, E., & Bosselmann, P. (1989). Wind, Sun and Temperature: predicting the thermal comfort of people in outdoor spaces. *Building and Environment*, 315-20.

Banerjee, T., & Southworth, M. (1990). The Life and work of Kevin Lynch. In T. Banerjee, & M. Southworth, *City Sense and City Design* (p. 18). Cambridge, Massachusetts: MIT press.

Bauer, C. (1934). *Modern Housing*. Boston: Houghton.

Bosselmann, P. (2018). Kevin Lynch and his legacy on teaching professional planners and designers. *Journal of the American Planning Association*, 84(3-4), 284-292. doi:https://www.tandfonline.com/doi/full/10.1080/01944363.2018.1528172

Bosselmann, P., & Arens, E. (1995). *Urban Form and Climate. Journal of the American Planning Association*, 226-39.

Bosselmann, P., & Craik, K. (1986). Perceptual Simulations of Environments. In R. Bechtel, R. Marans, & W. Michelson, *Methods in Environmental and Behavioral Research* (pp. 162-190). New York: Van Nostrand Reinhold.

Bosselmann, P., & Macdonald, E. (1999). Livable Streets Revisited. Journal of the American Planning Association, 186-81.

Bosselmann, P., Kondolf, M., & Webb, P. (2019). An Island in Transition, adaptation of urban form Pazhou Island in the Pearl River Delta. *Landscape Architecture Journal*.

Gropius, W. (1978). Program of the Staatliche Bauhaus in Weimar. In H. M. Wingler, T*he Bauhaus: Weimar, Dessau, Berlin, Chicago* (p. 32). Cambridge, MA: MIT Press.

James-Chakraboty, K. (1997). *Erich Mendelsohn & the Architecture of German Modernism*. Cambridge, UK: University of Cambridge Press.

Lowell, W. e. (2009). *Design on the Edge, a century of teaching architecture at the University of California, Berkeley*, 1903-2003. Berkeley: College of Environmental Design.

Neis, H. J. (2019). Shifting values in architecture and urban design. In E. Guttman, G. Kaiser, & C. Mazanek, *Christopher Alexander and the Eishin Campus* (pp. 123 - 142). Zuerich: Park Books.

Peters, R. (2009). W.W.Wurster. In W. Lowell, E. Byrne, & Frederick-Rothwell eds, D*esign on the Edge, a century of teaching architecture at the University of California, Berkeley*, 1903-2003 (pp. 60-70). Berkeley: College of Environmental Design.

Peters, R., Reichek, J., Stoller, C., & Temko, A. (2011). *James L. Prestini 1908-1993*. Retrieved from Calisphere, University of California.

Sachs, A. (2018). *Environmental Design*. Charlottesville: University of Virginia Press.

Schaefer, H. (1970). *The roots of modern design functional traditions in the 19th century*. London: Studio Vista.

Southworth, M., & Ben-Joseph, E. (1997). *Streets and the Shaping of Towns and Cities*. New York: McGraw-Hill.

Notes for the Foreword

[1] Accessed June 5, 2020: http;//ema.smb.museum/de/briefe

[2] Accessed June 8, 2020: http;//ema.smb.museum/de/briefe

[3] Accessed June 8, 2020: http://www.transatlanticperspectives.org/entry/.php?rec23

[4] Visual Resources Archive, College of Environmental Design, UC Berkeley.

[5] http://www.getty.edu/art/collection/artists/1545/william-a-garnett-american-1916-2006/

[6] Walter Gropius (1919): retrieved June 12,2020, https://www.stmarys- ca.edu/sites/default/files/attachments/files/Anna_Novakov_Synthetic_Spaces_Essay.pdf

Peter Bosselmann is a Professor of the Graduate School in Architecture, City and Regional Planning, Landscape Architecture and Urban Design at the College of Environmental Design, University of California, Berkeley.

Let America be the dream the dreamers dreamed—
Let it be that great strong land of love,
Where never kings connive nor tyrants scheme
That any man be crushed by one above.

O, let my land be a land where Liberty
Is crowned with no false patriotic wreath,
But opportunity is real, and life is free,
Equality is in the air we breathe.

— Langston Hughes, "Let America Be America Again", 1936

Introduction

Image A: American settlers moving towards the West: a painting by German-born painter John Gast entitled "American Progress" (1872). This painting has become a seminal example of American Western art that portrays the westward expansion (which occurred from 1812 to 1860). This 19th-century movement of settlers into the West, began with the Louisiana Purchase and was fueled by the Gold Rush, the Oregon Trail and a belief in "manifest destiny." Many of the settlers were immigrants from Germany. The figure of Progress is ushering an era of modernisation, development and advancement to the West, leading white settlers who follow her either on foot or by horseback, coach or train. Progress lays a telegraph wire with one hand and carries a school book in the other. As she moves westward, indigenous people and a herd of buffalo are seen fleeing her.

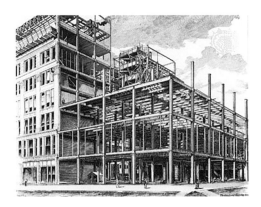

Image B: The steel-frame high-rise building was invented in Chicago in the 1880s. As steel is stronger and lighter in weight than iron, the use of a steel frame made the construction of truly tall buildings possible. William LeBaron Jenney's 10-story Home Insurance Company building (1884–1885) was the first to use steel-girder construction, and also the first to employ a curtain wall façade (an outer covering of masonry or other material that bears only its own weight and is affixed to and supported by the steel skeleton). It is considered the first modern high-rise building. It was not until the invention of the passenger elevator in 1852 that high-rise towers became possible and practical.

Image C: Suburbanisation, the rapid growth of US suburbia: in the post-war era, many Americans moved away from cities, into car-dependent suburbs. Techniques of mass production made it possible to build homes faster and more affordable than ever before, using one- or two-storey timber construction and assembly-line systems. Since the late 19th century, Americans as well as immigrants had flocked to American cities in search of factory work. In the post-war era, however, that trend reversed thanks to low housing costs: even working-class Americans could now afford to own a home in the suburbs.

Image D: Ground floor with the buildings set back behind a series of columns, creating a visual effect of the buildings "floating" above the site: The 26-floor apartment buildings at 860-900 Lake Shore Drive in Chicago (1949—1951), an elegant composition of four minimalist glass-and-steel towers designed by Ludwig Mies van der Rohe.
(Photo by the author, 2020).

Trans-Atlantic Engagements

Introduction

Today, in the United States and Canada alone there are more than 140 professional degree programs in architecture with over 6,000 academic faculty members educating more than 40,000 students. The subject of this book is the history of architectural education, in particular the evolution of architectural education in the United States today. "Trans-Atlantic Engagements: German Educators' Contribution to and Impact on US Architectural Education" is a publication project that explores the influence of pedagogical concepts of German-born professors on architecture schools in the US. Historically, the German architectural training has always been historically different from the Franco-Italian or British traditions.

It's not often that the history of architectural pedagogy is the subject of study. This report and study conducted for the ACSA traces the significant, influential and sometimes controversial contribution of German professors of architecture and design, from the 1930s to today, at universities in the US. With over two centuries of significant cultural exchange between both countries in the fields of architecture and design, there has been a considerable German influence on American architecture as well as on architectural education (and vice versa). The study takes a critical look and explores the important role that the Bauhaus—as a place, idea and culture—played in the formation of one of the most influential intellectual projects in 20th-century architectural pedagogy. The historical impact of Bauhaus pedagogy on the teaching and learning of design cannot be overstated. Over a century ago, starting out in Weimar in 1919 as an avant-garde academy of arts and crafts led by Gropius, the school progressively transformed, over its 14-year lifespan, into a lived experiment in the combination of technology and art – an endeavour fuelled by the optimism of the emerging Modern Movement.

The ideals of the Bauhaus School shaped more than just design and architecture around the world. Its guiding principles also transformed teaching. Not limited to the personalities of the generation of 1930s immigrants Walter Gropius, Ludwig Mies van der Rohe, Ludwig Hilberseimer, and Erich Mendelsohn, there has been a constant flow of eminent German architects crossing the Atlantic. After the Bauhaus's closing in 1933, several of its protagonists moved to the United States and their influence can still be felt today in numerous buildings, artworks, concepts and curricula. Frequently, they have led the innovative development of US curricula, effected significant impact on architectural education and were subsequently influential both in their capacities as educators and as practitioners. Some of these schools operated according to the new pedagogical principles introduced by the Bauhaus's legacy and had a lasting influence on the entire American system.

Remarkable mid-century figures of charismatic architects with strong principles come to mind, who were influenced by the Bauhaus model of interdisciplinary education. This book examines a couple of key questions: What makes these architects come to the US, and do they consider themselves German or American architects? What are the particular qualities that German architects might bring to the education of architects in the US? Are such national attributes, specialisations and identities, including preserving German cultural values, still relevant in a globally inter-connected society and profession? Which concepts do they import, and how do these architects assimilate to their new home country?

While the historic cases of the last century (the Bauhaus, Gropius, Mies, Mendelsohn, and others) have previously been well covered by numerous authors, and there is an extremely rich body of scholarship available in German and English language, the main contribution of this book is in the discussion concerning the current context. It examines not only their many built works and projects but also their contributions to teaching and writings. Therefore, the key questions for the second part of the book and following interviews with selected educators, are:

- How have early German-influenced pedagogies changed or transitioned, and what is their relevance between contemporary German-born educators today?
- How are more recent German-trained transplants influencing US schools now?

The book profiles 52 historical cases of German-born architects, and 39 contemporary German-trained professors currently active in the US; it concludes with a feature of conversations with selected influential educators, devoting their careers to the education of architects. These German-born architects had their upbringing, education and cultural formation in Germany, and frequently had a successful career before immigrating to the United States, where they took up important teaching positions. Their biographies are accompanied by in-depth conversations on their educational philosophies and strategies. This is a generation that is actively shaping architectural education today.

The study is relevant to the educational sector and the general public. It brings together available (but currently fragmented) knowledge to address relevant questions about the education of architects, and enables a better understanding of imported pedagogical models that were contributing to the future of US architectural education. Hence, the aims of this study are: to develop relevant research that gives an overview of German-trained educators in the US (historical and contemporary); and gathering, analysing, and synthesising the knowledge, connecting researchers to create dialogue and develop future joint research initiatives. The goal is to make a meaningful contribution to the discourse by producing a high quality scholarly book to widely communicate the project findings. The project audience is likely to include people interested in design education, academics and students in the US and Germany, and German Americans. The book fills a current knowledge gap. The book is different from earlier work, tracing the sometimes controversial contributions of German professors at US universities since 1930s.

The evaluation of German influences post-Bauhaus on US schools of architecture highlights the imported excellence in design and architecture and celebrates the individual contributions that German-trained architects have made and keep making to the North American vibrant educational scene trough their design research, teaching and pedagogy. This generation is as diverse as the country. The in-depth interviews with six selected architecture professors shed light on their intentions, and showcase their different educational philosophies and accomplishments, while providing an overview of their unusual international careers. The book argues that, although the educators' positions in between two cultural spheres creates discontinuities in their work, it also facilitates a mutual exchange between their European backgrounds and their North American peers, and thereby helps to shape the development and reception of the educational projects on either side of the Atlantic.

The pedagogical experiments of the Bauhaus, first imported by Gropius, Mies, Albers and others to the US system, challenged traditional Beaux-Arts thinking and played a crucial role in reshaping modern design education over the last eighty years. Their move to the United States led to a change in American architectural education, away from historicism and Beaux-Arts ideas to an architecture that relied on craft, innovation and modern industrial techniques. These new modes of teaching architecture and design had a long-lasting impact, however, are now being again transformed. The book's research outcomes respond directly to current and future educational and societal challenges by untangling legacies that started in 1937, with Gropius and van der Rohe's arrivals, and that continue with German educators today. Overall, the research aims to contribute to the better understanding of architectural education in the United States and advances the knowledge of architectural education by illuminating various educational strategies deployed at a range of architecture schools.

Authored by an established scholar with personal insight into the topic, the selected educators profiled in this volume render visible a broad array of discursive pedagogical strategies that partially build on the seminal educational model of the Bauhaus. The study provides insight into the ways in which these German-trained educators have influenced architectural and design education in the United States to this day.

PART I
Early German Influences, Immigration and Assimilation

1. Drawing from Two Different European Systems of Architectural Education

Immigration from Europe

Beginning in the 1880s, the arrival of immigrants from mostly southern and eastern European countries rapidly increased, while the flow from northern and western Europe remained constant. The previous waves of immigrants, particularly from Germany, Great Britain and the Nordic countries, were relatively well off, arriving in the country with some funds and education, often moving to the newly settled western territories. In contrast, the newer immigrants from southern and eastern European countries, including Italy, Greece and several Slavic countries (including Russia), were "pushed" from their countries by various reasons, including ongoing famines or the need to escape religious, political or racial persecution. The number of immigrants peaked between 1900 and 1910, when over nine million people arrived in the US.

Following the Revolutions of 1848 in the German states, a large wave of political refugees fled to North America. In the 19th and 20th centuries, German immigrants have been one of the three largest population components of American society, and several became prominent businessmen, scientists or visual artists in the New World. Many German Americans have played an important role in US industry and agriculture. Some German-Jewish immigrants became successful businesspeople and founded banks and financial service companies, like Lehman Brothers, or Marcus Goldman (1821—1904) who founded Goldman Sachs; or, for instance, Johann Jakob Astor (1763—1848), who was a German-American businessman, merchant, real estate mogul and investor who made his fortune mainly in a fur trade monopoly and by investing in real estate in New York City. Johan Jacob Bausch (1830—1926) was a German-American maker of optical instruments who co-founded Bausch & Lomb; over six decades, he transformed his small optical shop in Rochester into a large-scale international enterprise, pioneering the American optical industry. Others built the American beer brewing industry. But the majority were peasants and land grants were made available for them to settle as farmers.

German Americans are Americans who have full or partial German ancestry. In 2016, there were around 44 million German Americans nationwide (it is estimated that German Americans represent 17 percent of the total US population), which makes them the largest of the self-reported ancestry groups in the US. Immigration records show that Germans began to arrive in North America in the 1670s, and very large numbers immigrated in the 19th and 20th centuries, often attracted to the US by the promise of affordable agricultural land, religious freedom, endless economic opportunities and the promise of consistent, wage-earning work. Pennsylvania and New York have the largest population of German Americans (due to their role as arrival ports), and there are some small towns in North Dakota, Minnesota, Wisconsin and Ohio where the population of people with German ancestry is over 80 percent. Between 1875 and 1915, the German American population in the United States doubled, and many of the immigrants insisted on maintaining parts of their culture.[1]

In the US we can find plenty of imported cultural influences: German Americans established the first kindergartens in the US, introduced the Christmas tree, Oktoberfest and beer garden traditions, and introduced popular foods such as pretzels, hot dogs and hamburgers, and the skills of beer brewing. A steady influx of German-born musicians and conductors spurred the reception of German classical music in the United States. German architects have immigrated to the US for over 200 years, and the Appendix of Part I lists fifty biographies of eminent German-born architects who moved to the United States in the 19th and 20th century for a second career.

It is of great interest to analyse the different educational systems, their development and the spread of architectural programmes and networks in the US and in Germany to determine what has become of the initial intentions, and to examine the history of architectural education. The common element in the evolution of architectural education was the question whether it should reflect the practical or the artistic. Historically, architectural education in Europe and the US has evolved very differently, with different systems in Germany, France, Italy, and Britain. Various elements of architectural education were drawn from different countries and placed into the American institutions, partially out of context. From Germany, the concept was adopted that there should be a linkage between teaching and research, and that both occurs in universities; from France came the notion of formal state-certified degrees in architectural education. The two elements were synthesised and overlaid over an earlier apprenticeship system that was inherited from medieval Britain.

The Evolution of a Profession
Until the mid-17th century, before the first schools of architecture in Italy and France, there was no established way to become an architect. The word "architect" comes from the ancient Greek word for "chief carpenter", architektōn. The great Gothic cathedrals in Europe were built by tradesmen: masons, carpenters and artisans. The profession of architect is traditionally generalistic: the builders of bygone days created the design and the statics and oversaw the entire construction process. During the Roman Empire, architects were mostly military engineers (such as Vitruvius); in the Middle Ages, they were mostly craftsmen and sculptors; and during the Renaissance, mostly artists and scientists. Over time, wealthy, educated aristocrats became active as designers of new buildings. Some of the first "architects" were mathematicians or scientists who educated themselves through reading, travel and meeting other designers. They achieved their training informally, without established standards. Any talented and skilled person could become an architect through reading, apprenticeship and self-study. The famous Italian Renaissance architect Andrea Palladio, for example, apprenticed as a stonecutter and learned about the classical orders from scholars of ancient Greece and Rome (e.g., from Vitruvius), embracing ideas of symmetry and proportion.

The main method of architectural education in the 18th and 19th century US, before the adoption of predominantly school-based education, was "pupillage". This only changed in 1868 when the first departments of architecture commenced their programmes.

Articled pupillage, or paying to learn to be an architect in an established architect's office, rather than apprenticeship, was the usual method of becoming an architect before 1868. There were no described standards: what each student would learn in the office was entirely in the hands of the office owner. The traditional concept of on-the-job training, paid for by the pupil (and sometimes supported by classes and travel) was integral to the history of architectural training. Charles Dickens's parody of the exploitative architect, Mr Pecksniff, making money from tuition fees without providing any tuition, as described in the novel *The Life and Adventures of Martin Chuzzlewit* (1844), undermined its perception as a method of education for a professional qualification. Training at the sole hands of professionals was possible when architects made sure they were truly providing their self-learning pupils with practical, artistic and intellectual knowledge, while others simply exploited them.

Pupillage, a four-hundred-years-old model, is now again discussed as a contemporary form of possible architectural education (as an integrated workplace-based pathway). The idea is that design will be taught through participation in real projects and learned through direct practical experience. Peter Buchanan suggested in the *Architectural Review* (2015) that architecture students learn most not from university studio or critique situations but from watching an experienced designer unravelling and resolving a problem at the board. He contends that "pupillage once offered this essentially intimate experience." (Buchanan, 2015)

Comparing the German and French Models
Architects in the US carefully compared the two most established models: the German and the French systems on architectural education. There was a marked contrast in the artistic production of the two countries, in literature and in architecture, as the result of deep political, moral and cultural differences. Their pedagogical models have often been opposed to one another as reflecting different conceptions of architecture.

With the establishment of new institutions, there was a concerted effort to shift architecture solely into full-time studies at higher education institutions. But which model should the US universities adopt? There were three different directions of approaches: the French Beaux-Arts, British Arts and Crafts, and German scientific models (with, from the 1920s on, modernism inspired by the Bauhaus). Added to these approaches was the legacy of the German technical universities, which treated architecture as a technical science akin to engineering, with an emphasis on scientific research. This model was particularly influential in the university development in the US but was also found across Europe. In Italy, for example, qualification as an engineer-architect was common, such as a degree in civil architecture from the Milan Polytechnic.

US institutions were studying the different training systems in architecture at a time when they were looking for models to develop their own architectural training curriculum. Great Britain was less interesting, as it was late in having schools like those in France and Germany and still used the traditional apprentice system.

The German System

The polytechnic schools were already well-established in Germany (Karlsruhe, Stuttgart, and Berlin); these offered to train students as engineer-architects with a solid scientific background and used a more traditional form of pedagogy with lectures and graded exercises. The German system, which was also offered in Zurich, was based on a solid, rigid curriculum of technical and scientific training, which many saw as inadequate to develop true artistic personalities.

In Germany, starting with the University of Berlin, professors were expected to conduct scholarly research (Forschung), communicate it to various audiences, and integrate it into their teaching (Lehre). Between 1870 and 1900, most of the polytechnics and arts and crafts schools, where architecture was taught, were transformed into technical universities, the Technische Hochschulen (Lewis, 2012). Structurally, the German universities were organised as colleges or institutes of professors where research was carried out in institutes organised as the domains of the appointed chairs. These professors were appointed and tenured for life. In typical Teutonic fashion, the chair was given much autonomy and considered to represent the totality of his or her discipline; the employees in the institute were more or less assistants, helping to further elaborate the "world-system" he or she had devised. One effect of this structure was that German professors tended to view themselves as academics first, constantly involved with the life and governance of the university, and members of their discipline only second. Even today, German professors are appointed by the Ministry of Education (not by the universities), and their appointment brings lifelong tenure, which puts them into a very powerful position. Different form the Angle-Saxon model, at German universities, it is expected that professors of architecture maintain a practice on the side and stay involved in the construction of real projects, to ensure that their teaching and research remains fresh and relevant to the profession.

Based on their advanced methods and training, 19th century German-born and -trained architects coming to the US were highly respected. The careers of Adolf Ludwig Cluss, August Gottlieb Schoenborn and Detlef Lienau in the US, for example, illustrate the significant contributions made by the professionally trained German architects to American culture from arriving around 1848. With the outbreak of the German Revolution (1848—1849), liberals were forced into exile to escape political persecution, many immigrating to the US. Like few other architects of their time, they were influential in introducing a range of architectural styles to the US. For example, Lienau's importance to American architecture of the period from 1850 to 1890 lies not in his use of the Second Empire mode per se, nor in his general eclecticism, but in the classical orientation of his entire practice. His work represents a continuing current of conservatism in North American architecture, which for a time was submerged beneath the more dominant picturesque modes of the period, such as the Victorian Gothic and Second Empire styles. Lienau and the others served as a bridge between the neo-classical traditions of design and their re-emergence led in New York by the firm of McKim, Mead & White. Following the Great Chicago Fire of 1871, another wave of German architects arrived in Chicago to participate in the reconstruction of the destroyed city.

The French System
During the 1700s and 1800s in France, prestigious art academies, the École des Beaux-Arts provided training in architecture with an emphasis on the classical orders. The French academies were formally established to ensure a certain level of competence and responsibility, and that there was some cultural value to what architects were doing. Important architects in Europe and the American colonies would travel there to spend time in Paris for an education at École. At this time, architects were not yet required to complete any formal educational programme, and there were no required exams or licensing regulations.

France is a centralised state and in the early 19th century, with the ascent to power of emperor Napoleon Bonaparte (1769–1821), the state started to tightly control all the professions, and the Écoles des Beaux-Arts became state-certified elite schools which were made responsible for the education and degrees in architecture. The Napoleonic reformation of higher education established a defining characteristic of the professions: to be able to enter public service for the state, state-certified academic credentials from one of the elite *grandes écoles* were required. Graduates from the grandes écoles had a much greater status than all the others trained at universities or other institutions, a perception that persists even today. France invented academicised architectural education with the École des Beaux-Arts model and its system of ateliers. The dominant teachers were "patrons", the leaders of the twenty or thirty ateliers into which students were organised and which were the centre of their educational lives. Patrons were invariably practising architects.

The French system created architects who were formally certified by the state for work on government buildings, which offered status and legitimacy. The École des Beaux-Arts, which was established by Louis XIV, was maintained by the state and no admission fees were charged, hence competition for entry was high. In the US, the French model was adopted early: up to the early 20th century, the École had a reputation for leading architectural education. Many students from the US travelled to Paris to study there. The more artistic model promoted by the architecture section of the École des Beaux-Arts emphasised skills in composition above all else. It operated in the tradition of *ateliers* and competitions that fostered emulation among students. A great deal of artistic autonomy was given to students through the system of ateliers and concours, and the importance of the debates triggered by public competitions.

Architectural courses established in the United States and Canada following the Beaux-Arts model often employed French design critics, many of whom became synonymous with the schools. The Beaux-Arts Society of Architects was established in New York in 1894. Although it failed to establish a national school, it did influence architectural education. The Parisian, state-controlled, Beaux-Arts model entailed a five-year programme, primarily in design, but which also included classes in English and French reading, literature and composition. While the school held strong control over the nature of the work, it was up to the students to choose how and when they worked. They progressed from the entrance examination to the award of a diplôme by winning design competitions. In the North American versions, predominantly the design teaching was imported from the École (Lewis, 2012). Despite the decline in popularity of a Beaux-Arts education in the

1950s (caused partially by the popularity of the Bauhaus model), many of its elements are still recognisable today as elements of a French architectural education, such as the atelier or studio model, quick sketch design projects, the "charrette" and "crit" or critique, where a student's work is publicly examined and criticised by others. A "charrette" today is an organised intense brainstorming session that planners and architects use to initiate a project and involve different stakeholders and citizens. Students at the École would be on a deadline to finish their projects, and they would still be working on it when it was due, as they would hop on a cart or wagon (a charrette) and keep working on the project all the way to school.

During the 19th century, the École des Beaux-Arts was much engaged in theorising over typology and composition in architecture. Quartremere de Quincy began to discuss the idea of typology by classification, such as the tent, cave and hut (de Quincy, 1803), while Jean-Nicholas-Louis Durand codified architecture within type (Durand, 1802), exploring how the form fits the building type (e.g., a church, or a museum) and how to answer the pragmatic questions of an architectural programme, touching the ground, and façade openings. Only much later, Adolf Rossi's reclassification of typologies further developed these theories through the type of geometric form and historical archetypes (Rossi, 1966). However, an important part in the curriculum was allocated to architectural composition: students learned how the different parts were subordinated to the overall composition and how the various elements of the programme were distributed hierarchically according to their relative importance or the symmetrical and hierarchical modes of composition (Drexler, 1977; Middleton, 1982).

The Situation in the US
In an attempt to legitimise architecture as a profession, alongside those such as medicine and law, architectural education in the US became increasingly formalised through the 19th and early 20th centuries. In the 18th and early 19th century, before any US school of architecture was established, pupillage was still the common way to become an architect; it was the natural mode of education in the Anglo-American system of professions, adopted from the British system. Pupillage with established practitioners, as it had emerged from the medieval apprenticeship system and building trades, would last around five years and often include some time of attendance at a local arts academy and perhaps foreign travel. Professional education in the UK has always been dominated by practitioners, handing on their knowledge from generation to generation. Competition was a very common means in 19th century Britain for selecting designs, and winning a competition after a few years in pupillage was the rite of passage for a young architect competent to practice by him or herself.[2] Stevens (2014) notes that "the only universities in England in the early 19th century, Oxford and Cambridge, regarded the concept of vocational training as repugnant to the whole idea of a university, and were quite content to leave the new professions (such as architecture) to educate themselves. In the US, a system of state-certified education, which existed from the beginning in France and Germany, was entirely absent."

After the American Civil War (1861—1865), the professions were left without state support, and there was no licensing system for either medicine or law. Equally, no architect needed to be licensed until the State of Illinois introduced the first such legislation in 1897. The professional associations in the US were weak compared to their European counterparts, and they had been less involved in shaping education. Professional education started in the public land-grant universities of the post–Civil War period, driven not by the demands of practitioners, but by the universities themselves. Compared to the practitioner-dominated system of professional education in Britain and the state-dominated system of France, the American professional education system was much more university dominated (Woods, 1999).

In the late 19th century, several prolific German-born architects established their successful practices in the US — including Adolf Ludwig Cluss and August Gottlieb Schoenborn in Washington, D.C., Albert Kahn in Detroit, and Dankmar Adler in Chicago, and Frederick Sauer in Pittsburgh. They became sought-after architects, recognised for their sophisticated design expertise in the construction of churches, villas, public buildings, factories and office buildings. At this time, intellectual life and architectural debate was something that happened outside the universities, in the circles of the leisured aristocracy, the bourgeoisie and the elite members of the professions. Many of these were educated in the elite universities, but very few were employed by them to teach.

Between 1930 and 1940, a large number of Germans fleeing Nazi oppression escaped to the US (over 110,000 people), including well-known intellectuals such as Albert Einstein, Bertolt Brecht, Lion Feuchtwanger, Henry Kissinger, Thomas Mann, Hannah Arendt, Walter Gropius and numerous others who moved into US exile. With the immigration of Northern European and Jewish-German intellectuals into the US schools, the influence and popularity of the French Beaux-Arts model quickly declined. This is remarkable, because during the two world wars, anti-German sentiments grew in opposition to German culture. In 1941, following the attack by Japan on Pearl Harbor, the United States entered the war against Nazi Germany, which led to many restrictions for the American Germans. Following the war, German schools were not reopened, the use of the German language became restricted to the home and the older generation of immigrants, and the German-language press permanently disappeared. In addition, assimilation led to a steady loss of German culture (especially the language), as the Germans were quick to give up their former cultural characteristics to melt into a common American nationality and culture. As such a diverse and heterogeneous group, German Americans assimilated relatively rapidly. In the aftermath of World War II, millions of Germans came as refugees to the United States in the late 1940s and '50s, and once settled, some re-established modest cultural centres in their new hometowns. German Americans who immigrated after World War II were mostly professionals or academics who came for work reasons, and after 1970, the anti-German sentiment aroused earlier by the wars had slowly faded away.

The Knowledge Gap and Purpose of this Study
This study aims to trace the significant, influential and sometimes controversial contributions of German professors of architecture and design at US universities, from the 1930s to today. There has been a considerable German influence on American architecture as well as on architectural education (and vice versa—American culture influenced Germany). Like before, in 1848, intellectuals were again in the 1930s forced into exile to escape political persecution, many immigrating to the US. However, there has been surprisingly little research on the topic of educational influences and only limited scholarship is available. *The Bauhaus and*

America, 1919—1936 (Kentgens-Craig, 2001) focused exclusively on the Bauhaus school, where Margret Kentgens-Craig noted that "the transfer of artistic, intellectual, and pedagogical concepts from one cultural context to another is a process of transformation and integration". The 2012 exhibition *Made in USA: German Architects in New York* offered a limited overview of seven practicing architects from Germany based in New York City. Since then, no broad or updated evaluation of the German progressive design theories and their influence on architectural education in the US has been conducted. The limited available literature deals with various elements in the history of architectural education and the influence of German educators, but does not bring them together into a cohesive history of education in this field, nor does it tackle the influence of changing approaches to that education.

In setting the context for the history of architectural education in the US, the following three comprehensive works offered great insight: Crinson and Lubbock's *Architecture: Art or Profession? Three Hundred Years of Architectural Education in Britain* (1994); Ockman and Williamson's *Architecture School: Three Centuries of Educating Architects in North America* (2012); and Kostof's *The Architect: Chapters in the History of the Profession* (2000).

We must also remember that not all immigrating architects ended up teaching. For example, German-born architects Albert Kahn and Helmut Jahn did not become educators, as their main interest was in their busy practices and the construction of buildings. The work of recognised practicing architects, such as Dankmar Adler, Brigitte Peterhans and Annabelle Selldorf, as well as the German-speaking, Austrian-born practicing architects Rudolph Schindler and Richard Neutra in California, Austrian émigré Frederick Kiesler in New York, and Swiss architect Albert Frey in Palm Springs, has been widely published—but what about the teaching architects, committed to education?

This study focuses on the noble profession of the architectural educators. The German-speaking educators had their upbringing, architectural training and cultural formation in Germany or Austria or Switzerland, and frequently had already successful careers before immigrating to the United States, where they assumed influential teaching positions. After arriving in the US, these educators were able to pursue a second career and influence generations of American architecture students. Thinking about these educators, charismatic architects with strong principles come to mind, like Gropius and Mies, who imported the Bauhaus model of interdisciplinary design education. Does this image still hold up in reality today?

2. The Development of German Architectural Education in the 19th Century

The subject of this book is the history of German influences on architectural education, and in particular on architectural education in the US today. As described earlier, German architectural training has been historically different from the French Beaux-Arts tradition. Military architecture, archaeology, anatomy and geometry were all taught as part of the formal architectural education at the Academy of Berlin since 1696, where architecture was combined with engineering (in contrast to the artistic curricula of France and Italy, where architecture was seen as an autonomous art form).

Our current method of architects receiving their training at an institution that conducts systematic research and scholarship in a wide variety of intellectual areas is of quite recent date. After the victory in the Franco-Prussian War and the unification of Germany (1871), Berlin was emerging as a thriving, fast-growing and powerful European capital, alongside Paris, London and Vienna. The brothers Alexander and Wilhelm von Humboldt in Berlin were the first to lay the groundwork for the "true purpose and principles of the modern university" where teaching and research was recognised as of equal importance, influencing and cross-fertilising each other. The University of Berlin, founded in 1810 (and later renamed Humboldt University), spearheaded what is called the "modern" university. The Humboldt brothers encouraged the University of Berlin to operate according to scientific (as opposed to market-driven) principles, including "curiosity and freedom of research". They convinced the king of Prussia to build a modern university in Berlin based on Fichte and Schleiermacher's liberal ideas (Anderson, 2004). Wilhelm was the older brother of Alexander von Humboldt, the influential scientist-adventurer and natural geographer whom Charles Darwin called "one of the greatest men the world has ever produced". The Humboldt brothers and Darwin laid the foundation for the scientific formulation of numerous fields, including ecology. Today's environmentalists develop thoughts expressed by them when they described life as a process emerging from interactions between living beings and their surroundings.

Since the Middle Ages and the Enlightenment, scholarly activities had only been loosely tied to universities and most scholarship was conducted separate from them. Prior to the foundation of the University of Berlin, research in Europe had been conceived of as a strictly private undertaking, conducted only by talented individuals with the private financial means to do so. The concept of the new Humboldtian University was very different from all previous institutions: learning was not just about conveying current knowledge; it was also about generating new knowledge and watching that process of generation in action. It was about being part of a community of knowledge generation. The Humboldt brothers strongly argued that research should play a central role in any modern university — and that teaching students how to think, be responsible and communicate effectively should be accomplished through the integration of research and teaching. One of the key goals of the modern university was to develop scientific inquiry and critical thinking, and specifically to use scientific reasoning to interpret the world. It included the use of evidence-based reasoning and rational thought as well as curiosity and self-reflection. This ideal led to modern public universities that were more than just teaching institutions, based on the principle that the government supports the modern universities as places of great scholarship where, in return, both students and society as a whole would benefit in the long run.

However, the Humboldtian educational model did not extent to the technical fields—one of the reasons why architecture education in Germany never rose to a high level of academic standing (compared to France or Italy). The study of architecture was limited to the new Technische Hochschulen, polytechnics, or art academies. It was this Humboldtian model of research and teaching that was finally adopted by the US universities. As Stevens (2014) notes,

> "the notion that research was a fundamental mission of a university did not
> appear until the importation of the German model in the latter part of the
> 19th century. However, several important changes were made to the model

as it crossed the Atlantic. Firstly, the chair-institute structure was dropped in favour of a departmental structure, replacing the German autocratic polymath closely directing the research of a group of assistants with a more egalitarian system, in which the departmental chair handled administration and finance for a group of academics who more or less set their own intellectual agenda. Secondly, where the Germans had left applied research to industry or the lower-status polytechnics, the Americans brought it into the universities. Thirdly, the academics at these new universities tended to see their primary loyalty and milieu as that of their discipline or profession, not to the university, which meant the reverse of the German model." (Stevens, 2014)

Germany, due to the federal structure of the German Empire, has never been a homogeneous country, and there are significant and subtle differences between the various regions, including the liberal traditions in the arts in places like Munich and Dresden. Both cities were always very different from Berlin. Germany was culturally and politically diverse, and the local artistic traditions influenced how architects responded to political and social change. Until World War II, Dresden and Munich were the centres of Baroque art and retained a high degree of political autonomy from Berlin; by 1898, Munich was also the burgeoise capital of the Jugendstil movement, a cosmopolitan art of design that appealed to the educated middle class. Berlin was the opposite from Munich or Dresden: a workers's city, with dense perimeter blocks and cramped courtyards that lacked daylight. In 1910, the art and architectural critic Karl Scheffler memorably described Berlin as a city "condemned forever to becoming but never actually to be": a city in perpetual and restless flux, ever-transfiguring itself into something new. Scheffler wryly observed that Berlin is not a city that can simply be, but a work in progress, "eine Stadt, verdammt dazu, ewig zu werden, niemals zu sein."

How Did the German Model Evolve?
The Baroque period (1600—1720) was one of the most fertile times in German literature, music and architecture. The German Baroque architects, however, did not care much for pursuing education at the academies; they trained apprentices in their craft directly through hands-on practice on projects on site, leaving formal architectural education to the rationalising neoclassicists. Consequently, the 19th-century education of architects was mainly led by the classicistic architects, including Leo von Klenze, Friedrich Gaertner, Karl Friedrich Schinkel und Gottfried Semper (Zucker, 1942). In 1799, the Department of Architecture at the Academy of Berlin was separated from the rest of the university and set up as the Preussische Bauakademie. It was a specialised school for educating architects, housed since 1836 in its own building, designed by Schinkel, in the centre of Berlin (see Image 1). Of such national importance was the education of architects that the Bauakademie in Berlin was specifically founded as a new model of higher education for the art of building and to train master builders. The reason was that the discrepancy between practical needs and architectural expression was much greater in the 19th century than it had been one hundred years before. "Civil architecture" emerged as an important field, fuelled by the Industrial Revolution and the rapid development and growth of cities. As part of this educational model, Schinkel introduced the idea of the architectural workshop (called *"Meisterklasse"*); these workshops were mostly conducted within the private offices of leading architects (the *"Meister"*), where students were considered apprentices.

Until then, the key 19th-century concept was historicism and eclecticism, concerned with styles and the idea of "the spirit of the age" as form giver. The German educational system emphasised architectural science and construction. Since 1870, almost all architectural education in Germany was based in universities. It involved two, two-year courses sandwiched around three years under government employment, as inspector or clerk on a government building, which gave eligibility for a state diploma. Described as "long, rigid and technical, with little opportunity for individual freedom or originality in design", its influence can be seen in the debates about architecture as a science that followed and in the influence German émigrés had on US architectural education in the 1930s (Ockman and Williamson, 2012).

When engineering sciences and the proper planning of cities had become increasingly important due to rapid urban growth and the Industrial Revolution, the Technische Hochschule was founded in 1871 as a new type of institution. Architectural education was now taught at technical universities and this new type of institution educated 90 percent of German architects. It was here where the architects were educated who later would enter the civil service of the German states and the German Reich. There was dry, rational, scientific teaching with a technical emphasis on structures and construction, but with little focus on the artistic component in the curriculum (in contrast to the artistic methods carried out in Paris at the École des Beaux-Arts led by Eugene Viollet-le-Duc; and at the École Polytechnique led by Jean-Nicholas-Louis Durand). Gottfried Semper's educational influence at this time cannot be overestimated. He was a professor at the Academy in Dresden and developed theories still relevant today. In 1852, he published the seminal manifesto *Der Stil in den technischen und tektonischen Kuensten*, emphasising the connection between the machine and its products, and writing about the influence of material selection and techniques upon the final form. Long before functionalism, Semper recognised its principles and described the functional needs of buildings as form giver, shaping the resulting design). Semper moulded a generation of students who became recognised architects at the beginning of the 20th century, including Alfred Messel, Ludwig Hoffmann, Friedrich von Thiersch and Paul Wallot (Froehlich, 1974; Tschanz, 2015). [3]

The Bund Deutscher Architekten (BDA, the Association of German Architects) was founded in 1903 to protect the interests of freelance architects against real estate speculators and building contractors, and to promote the quality of architecture. The association created the member title "Freier Architekt BDA." The title means for clients that they can be sure their architect works independently and is free of interests of commercial nature, which otherwise could lead to counteracting the interests of the client (the architect's fee is usually a percentage of the construction costs, which could be seen as a reason why the architect might not be interested in cost-savings).

Image 1: The Preussische Bauakademie in Berlin,
drawing by K.F. Schinkel, 1831—1836; a specialised school for the
education of architects

The Emergence of Modern Architecture in Amsterdam, Chicago, Paris, Moscow and Vienna

It is important to note that the modern movement was not exclusively a German movement and that early modern buildings in other countries preceded the work of the German architects. The avant-garde emerged aside new technical possibilities and construction processes, as expressed in the innovative work of French architect Auguste Perret (1874—1954), the high-rise towers in Chicago by architects Louis Sullivan (1856—1924) or John W. Root (1850—1891), and through the ambitious urban planning projects by Charles Garnier (1825—1898), Ebenezer Howard (1850—1928), Hendrik P. Berlage (1856—1934), Michel de Klerk (1884—1923), and others. In the arts, the Russian movements of *Suprematism and Constructivism* (with protagonists including El Lissitzky, Malevich and Tatlin) and the Dutch movements of *Neo-Plasticism and De Stijl* (with protagonists, including Van Doesburg, Mondrian and Vantongerloo) were ahead and influential for the events that would follow in German architecture. Pre-1914, architects at the forefront of the modern movement in Europe included Dutch architects Hendrik Berlage, Gerrit Rietveld (1888—1964), and Jacobus J. P. Oud (1890—1963); Austrian architects Otto Wagner (1841—1918), Joseph M. Olbrich (1867—1908), both of the Vienna Secession, and Adolf Loos (1870—1933); Swiss architect Le Corbusier (1887—1965); and Scottish architect Charles Rennie Macintosh (1868—1928). This means that by 1914, there were already numerous precedents of European modern architecture around—and these were known to Gropius, Mies and the others.

The functional clarity of the Kuenstlerkolonie Mathildenhoehe, an artists' colony in Darmstadt (1899—1914), designed by architects Peter Behrens and Josef Maria Olbrich, laid the basis of modern architecture in Germany. Educationally, the influential teaching by Austrian architects Otto Wagner and Adolf Loos in Vienna was immensely relevant. In 1896, Otto Wagner's historic manifesto *Moderne Architektur* [Modern Architecture] shocked the European architectural community with its impassioned plea for an end to eclecticism and for a "modern" style suited to contemporary needs and ideals, utilising the nascent constructional technologies and materials.

Beside Amsterdam and Berlin, the city of Vienna emerged in Europe as a place of progressive architecture and heated debate. There were opposing views on the urban future of the city: on one hand, the picturesque and romantic theories of town planning as proposed by Austrian city planner and painter Camillo Sitte (1843-1903), put forward in his influential book *City Planning According to Artistic Principles* (*Der Städtebau nach seinen künstlerischen Grundsätzen*, 1889). Sitte traveled extensively to Italy, seeking to identify the factors that made certain towns feel "warm and welcoming". Modernists rejected his romantic ideas and Le Corbusier, in particular, is known for the dismissals of Sitte's work. On the other hand, the classical-rational urbanism point of view as it was proposed by Otto Wagner, who was strongly influenced by the Parisian model of Baron Haussmann—who was chosen by Emperor Napoleon III to carry out a massive urban renewal programme of new boulevards, parks and public works. From 1958 to 1870, the city of Paris had created wide boulevards through the old labyrinthine city, with the intent of modernising traffic and waste management, as well as enabling public health programmes and the greater social control of the population.

We can assume that most of the European architectural publications and discussions found their way quickly across the Atlantic through English translations by American students soon after their first appearance in Europe. For example, Rudolf Redtenbacher's 1883 classic *Architektonik der Modernen Baukunst* was already translated into English in the following year by Nathan Ricker in Chicago and disseminated as essential reading to his students at the University of Illinois. A periodical published in Chicago, the *Building Budget*, was dedicated to disseminating the latest news in European architecture in North America; it promoted European culture by translating into English excerpts from French and German authors, for instance, from Viollet-le-Duc and August Thiersch.

3. Modest Beginnings: The First US Departments and Curricula of Architecture

In the 19th century, American architects were either trained as apprentices through pupillage or pursued studies abroad. In 1857, a group of prominent architects launched the American Institute of Architects (AIA) to "promote the scientific and practical perfection of its members" and "elevate the standing of the profession" (AIA). But the nation was on the brink of the Civil War and, after years of economic prosperity, America plunged into depression in the Panic of 1857.

The profession's growing awareness of the need for a professional architecture school was first evidenced by the report of the Committee on Education at the annual convention of the AIA in 1867. Until 1868 there were no architectural schools in the United States, although American statesman Thomas Jefferson had proposed one at the University of Virginia in 1814. Kruty (2004) notes that "in the US, public institutions of higher education had taken form slowly, following Jefferson's concept of a public university for each state—a concept exemplified by Jefferson's architectural masterpiece, the University of Virginia, which opened in the mid-1820s." Jefferson had learned about architecture through books by Renaissance masters like Andrea Palladio and Giacomo da Vignola.

As mentioned earlier, formal architectural education in the US had its modest beginnings in 1868 in the creation of new departments of architecture at the Massachusetts Institute of Technology (MIT; 1868), Cornell University (1871), the Illinois Industrial University (now: the University of Illinois at Urbana—Chapmpaign; 1873), and Columbia University (1881). To be precise, the first school of architecture in the US was founded at the Polytechnic College of Pennsylvania already in 1861; this became the first collegiate school of architecture in the US, but it was only short lived and had to close in 1885 due to a lack of interest by students. While it post-dates the course at the Polytechnic College of Pennsylvania, the school usually recognised as the first school of architecture in the US was established at MIT in 1868 based on the Beaux-Arts model. It was run by William Robert Ware, who had attended an atelier led by the first American student to graduate from the École des Beaux-Arts in Paris, Richard Morris Hunt.

The first architectural curriculum in the country had only recently been established at MIT in 1868, followed by the University of Illinois curriculum in 1870. Already in 1865, MIT had recognised the need for formal professional training in architecture and appointed William Ware for the specific purpose of establishing the first such curriculum. Ware spent a year in Europe preparing the programme and in October 1868 the MIT architecture department opened with four students in the four-year course. Around the same time, the Illinois Industrial University also realised the need for formal professional training in architecture, and it presented this idea to its trustees in 1867.

This is where the formal architectural education of architects in the US commenced in 1868. Prior to these three initiatives to formalise architectural education, there was no academic instructional method available for studying architecture in the US.

Architects in America in the 18th and 19th centuries were taught through apprenticeship with other architects, not by instructors at institutions of higher learning. Both models, the German and the French/Franco-Italian institutional model, were imported to the US at the end of the 19th century, around the same time. It is no coincidence that the first architecture schools were in new universities. These institutions were the first to offer a programme in architecture, and they introduced a four-year architecture curriculum. The University of Illinois drew its inspiration from German architectural education and the system as it was taught at the Bauakademie in Berlin. It followed the rigidly structured, thorough German curriculum with an emphasis on technical and structural studies, while MIT adopted the traditional atelier system of the French École des Beaux-Arts.

With over one hundred schools of architecture today, the expansion in the number of architects in the US has been driven by the considerable increase in the number of universities offering architectural programmes. Today, in the United States and Canada alone, there are more than 140 professional degree programmes in architecture, with over 6,000 faculty educating more than 40,000 students.

Nathan Ricker in Illinois: Educator and Pioneer

The first student in the programme at the Illinois Industrial University, Nathan Clifford Ricker (1843—1924), arrived in Urbana in 1870. One of his teachers was Harold Hansen, a Swedish architect who had studied for two years at the Preussische Bauakademie in Berlin. Ricker found Hansen a stimulating mentor, and he responded well to the practical and rigorous course of instruction based on the German model. Ricker graduated in March 1873, making him the first person to receive a formal degree in architecture in the United States. Soon after this, MIT and Cornell University celebrated their first graduates in June 1873. Following his graduation, Ricker was offered a teaching position at the university. The historical archives of the University of Illinois note that

> "as a condition of his appointment, the university's regent insisted that Ricker spend six months in Europe. There he attended the Vienna Exposition of 1873 and visited a Russian carpentry shop. His most impressive experience, however, must have been his tour as a special student at the Bauakademie in Berlin. Ricker chose the Bauakademie over the École des Beaux-Arts in Paris because he considered the quality of its programme and pedagogy superior to the individualistic and competitive French system. The influences of Ricker's travel abroad reverberated throughout his career."

Influenced by the study of the German model that he was able to observe in Berlin, Ricker created the new department and its curriculum at Illinois. He returned to the University of Illinois in 1873 to take up his duties as head of the new Department of Architecture, which had an average programme enrolment of eight students during its first decade. Until 1885, Ricker continued to teach all courses in architecture himself and produced his own texts when those available proved unsuitable. Ricker firmly believed that research was essential to the education of an architect. In 1880 he translated the first of more than thirty German books on architecture into English—an undertaking that extended over forty years.

Kruty (2004) describes Ricker's practical curriculum as follows: "Ricker came to believe that an architect should, first and foremost, be a safe and economical builder, and, second, a capable businessman. Lastly, he should be a designer of pleasing forms." In 1899, Ricker explained his pedagogical goal in the *Inland Architect* magazine as creating "builders of good architecture," which he explained, "must largely consist of good and honest construction, obtaining the best results possible for the means available for the purpose, employing all improvements in the system of construction and materials, and in the protection of the life and health of inmates of the buildings." Regarding the importance of aesthetics in design, he noted, "The highest perfection of style is demanded by comparatively few buildings." The entire method was derived from Ricker's personal values and his exposure to the Germanic principles, as taught by Hansen and observed at the Bauakademie. Ricker's method was diametrically opposed to the more popular French system with its strong emphasis on design, representation and rendering, a system followed by the majority of new American architecture schools created in the following decades. Ricker believed that students fell into two major categories: those with design ability and those with the technical ability for structural analysis and synthesis.

Nathan Ricker was a dedicated professor and architect; he served the University of Illinois for forty-five years (from 1872 to 1917), creating a department and curriculum that influenced generations of American architects. He chaired the Department of Architecture from 1873 to 1910 as the first US chair of a department of architecture. Recognising that architects needed to have more technical knowledge, he also established the first US curriculum in architectural engineering in 1890. From 1878 to 1905, he served as dean of the new College of Engineering while continuing to serve as the head of the Department of Architecture. He also served as university campus architect, designing four major buildings. He introduced a four-year curriculum in architectural engineering, which arose from his close involvement with Dankmar Adler and other Chicago architects and engineers responsible for the first steel-skeleton high-rise buildings.

The basic idea of these early programmes was that architecture reproduces itself through a formal system of education which is properly located in universities. The university would credential graduates, formally certifying them as sufficiently competent, and rely on professional proxies to monitor the quality of the educational programmes. After establishing the first formal architectural education, Ricker didn't stop there. Kruty notes that "having set the standards for a professional architectural education in America, Ricker was greatly concerned about raising the general level of professional competence in architecture. He joined forces with Dankmar Adler to promote a state law to license architects." (1997; 2004). Ricker was also actively developing new legislation for licensing to protect the profession of architecture, following the model of medicine and law. In 1897, he and Dankmar Adler lobbied to move the Architectural Registration Act of Illinois through the state legislature; the first Architect's Registration Board exam was introduced in 1898. Illinois was the first state in the US to adopt a licensing law for architects. Other states followed slowly over the next fifty years, and today, a professional license is required of all architects who practice in the US. Standards for licensing are regulated by the National Council of Architectural Registration Boards (NCARB).

Goddard (2019) notes that discussions about the status of the profession, the professionalisation of architecture, and the protection of title for the practice of architecture were long-running initiatives: architecture was not recognised as a distinct profession until the establishment of the Royal Institute of British Architects (RIBA) in 1834 and the AIA in 1857. These were manifestations of recognition driven by the desire of architects to be seen as professionals alongside doctors and lawyers, with appropriate safeguards against pretenders, and closely tied to the wish for controlling educational standards. The RIBA and AIA sought to represent the interests of the profession and to control what constituted an appropriate architectural education and how architecture should be taught (including testing for competency and acceptability for admission to the profession). Hundred years ago, the emphasis was on moving architectural education into universities, with properly regulated courses, seeking to match the perceived status of lawyers and doctors.

This means that the rise in credentialed architectural education in the US began in 1898 with the introduction of the licensing regulation for architects in Illinois (as spearheaded by Nathan Ricker and Dankmar Adler), and soon other states followed. Ricker and Adler applauded professional institutions taking action to set up a more formalised licensing system. For Ricker, the licensing law was a personal vindication of his life's work to establish what was perhaps the country's most thorough and rigorous course of architectural education. In 1901, he proudly reported, "The Board has had every opportunity to see the beneficent results of the establishment of the School of Architecture at the University of Illinois, which was one of the earliest, and the forerunner in making architecture a part of university education, an example that has been followed by many other states." (Ricker, as cited in Laing, 1973, and Kruty, 1997). To ensure a degree of parity and reciprocal arrangements between the states, the NCARB was established in 1919.

The Rise of American Cities in the Late 19th and Early 20th Century

By 1920, the urban population in the US became larger than the rural population. Urbanisation occurred rapidly in the second half of the 19th century for a number of reasons. Many Americans moved to the cities, leaving behind the declining prospects of agriculture in the hope of better wages in industrial labour. The new technologies of the time led to a massive leap in industrialisation, requiring large numbers of factory workers. New electric lights and machinery allowed factories to run twenty-four hours every day, requiring the workers to live close to the factories. Furthermore, immigrants from Europe arrived in large numbers: the number of immigrants peaked between 1900 and 1910, when over nine million people arrived in the US. Many of them settled close to employment opportunities and found work in the cities where they first arrived. Philadelphia, Boston and New York experienced an explosion in urban population. These cities developed their own unique characters based on the core industry that spurred their growth: in Pittsburgh, it was steel; in Chicago, it was meat packing; in New York, the garment and financial industries dominated; and in Detroit, by the mid-20th century, it was the automobile industry. This led to a rise in ethnic enclaves within the larger city, for example, Little Italy, Chinatown and other communities developed in which immigrant groups could find everything to remind them of home, from local language newspapers to ethnic food stores.

The surveying grid established by the Land Ordinance in 1785 organised the country for rapid expansion towards the West, with little concession to topography. It was set up as a standardised system whereby settlers could purchase title to farmland in the undeveloped west. The Ordinance of 1785 provided for the scientific surveying of the territory's lands and for a systematic subdivision. Land was subdivided according to a rectangular grid system; the basic unit of land grant was the township, which was a square area measuring six miles on each side. This law was an excellent way to organise the sale of western land that generated a constant revenue for the government. This surveying grid still defines much of the United States today. The city of Chicago emerged as the centre of a new architecture, with its main protagonists Daniel Burnham, Louis Sullivan and Frank Lloyd Wright. The architecture of Chicago was always very different from New York. Alexander Eisenschmidt notes in "Chicagoism" (2018) that

> "while in the early 19th century, Chicago was only a frontier village with a few settlers, it had materialised by 1870 as one of the largest markets in the world, supported by an unparalleled railroad junction and a harbor that connected the center of the US with the rest of the Western world and beyond. By 1890, its population had passed the one-million mark, and the city sprawled over more than 180 square miles, making it the largest urban footprint in North America. What made all of this possible was the implementation of the gridiron by James Thompson in 1830 on land south of the Chicago River.

> The grid laid the foundation, both figuratively and literally, for Chicago's rise as the archetypal metropolis. (...) The nonhierarchical avenues and streets run straight through the town, into the prairie, and continue their way across the US."

Even a disastrous event like the infamous Great Chicago Fire of 1871 was turned into an opportunity, allowing the city a new urban beginning and to continue its relentless expansion with new opportunities for renewal. The fire provided early modern architects the sites and projects to experiment with steel-frame construction and make their mark. Chicago was laid out in a rectangular grid with large urban blocks. On Chicago's famous urban grid, Eisenschmidt comments that "with the regulating spaces of the grid newly exposed and the rubble pushed into the lake to expand Chicago eastward, massive buildings began to emerge that soon lined entire blocks of the downtown grid turned vertical. The new building code, combining the advances in fireproof iron- and steel-frame construction with inventions such as Otis's elevator, contributed to remaking the city as a built experiment." (2018) The safety elevator with electric motors, originally designed by Elisha Otis in 1852, was a pivotal advancement for tall buildings which enabled it to carry passengers comfortably beyond 20 stories – heights unreachable by older elevator models that used steam or hydraulics. Eisenschmidt identifies the main drivers as a commitment to commercial progress, openness to technological experimentation, and a willingness to reinvent itself, providing the ground for structural experimentation and off-site prefabrication methods.

William LeBaron Jenney (1832—1907) was an engineer and architect who designed most of Chicago's first skyscrapers. His office became a training ground for the next generation of tall building architects, including Holabird & Roche, Adler & Sullivan, and others. The Great Chicago Fire created an opportunity for many immigrating architects as the city was rebuilding in earnest but in 1871 had only sixty architects in town. The reconstruction efforts lasted the following two decades and attracted a large number of architects to come to booming Chicago, including the German architects Paul Huber and his son Julius H. Huber (the founder of the Illinois Society of Architects in 1897), Edmund Krause, Frommann & Jensen, George & Cornelius Rapp, Julius Ender, and numerous others. Chicago had soon the reputation of being the most modern and advanced city in the world with an elevated modern transport system: the city built its first elevated tracks in 1892 in connection with the World's Columbian Exposition to help move its booming population around the city. The elevated railway was a rapid transit system built by various private companies between 1892 and 1931. In addition, new building technologies—including skeletal steel framing and elevators that could reach 10 or more stories—gave developers, architects and engineers the tools to quickly build in service of a booming population and economy. The architect Adolf Loos visited Chicago in 1893, Max Weber in 1904 and Eliel Saarinen in 1922, all in order to see what this modern reality was like, calling Chicago the "prototypical American city" (Weber).

In the meantime, while American cities along the East-Coast grew rapidly, new cities were founded in the West. Greater Los Angeles, for example, has become famous for its sprawl. Today, it is the second-largest urban region in the US, behind the New York metropolitan area. Throughout the 20th century, it was one of the fastest-growing regions in the US, although growth has slowed since 2000. During the 20th century, the population of Greater

Los Angeles experienced an enormous growth: in 1900, there were only 250,000 people; by 1920, this number had already grown to 1.150,000; and by 1950, Greater Los Angeles had reached almost 5 million population. As of the 2010 US Census, the Los Angeles metropolitan area had a population of almost 13 million residents, while the larger metropolitan region's population is over 18.7 million people (2015 data).

4. Other German Influences

There has been almost two centuries of significant cultural exchange between Germany and the United States in the field of architecture and architectural education, which commenced around 1850, long before the 1930s introduction of modern architecture to the US by Gropius and Mies van der Rohe. The previous chapter described the adaptation of the German model by Nathan Ricker and others, and there are plenty of other areas where German cultural influence is visible. For example, the prominent architect and civil engineer Dankmar Adler practiced in a fifteen-year partnership in Chicago with Louis H. Sullivan (a partnership that lasted from 1883 to 1898), as Adler & Sullivan. Together they designed some of the first steel high-rise towers in the US. This partnership succeeded through combining the architectural design skills of one partner with the entrepreneurial and social skills of another: one mainly designed (Sullivan), while the other courted the wealthy to bring in commissions (Adler). During their long and distinguished career, their firm also employed other German immigrant architects who would later become well known themselves, including Hermann Gaul (1869–1949). However, their most famous draftsman was Frank Lloyd Wright (1867–1959). The ambitious young architect Frank Lloyd Wright joined the firm Adler & Sullivan in 1888 and worked there for five years, before he went on to become one of the most influential American architects. Frank Lloyd Wright later acknowledged the German influences on his own philosophy, including his time with Dankmar Adler and Louis Sullivan, and the geometry of Froebel blocks.

The Froebel blocks were popular wood block toys, educational play material for children originally designed by the educational theorist Friedrich Wilhelm August Froebel in 1837. Froebel laid the foundation for modern education based upon the unique attributes and capabilities of children. German kindergartens used the toys to nurture the child's creative three-dimensional instinct and understanding of spatial relationships, abstract geometries and construction. The children can use the sets to explore systems of tectonic order. Frank Lloyd Wright was given a set of Froebel blocks at about age nine, and in his biography, he cites them as an important influence, explaining that he learned the geometry of architecture in kindergarten play: "for several years I sat at the little table-top ruled by lines about four inches apart each way making four-inch squares; and, among other things, played upon these unit-lines with the square (cube), the circle (sphere) and the triangle (tetrahedron)—these were smooth maple-wood blocks. All are in my fingers to this day" (Alofsin, 1993; see Image 2).

More recently, there has been extensive scholarship on the influence of the Froebel blocks on architects and the relationship of toys to 20th century architectural education (MacCormack, 1974; Rubin, 1989; Lerner, 2005; Ginoulhiac, 2013). Ginoulhiac notes that "Froebel's architectural toys represented a particular part of a materialistic culture that contains educational, artistic and ideological values" (2013). Other prominent people educated with the Froebel blocks who noted them as an important influence in their childhood include Josef Albers, Paul Klee, Albert Einstein, Charles Eames and Richard Buckminster Fuller.[4]

Image 2: The German Froebel blocks used in early childhood education

Johannes Itten was a Swiss painter and teacher at the Bauhaus school. His *Vorkurs*, a foundation course developed at the Bauhaus in the 1920s, had numerous similarities to Froebel's pedagogy: for both, students learned by doing, and play was considered key to important discovery, gaining knowledge of materials and the discovery of basic shapes. In the 1940s, a version of the Bauhaus *Vorkurs* re-emerged under Gropius's leadership at Harvard University's Graduate School of Design (GSD; there called "Design Fundamentals") as a versatile, enduring prototype for combining art, design and architectural studio education (Lerner, 2005). Itten was an extraordinary pedagogue, and his methods had a liberating effect on his students. He was the first to recognise the importance of the sub-conscious in creative work and the first to introduce into his Vorkurs compositions using different materials: wood, glass, metal, fabric or simply things available in scrapheaps.

The ideals of the Bauhaus school shaped more than just design and architecture around the world. Its guiding principles also transformed design teaching. Not limited to the personalities of the generation of 1930s immigrants Walter Gropius, who led the architecture school at Harvard University in Cambridge; Ludwig Mies van der Rohe, who led the architecture school at the IIT in Chicago; and Erich Mendelsohn, who lived from 1945 to 1953 in San Francisco, teaching at UC Berkeley, after spending some years in Palestine and New York, there has been a constant flow of eminent German educators working at schools of architecture in the US. Frequently, they have shaped the innovative development of these schools' curricula and effected significant impact on the architectural curriculum. Some of these schools operated according to the pedagogical principles of the seminal Bauhaus, a legacy which had a lasting influence on the American system of art and design schools. After the Bauhaus's final closing in 1933 in Berlin, several of its protagonists moved to the United States. Besides Gropius and Mies, who both arrived in the US in 1937, other Bauhaus teachers followed, including the Hungarian-born architect Marcel Breuer, the artists Josef and Anni Albers, and the Hungarian photographer and designer László Moholy-Nagy. Their influence on US schools can still be felt today in educational concepts and school curricula.

5. The Legacy of Gropius and Mies and the Influential Bauhaus Methods

The legacy and impact of Walter Gropius (1883–1969) and Mies van der Rohe (1886–1969) as influential teachers and pioneers of new educational models in the US has been previously documented by scholars including Wick, Kentgens-Craig, Schulze, Neumeyer, Lambert and Pearlman, amongst others. An extremely rich body of scholarship on the Bauhaus is available, and the work of Gropius and Mies has already been well discussed. Therefore, this study looks at their work as educators, which formed the basis of modern architectural education programmes of the 20th century, not only in the US but worldwide; their influence changed the pedagogical methods and approaches of others. The two Bauhaus architects flourished after leaving Germany: in the US, the principles and ideals of the Bauhaus received the freedom to further evolve in the 1940s and '50s, particularly at the IIT in Illinois; at Harvard in Cambridge, Massachusetts; and Black Mountain College in North Carolina, but also at design schools in Michigan and New York.

At just thirty-six years of age, architect Walter Gropius was appointed in 1919 as professor at the Weimar Academy of Fine Arts, which gave him the opportunity to relaunch the school as the newly created Staatliches Bauhaus. Right from the beginning, Gropius knew exactly where he wanted to take the new school. Much of his vision had to do with a newly defined role for the architect in society, centred on working collaboratively and using the latest construction technology. He was an ideas man and his aim was nothing less than a *Gesamtkunstwerk*. A *Gesamtkunstwerk* is a total work of art that unites and synthesises various elements, as defined earlier by musician Richard Wagner. The ideal was a total work of art, in which all the elements would be integrated and nothing was left to chance; all elements would be directed towards the same single, unified and harmonious ensemble. Gropius's concept was that of a new school integrating all art forms and disciplines into architecture. In the 1919 *Bauhaus Manifesto*, Gropius wrote: "Let us strive for, conceive, and create the new building of the future that will unite every discipline, architecture and sculpture and painting."

This interdisciplinary approach sought to bring the fine arts together with the applied science of architecture, with the spotlight on the building itself as the goal of all art. Gropius noted, "The goal of the Bauhaus is not a style, system, dogma, canon, recipe or fashion. It will live as long as it does not depend on form but continues to seek behind changing forms the fluidity of life itself" (Gropius, 1919).

Using radical pedagogy, open debate and a "thinking through making" ethos, the Bauhaus challenged and redefined the way art, design and architecture were taught, moving towards a more collaborative and interdisciplinary mode of operation, with a hands-on approach in workshops and incorporating technological innovation and mass production techniques into the syllabus. Presentations of design projects were held in the format of "open juries" accompanied by public debate—a format that is still practiced at most schools today. The emphasis was on functionalism and the abstract aesthetic of mass production; efficiency and simplicity; ethical, affordable design, and decent housing for all—topics that remain relevant today.

Gropius called for a return to basic shapes and simple geometries, simplicity in replication, and the optimal use of space, material, time and money. While this is widely accepted today, it was a ground-breaking credo at the time. Mulke notes that "today, these principles are practically universal in product development for everything from the smartphone to the modern office building" (2018). After the long historicistic 19th-century battle of the "styles" and Adolf Loos's provocative, critical essay "Ornament und Verbrechen" [Ornament and Crime] (1910), the eclectic and hollow historicism had finally run out of steam. Loos criticised the application of ornamentation in useful objects and utilitarian buildings—it was a refreshing view and "sign of spiritual strength" (Loos) which helped to lay the groundwork for and define the ideology of modern architecture. Loos famously denounced building ornament as immoral.

The principles of functional design were first articulated by German architects Gottfried Semper (1803–1879) and Peter Behrens (1868–1940). Semper, in his pivotal book in 1861, articulated a new understanding of materials and tectonic order, an approach that was later promoted by Peter Behrens. Both were an immense influence on Gropius's and Mies's thinking. Semper, whose credo was "if it is practical, it is beautiful", taught at the University of Dresden and wrote extensively about the origins of architecture. Especially his books *Die vier Elemente der Baukunst* [The Four Elements of Architecture] (1851) and *Wissenschaft, Industrie und Kunst* [Science, Industry and Art] (1852) were widely influential and would ultimately provide the groundwork for his most regarded publication, *Der Stil in den technischen und tektonischen Künsten oder Praktische Ästhetik*, which was published in two volumes in 1861 and 1863. Here, he argues ahead of his time, that the three factors of material, technique and theory needed all to come together in balance to produce the Gestalt of the new building or product.

Much of the principles of functionalism goes back to Semper's early observations of the relationship between material and technique, and the correlation of function and form, describing how function generates shape and plan independently from ornament (paving the way for Sullivan's "form follows function" credo). The phrase "form follows function" was coined only much later by Louis H. Sullivan in his 1896 essay "The Tall Office Building Artistically Considered." Frank Lloyd Wright, Adler & Sullivan's assistant at one time, also adopted the principle. The debate on just how the principle is to be applied, as well as the validity on any interpretation, dominated much of 20th century architectural discussion.

Around 1900, the closely related concepts of functionalism and "Neue Sachlichkeit" were shaped by Peter Behrens, the influential architect and industrial designer important to the Jugendstil and early modernist movement. The shared idea promoted by Semper, Behrens and Sullivan was that a building's exterior design should primarily reflect its different interior functions. Industrial designers later adopted this design principle, insisting that the shape of an object or device should primarily and honestly relate to and express its intended function or purpose.

The question of what should generate architectural form, and the form's relationship to the architectural concept, is of course still today a valid one which has occupied architects for centuries and appears to remain unresolved. Theorist and architect Bernard Tschumi asked in 2015, "Is it the form that generates a concept, or the concept that generates a form?" An essential part of the history of architecture in the last 150 years is the philosophical dispute about how far function should determine form and form should determine function, and it is probably around this question that the differences between architects of the late 19th century and the modernists are best understood. Architecture is different from a functionless artefact, such as a sculpture. Functionality (purpose, utility, practicality) is a necessary part of architecture. Adolf Loos's functionalism, as implied in his claim in "Ornament and Crime", is ethically as well as architecturally grounded.

While some architectural theory remains focused on Vitruvius's three elements and the relationship between form and function, more recent debate about the relationship between architecture and ethics has refocused the discussion. Louis Sullivan, the architect responsible for developing the typology of the late 19th century high-rise tower, argued against architectural features unrelated to the purpose of a building. "Form follows function" was seen by some as an inviolable principle offering unique design solutions. For Sullivan, the principle was metaphysically grounded—a kind of law of nature that was normative.

Peter Behrens was one of the early leaders of architectural reform and instrumental for the transition from Art Nouveau to the rationalism of the Bauhaus period. He worked in numerous design disciplines and is often called the pioneer of modern industrial design. After he had accepted smaller design projects for the German energy company AEG, he was appointed to the company's Artistic Advisory Board in 1907. In the following years he worked for AEG in almost all disciplines of design, from graphic design works such as advertising brochures to product designs for household appliances to large factory and administration buildings. In 1918, he published the book *Vom sparsamen Bauen* [On Economical Building], in which he advocated the use of inexpensive materials such as concrete. During the 1930s, Behrens was particularly active with urban planning tasks in Berlin, where such assignments became necessary due to the rapid development of the city and the issues of mass transportation. Several of the modern movement's leading names worked in Behrens's atelier in Berlin in the early stages of their careers, between 1907 and 1912, including: Walter Gropius, Ludwig Mies van der Rohe, Le Corbusier, Carl Fieger and Adolf Meyer, amongst others (young Le Corbusier joined the office in 1910, the year Gropius and Meyer left, and their time at the Behrens Atelier overlapped only shortly).

Behrens wrote, "Design is not about decorating functional forms—it is about creating forms that accord with the character of the object and that show new technologies to advantage." Behrens was also an important teacher, and after 1921 he focused more on his work as educator. He was appointed to the Düsseldorf Art Academy, and in 1922 he succeeded Otto Wagner as head of the Graduate School of Architecture at the Vienna Academy of Fine Arts, where he remained director of the architectural department until 1927. In 1936 he taught architecture at the Prussian Academy of Arts (now the Akademie der Künste in Berlin), in succession to Hans Poelzig.

The concept of design as an expression of form, or in German *Gestaltung* (form giving), was also a framing concept for this period of design theory development. Behrens was an influential force for so many architects through his teaching, writing and built works, and working closely with him laid the foundation of many of the beliefs shared by Gropius and Mies. It was here that they were exposed to the current design theories and to progressive German culture; it was also here that the cordial rivalry between Gropius and Mies began. It was at Behrens's studio where Gropius met Adolf Meyer and they worked side by side from 1908 to 1910, until they decided to establish their own practice. They both left and formed the partnership Gropius & Meyer to build the Fagus factory building (completed 1913), a shoe last factory in Alfeld an der Leine, which turned out to be an iconic building of great influence, establishing Gropius's name as a radical young architect early. Numerous articles have been written about its ingenious glass façade and transparent corner solution, and most architectural historians connect 1913, the date of completion of the Fagus Werke, as the year that marks the beginning of the modern movement in Germany (see Image 3).

Image 3: Fagus Werke, a shoe last factory building designed by Walter Gropius and Adolf Meyer in Alfeld an der Leine, Germany, built 1911—1913. It's an important early example of modern architecture that established Gropius's name as leading architect. The beginning of modern architecture in Germany is often connected with the year when this building was completed

In *Gropius: The Man who Built the Bauhaus*, Fiona MacCarthy remembers her encounter with Walter Gropius:

> "By 1968 he had experienced three disparate lives: first in Germany as a radical young architect, and then as the founder and director of the Bauhaus, the flight to England via Rome in 1934, followed by yet another emigration. He had now lived in America for more than thirty years. Gropius had experienced the long life of a wanderer, albeit an especially distinguished one. [...] Gropius at this point was still valiant and impressive, with a flickering arrogance. I could see why Paul Klee, one of the first Masters he appointed to the Bauhaus, referred to Gropius in his early Weimar days of authority and glamour as the "Silver Prince". [...] I see him as in many ways heroic, a romantic and optimist, a great survivor." (MacCarthy, 2019, 4)

6. The Bauhaus Movement's Transformative Pedagogical Ideals

Gropius issued the *Bauhaus Manifesto* in April 1919; his call to students was not an explicitly political document, but echoes the utopian hopes of the era. Significant facts and changes that loomed over the founding of the Bauhaus in 1919, included: the consequences of World War I (1914-1918), with an economy left in chaos; the post-war crisis that was deepening in 1923, when the inflation became a hyper-inflation; the Russian Revolution of 1917, a successful Marxist-led revolution on Germany's doorstep that overthrew a much-loathed Czar (igniting a wide-spread enthusiasm for revolutionary politics); and the German Revolution of November 1918, with the discredited German Kaiser fleeing the country and the monarchy collapsing; subsequently, the German Empire became the German Republic.

The Weimar Republic, officially the German Reich, was the name of the German state from 1918 to 1933. The term derives its name from the provincial city of Weimar, where its constitutional assembly first took place. The Bauhaus school that also commenced in Weimar, also lasted but fourteen years, the duration of the Weimarer Republik. The school's shaky history can best be categorised by four phases: first, its beginning years starting in 1919 in Weimar, which were marked by experimentation and an attempt to assimilate various avant-garde tendencies (such as Constructivism and Expressionism). In the 1924 local elections in Weimar, the Nationalists gained a majority over the Social Democrats, and with the change in local government all subsidies to the Bauhaus suddenly came to an end. The protests of internationally famous artists, architects and scientists, Einstein among them, were of no avail. The Bauhaus in Weimar had to close. Gropius was able to resurrect it in Dessau in the province of Anhalt in 1925, but when the Nazis came locally to power there, one of their first acts of state was the cutting of funding for the Bauhaus. From 1924 to 1925, the Bauhaus was forced to find a new home, and it was subsequently able to move to its new campus in Dessau, a complex masterminded and designed by its director Walter Gropius. This is called its second phase (see Image 7).

Until 1927, the Bauhaus had no formal department of architecture and the focus was generally on creative, artistic disciplines that worked across conventional disciplinarian boundaries. Teaching students to build was always the ultimate aim of a Bauhaus education, which originated in the Arts and Crafts movement's idea of "making things". However, it was only in Dessau in 1927 that an independent department of architecture was created; until then, students occasionally had participated in projects in the private practice of Gropius. The students disapproved of the lack of classes in architecture. But in the opinion of Gropius, the Bauhaus in Weimar was still too young to embark on teaching architecture, and he thought it essential to first learn a solid basis of crafts in the workshops.

The third phase commenced in 1928, when Gropius resigned and Swiss architect and urban planner Hannes Meyer was briefly in charge as director of the Bauhaus, until 1930. Meyer insisted on organising architectural processes according to logical scientific criteria. The school was active in Dessau until 1932, and during his directorship, Meyer introduced a series of important pedagogical inventions: he added vertical studios and new courses in subjects such as technology, humanities and natural sciences to a previously largely arts-based programme. In addition, Meyer initiated small "live" building projects, which were designed and built by Bauhaus students in the workshops. (This is the origin of design and build programmes common at architecture schools today.) After Meyer's dismissal, Mies van der Rohe became the next Bauhaus director. He was a much more apolitical Bauhaus director and careful not to be seen as connected to any political party, after the openly communist activist Meyer was removed in 1930. The last, fourth phase was from 1932 to 1933 in Berlin, where Mies attempted—as the Bauhaus's last director—to revive the school, until it was finally forced to close by the Nazis for good. In 1933, after the short time under Mies van der Rohe's leadership in Berlin, came the final end for the famous school.

Both Gropius and Mies were fundamental in shaping the avant-garde Bauhaus approach, and later in continuing its legacy by introducing the development of educational concepts through their influential teaching in the US for over twenty years. Few architects in the 20th century were more influential during their lifetimes (see Image 4). But they were not the only ones. Josef and Anni Albers and László Moholy-Nagy are often forgotten or fully acknowledged in studies, as they have been overshadowed by the common narrative of Gropius and Mies. In 1933, artists Josef and Anni Albers moved to North Carolina to teach at the new Black Mountain College, and other artists, musicians and academics soon followed their lead. The college emerged as a hugely influential artists' collective that gave instructors almost complete freedom in designing their lessons, which focused on methods rather than theory. By the 1940s, the school was a leading interdisciplinary art and design college; however, it was forced to close in 1957 due to financial reasons: some staff members were suspected of being communists during the Cold War, driving potential donors away. In 1934, Hungarian László Moholy-Nagy, one of the most important photographers and typographers at the Bauhaus, left for North America. In 1937, he became the founding director of the New Bauhaus Graduate School in Chicago, today the Institute of Design (ID) at the IIT.

What exactly made the Bauhaus pedagogical model so special? As is still common in schools of architecture today, Gropius, Mies and the other masters were appointed on the basis of their professional career, artistic skills and personality—not based on their teaching performance or pedagogical expertise, as they have not been trained as teachers. Rainer Wick has intensively studied the pedagogy and teaching methods used at the Bauhaus and argues that "the Bauhaus instruction was shaped by four basic principles: the first maxim was 'start from scratch', in other words, shake off all the old academic ballast and think afresh. The second was 'learning by doing', and 'trial and error' the third. Bauhaus students honed their abilities and skills working on actual projects and not just in the classroom. The school sought to eliminate the distinction between craftsmanship and academic education, which served as the fourth and final dictum" (as cited in Mulke, 2018). The Bauhaus curriculum involved experimentation with an emphasis on developing prototypes in workshops (for example, furniture and objects), an emphasis on research and method, problem-orientated (rather than solution-oriented) attitudes, and an adaptable, process-driven curriculum. It encouraged all students to tackle important real-world issues involving advanced technical, design and social parameters. The students were responding to new ideas about the meaning of science and technology in an age of rapid modernisation, inserting design into the narrative of epochal transformation. The radical Bauhaus pedagogy was based on timeless principles that are still relevant to the education of architects and designers today, including intensive collaboration, experimenting with new ways and the constant reframing of the issue or design problem, to focus on the process rather than the outcome. Initially, the Bauhaus was seen as an educational experiment; only later was it recognised as a style and a movement (Powers, 2019).

What made this school of art and design different from others? Naturally, the group of modern artists teaching there—Itten, Klee, Kandinsky, Feininger, Schlemmer and others—and the promise of their revolutionary teaching methods were a great attraction. For a short time, the Bauhaus brought together a fascinating and hugely influential group of educators who worked alongside each other and together left a lasting legacy despite existing for only just over a decade. All these artists were personalities in their own right and yet, though one could not by any means call them a collective unit, the common denominator, the idea and ideal of the Bauhaus, forged them together as it did the students (see Image 4).

In "Memories of a Bauhaus Student", George Adams (1968) remembers that
> "Gropius was immensely active, full of ideas and ideals, and a splendid organiser. With his enthusiasm he carried us all away. Itten was in charge of the compulsory preliminary Vorkurs. At its end you were either admitted as a full Bauhaus student, or not. There were no school fees, no registers. We were at complete liberty to come and go as we liked. Only one day per week was set aside for compulsory tuition in the preliminary Vorkurs. For the rest of the week, we were free to attend life and drawing classes and lectures. So we all eagerly looked forward to this one day of regular classes, which was always stimulating. We usually had to bring along what we had produced during the week, and we were given projects which were criticised when they had been completed. Much of our free time was taken up by discussion." (Adams, 1968)

Reception of the Bauhaus in the US

The interest of the Museum of Modern Art (MoMA) in New York in the Bauhaus commenced early. In 1930, New York–based curator Philip Johnson and MoMA director Alfred Barr were among the first Americans to recognise the ground–breaking importance of the Bauhaus and its innovative curriculum. Johnson and Barr acknowledged that it had the most innovative curriculum of all design schools at this time, and its pedagogical model would influence design education worldwide for the next decades. Progressive-minded American architects admired the Bauhaus and could learn about its concepts in three relevant exhibitions (in 1930, 1932, and 1938). Curators Barr and Johnson, along with architectural historian Henry-Russell Hitchcock, were seeking to create a suitable culture for a new modern architecture in America. In the same year, the first US exhibition of the Bauhaus (and the only exhibition during the school's existence), took place at Harvard University; subsequently, the show travelled to New York and Chicago.

Gropius developed a friendship with the much younger, ambitious New York architectural maverick Philip Johnson (1906—2005). From 1932 to 1934, Johnson was chair of the Department of Architecture at the MoMA; through this influential position, he would become one of the key promoters of Gropius and Mies's work and the theories of the Bauhaus. Ironically, later, in

1942, Johnson went back to school and joined the GSD to complete a degree in architecture as a student of Gropius.

In 1932, Philip Johnson and Henry-Russell Hitchcock were the curators of the seminal MoMA exhibition *The International Style*, which was accompanied by the publication of a comprehensive book. The exhibition also featured the work of Gropius and Mies and introduced them to a wider US audience. While Henry-Russell Hitchcock argued that modernism in architecture was a style, which he and Phillip Johnson dubbed the international style, it was increasingly seen as a new way of thinking, distinguishing itself from past practices by emphasising architecture as an artform that combined science and technology with the creative acts of design. It is often said that Johnson was the inventor of the international style, which is defined by the Getty Research Institute as "the style of architecture that emerged in Holland, France and Germany after World War I and spread throughout the world, becoming the dominant architectural style until the 1970s." It was Johnson and Hitchcock who sold modernism to America. They made it understandable by concentrating on the formal and spatial aspects of modernism, which is what interested the US public at large—different from the social agenda that was more important in the European context.

In 1938, the highly influential retrospective exhibition *Bauhaus 1919—1928* at MoMA (co-curated by Walter Gropius, his wife Ise Gropius and Herbert Bayer; see Image 6) introduced the Bauhaus's theoretical models and design theories in greater detail to a wider audience. The 1938 exhibition and catalogue introduced Gropius's ideas on housing for lower-income workers and his vision of the ideal dwelling for US cities (the apartment high-rise tower), displaying his white Siemensstadt housing complex as model. In the 1940s and '50s, Gropius became a strong protagonist and champion of high-rise living in the US, with concepts not dissimilar to Le Corbusier's "high-rise tower-in-the-park" vision. The exhibition was an immense success, as the aesthetics of Bauhaus, its architecture, graphic design, tubular steel furniture and objects resonated well with American culture. Some of its furniture and objects are still reproduced for sale at the MoMA shop today.

The fame and renown of the Bauhaus spread rapidly, and Crinson and Lubbock suggest that its greatest achievement was its "propaganda and the image, or myth, of itself" (1994). Bauhaus teachings were promulgated internationally through the formation of the Congrès International d' Architecture Moderne (CIAM) in 1928 and by professional journals such as *L'Architecture d' Aujourd'hui* and *Architectural Record*. CIAM promoted architecture as both an economic and a political tool that could be used to improve the world through the design of buildings and urban design. Publications such as Le Corbusier's *Vers Une Architecture* (1923) and *The City of Tomorrow and its Planning* (1929), and Gropius's *Scope of Total Architecture* (1962) and *The New Architecture and the Bauhaus* (1965), were also avidly read across the world and became classics between architects.

The Bauhaus had always a particular strong sense of its public presence (e.g., it published a series of fourteen *Bauhausbuecher* from 1924 to 1928, presenting itself as the cradle of European modernism). Information about the Bauhaus was regularly reported in American journals for the duration of the school's existence, and Gropius and Mies were media savvy. The marketing of the

Bauhaus as a "brand" was ahead of its time, and only one other architect was equally successful in promoting his ideas: Le Corbusier. Through a consistent flow of information and fine-tuned marketing information about the latest Bauhaus news, the ground was prepared for a welcoming US reception of the Bauhaus concepts, as these seemed to be available for post-war America at the right time and in the right place. The North American architectural context, the MoMA, and Harvard University's GSD were ready for welcoming the Bauhaus ideas, their new chair Gropius, and the enduring impact on education in the creative disciplines.

Le Corbusier was the first to use the power of media and publication to widely promote his own oeuvre. In 1923, he published *Vers une Architecture* (Towards a New Architecture, translated in 1927 into English), a bold manifesto that presented a collection of articles written by Le Corbusier for his own avant-garde magazine, *L'Esprit Nouveau*, to propagate his work and theories. As a consequence of the Bauhaus's intensive publication activities, there were few German architects with the international fame of Walter Gropius or Mies van der Rohe. In fact, other architects including Hugo Häring and Hans Scharoun were forced to play a role as "outliers" of the modern movement, caused by the dominance of the historiographic narratives that centred on the three dominating heroic figures Le Corbusier, Gropius and Mies (Blundell Jones, 1999). Häring's and Scharoun's organic architectural tradition was less accessible when they declared buildings as "living organisms". Architectural historian Julius Posener (1904—1996) argued that not Gropius or Mies but Hugo Häring (1882—1958) was the only early modernist architect who really had formulated an entire body of consistent architectural theory of his time, noting that "Häring was the one whose written oeuvre should have been the most important by far. Not only had he written considerably more than any other leading architect of the time, his theory was more consistent than the occasional manifestoes or essays written by his contemporaries" (Posener, 1972, 33).

A building boom in the post-war era attracted an increasing number of immigrant architects to the US, fascinated by the opportunities, scale and speed of development (not dissimilar to the architectural attraction of working in China in the 1990 to 2010 period). The influx of immigrating architects was also felt at the universities. In the 1950s, German educators and their influence in the arts and architecture was suddenly everywhere, although less prominent than in Gropius's and Mies's cases. There are plenty of cases for this; for example, American architect Antoine Predock remembers his life-changing encounter with a German architecture professor and chair of architecture at the University of New Mexico, Don Schlegel (1926—2019), who led him to transfer from engineering to architecture.

Image 4: Ludwig Mies van der Rohe reviewing students' work at the Bauhaus in 1931

Image 5: Group photo of Bauhaus masters in Dessau, 1926, with director Walter Gropius in the centre (Photo courtesy of Alliance AKG Images)

Image 6: The 1938 exhibition *Bauhaus 1919–1928* at the Museum of Modern Art in New York, co-curated in by Walter Gropius and Herbert Bayer, on invitation of Alfred Barr

German Philosophical Influences on Architectural Thinking

Architectural history is largely an offshoot of art history and important for evaluating the meaning of works of architecture. The writings of German art historians in the 18th and 19th century (e.g., Winckelmann, Semper and Wölfflin) contributed much to the formation of architectural canons and a critical historiography developed alongside Hegelian notions of zeitgeist (the spirit of the age manifest in art forms) and *Weltanschauung* (the notion that art represents a people's worldview). German philosophers and cultural critics have been influencing architectural thinking for centuries. The concepts propagated by the various philosophers had a direct impact on the conception of space and understanding of the discipline, as traceable in the writings of theorists Adolf Loos, Le Corbusier, Sigfried Giedion, Frederick Kiesler and others.

Since Plato, the Greek philosopher, and Vitruvius, the Roman builder and philosopher, philosophy has been closely connected to the ethical and aesthetic issues of architecture. Roman builder Marcus Vitruvius Pollio is often cited as the first "architect". As chief engineer for Roman rulers such as Emperor Augustus, Vitruvius documented building methods and acceptable styles to be used by governments. His three principles of architecture were used as model of what architecture should be, published in his book De Architectura. Vitruvius's three principles, namely: *firmitas* (durability, firmness), *utilitas* (practicality, function) and *venustas* (beauty, delight), are accepted as a timeless truth.

For most of the time, architecture is closely related to social theory and political philosophy. The movement of idealism had its origins in late 18th-century German philosophy, mainly in the writings by Kant and Hegel. The influence of idealism can be seen in Nikolaus Pevsner's writing on the origins of the modern movement, notably in *Pioneers of the Modern Movement* (1936).

The discourse and relationship between philosophy and architecture also concerns the meaning of human habitation and the degree to which social progress and human flourishing may occur. German philosophy was always particularly sensitive to revolutionary changes in society, culture and science. As Taylor and Levine (2010) point out, architecture can be conceived as an intrinsically philosophical activity, grounded in aesthetics and ethics, and also in elements of social and political philosophy. Architects, landscape architects, and designers are all responsible for creating spaces in which people live and interact, and in so doing promote certain values, understandings and concepts of living.

The most important German philosophers wrote in German, which was the language in which important scholarship was conducted. The key ideas and arguments of German philosophers, from Kant to Habermas, had a deep influence on architectural thinking. Some of the most prominent German philosophers and theorists who made significant contributions to a philosophy of architecture, include the following:

18th- and 19th-century German-speaking philosophers
- Immanuel Kant (1724–1804)
- Johann Wolfgang von Goethe (1749–1832)
- Georg Wilhelm Friedrich Hegel (1770–1831)
- Karl Marx (1818–1883)
- Friedrich Nietzsche (1844–1900)
- Max Weber (1864–1920)

20th-century German-speaking philosophers
- Martin Heidegger (1889—1976)
- Ludwig Wittgenstein (1889—1951)
- Walter Benjamin (1892—1940)
- Herbert Marcuse (1898—1979)
- Theodor Adorno (1903—1969)

Modern philosophical discourse on architectural practice and education can be traced to Kant and Heidegger. Their thinking influenced the writing of architectural historians including Wittkower, Pevsner, Giedion and others. Sigfried Giedion claimed that—based on Kant—the main task of architecture was "the interpretation of a way of life", suggesting that a building is capable of "expressing the spirit of an age." In *The Critique of Judgment* (1790), Kant noted that function limits the potential beauty of buildings. German philosophy has often focused on architecture's desire to articulate its identity and special relevance by expressing the social, political, economic and personal character of the times.

During the entire 19th and 20th centuries, the discourse by German philosophers deeply influenced the understanding of architecture and the history of architectural ideas. Gropius, Mies, Mendelsohn and the other immigrants were well aware of these debates and the different ideological concepts. The German philosophers had a profound and formative influence on their thinking. Mies was apparently particular fond of reading Plato, Nietzsche, Goethe and Schopenhauer. He read and quoted philosophy his entire life, and it is tempting to argue that the architect designed some of his buildings with the intention of expressing a philosophical position in built form.

Image 7: The new Bauhuas complex in Dessau designed by Walter Gropius, 1923-25. In 1925, the Bauhaus moved to its new facilities in Dessau.

APPENDIX PART I. The Historical Cases and a Timeline of 200 Years

Time Worked in the US

This timeline lists 30 immigrated architects and the period they worked in the US.

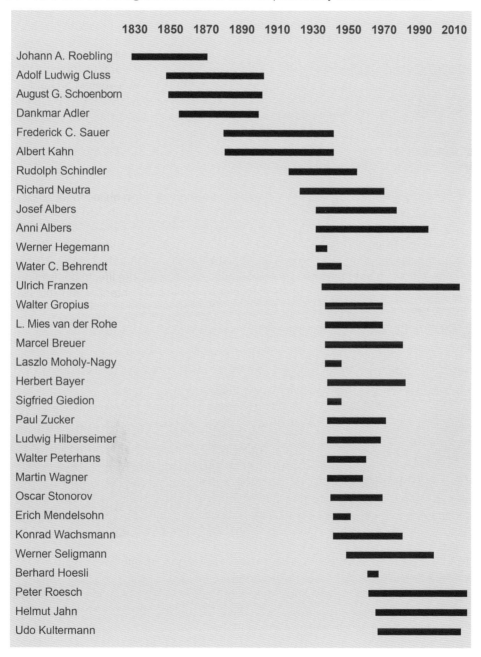

The Historical Cases

Biographies of 52 recognised 19th and 20th century German-speaking architects in the US who made important contributions over the last two hundred years—a long overdue survey of the continuous influence of these architects in the US (the listing is in alphabetical order. Please note: a few Austrian and Swiss-German cases are included, as they shared a similar cultural background and the German language).

Raimund Abraham *(Lienz, Tyrol, 1933—Los Angeles, 2010), New York City)* Abraham was an influential architect in his native Austria and part of the New York avant-garde. His poetic architectural vision was influenced by the Viennese tradition to understand architecture as sculpture, along with other Austrian masters including Hollein, Pichler and Domenig. Throughout a 40-year career, he created visionary and enigmatic projects and built works in Europe and the US. From 1952 to 1958, Abraham studied at the Technical University of Graz, and in 1959, he established a studio in Vienna. From 1960 to 1964 he worked in Vienna with Walter Pichler. Abraham's first book, the 1963 publication "Elementare Architektur" was made at a time of his transition from architecture studies to practice. In 1964, Abraham immigrated to the United States. After arriving in 1971 in New York, he taught at the Rhode Island School of Design and was a professor of architecture at the Cooper Union School of Art and Architecture in New York. He was also adjunct faculty at Pratt Institute in Brooklyn, and a visiting professor at numerous other institutions worldwide. He became known as a strong critic of mainstream architecture's preoccupation with style, its indifference to history, and the rigid definition of Modernism at that time. Abraham went on to influence generations of professional architects through his poetic architectural drawing style and teaching.

Dankmar Adler *(Lengfeld, Thuringia, 1844—Chicago, 1900), Chicago* Adler was an architect and civil engineer best known for his fifteen-year partnership with Louis Sullivan, as Adler & Sullivan in Chicago, during which they designed some of the first high-rise towers. Adler came to the US in 1854 with his father, who was a Jewish rabbi. He became a draftsman before working in the practice of architect Augustus Bauer in Chicago. In 1871, Adler formed a partnership with Edward Burling that ultimately created more than 100 buildings. In 1880, he eventually established his own firm; in the same year, he hired Louis Sullivan as a draftsman and made him a partner three years later. Adler's partnership with Sullivan was very productive but ended around 1895 due to a slump in their architectural practice brought on by the Panic of 1893. Adler & Sullivan produced more than 180 buildings and some of Chicago's most important architecture. With his partner Burling and thereafter, as a partner in Adler & Sullivan, he was instrumental in rebuilding much of Chicago following the Great Fire of 1871 (the city government improved building codes to stop the rapid spread of future fires, stopped timber construction, and rebuilt the city rapidly to higher standards). Buildings in Chicago have always been different from New York: tough, more durable and uncompromising. Adler is considered a leader in the Chicago school of architecture through pioneering accomplishments with steel-framed buildings and high-rise construction. Dankmar

Adler and Louis Sullivan were early employers and mentors of architect Frank Lloyd Wright. A victim of the financial depression, Adler left the partnership in 1895, but returned to architecture in partnership with his two sons; he never regained the prominence he had earlier. Sullivan continued to practice and died in 1924 penniless.

Augustus Bauer *(Darmstadt, 1827–Chicago, 1894), Chicago*
Augustus Bauer was among Chicago's most prominent early architects and one of the city's earliest professional architects. Quoting a *Chicago Tribune* article published in 1873, the writer notes that in his day, Bauer was considered one of Chicago's "best educated and most experienced architects." A German immigrant, Bauer graduated with high honours from the Polytechnic School in Darmstadt, and immigrated to New York in 1851, where he worked for the firm of Carstensen & Gildmeister on plans for the great Crystal Palace. In 1853, Bauer moved to Chicago at the suggestion of Frederick Baumann, who would later serve briefly as architect for the Chicago Board of Education. Bauer soon joined forces with Asher Carter, the second professional architect to practice in the City. Carter & Bauer designed many residences and public buildings, including Old St. Patrick's Catholic Church (1856), now a monument. Beginning in 1863, Bauer practiced alone for several years, during which time he became an expert in school buildings and designed numerous brick schools including the old Wells and Dore schools. These are among the oldest public school buildings in Chicago still in use. In 1866, Bauer became associated with Robert Loebnitz (young Dankmar Adler worked as a draftsman in their firm). They produced a great deal of work between 1871, immediately after the Great Fire, and 1874, when Loebnitz retired to Europe. Bauer again practiced solo from 1874 to 1881. Throughout this period, he designed twenty school buildings for the Chicago Board of Education (see image), including the Mark Sheridan and James Otis Schools. Bauer served as the president of the Chicago Chapter from 1879 through 1885.

Cajetan J.B. Baumann *(Ravensburg, 1899–New York City, 1969), New York City*
Brother Baumann was a Franciscan friar and architect. His designs were progressive, providing modern interpretations of Gothic architecture. He was born in 1899 in Baden-Württemberg in South Germany, and in 1922 entered the novitiate of the Order of Friars Minor in Sigmaringen, where he was given the name by which he is known. He remained a member of this Province throughout his life. In 1925, Baumann was sent to the US to help with his skills as a cabinetmaker and wood carver. He first served the community at St. Bonaventure Friary in Paterson, New Jersey for ten years (1926–1936); and then went on to earn a bachelor's degree from St. Bonaventure University (1941) and a Master of Architecture from Columbia University. He later served on the Board of Governors of Columbia's School of Architecture. He was active in the National Committee on Religious Buildings, the Architectural League of New York, the New York Building Congress and the National Council of Architectural Registration Boards. Baumann was the American representative of the International Commission for the Restoration of the Basilica of the Holy Sepulcher in Jerusalem. He became the first

AIA member of a religious Order. He headed an architectural firm based in New York City for the Order of Friars Minor, the Office of Franciscan Art and Architecture, designing numerous religious structures worldwide, including churches, convents, schools, college residences, retreat houses and seminaries. Although he was not engaged in general practice, Baumann's firm attracted a number of young architects who later earned national reputations, including: Paul Damaz, who worked on the UN headquarters, and German architect Gottfried Boehm, who received the Pritzker Prize in 1986.

Frederick Baumann *(Berlin, 1826—Chicago, 1921), Chicago*
Born and educated at the Berlin Polytechnic Academy of Arts, Frederick Baumann arrived in 1850 via New York in Chicago. In 1851, he joined the office of one of Chicago's first professional architects, John Van Osdel as draftsman. The following year, Baumann formed a partnership with his cousin, Edward Burling, and they built Chicago's first large office building, known as the Marine Building, located at Lake and LaSalle streets. The office building, with its cut stone front, rose to a height of seven stories. The Marine foreshadowed Baumann's later expertise in designing tall, heavy buildings in Chicago's difficult lakeside soil. He is recognised for his contributions to the development of the skyscraper typology through the publication of numerous articles, including *Improvement in the Construction of Tall Buildings* (1884), and for his innovative structural designs. He also designed the First Chicago Courthouse and other prestigious commissions. Baumann had an enduring relationship with the Chicago Board of Education. Between 1857 and 1859, he served on the Board and a decade later, he designed the Franklin School and the Hayes School buildings. Mid-way through his long and prolific career, in 1882 Baumann was named the first official Architect and Superintendent of the Chicago Board of Education. It is unlikely that any of his Chicago school buildings exist today.

Herbert Bayer *(Haag, Austria, 1900—Montecito, California, 1985), New York City; Aspen, Colorado*
Austrian-born graphic artist, painter, photographer and architect, Herbert Bayer taught at the Bauhaus and became influential in spreading European principles of advertising in the United States. Bayer was first trained as an architect, but from 1921 to 1923 he studied typography and mural painting at the Bauhaus. In 1924 he became a master of typography and advertising at the Bauhaus, and simultaneously was an art director with *Vogue*, the American-French fashion magazine. In 1928 he moved to Berlin, where he worked in advertising, painting, exhibition design, typography, and photography until 1938, when he moved to New York City and concentrated on advertising design. In the same year, he arranged the exhibition "Bauhaus 1919—1928" at the New York Museum of Modern Art (together with Gropius). He became an American citizen in 1944. In 1946, Bayer became chairman of the department of design of the Container Corporation of America; and a design consultant for Aspen Development, a corporation that stages an annual festival of the arts in Aspen, Colorado. In the latter capacity he designed several architectural projects.

Walter Curt Behrendt *(Metz, 1884—Norwich, 1945), Norwich, Vermont*
Behrendt was a German-American architect and active advocate of German modernism. From 1912-1933, Behrendt worked in Civil Service with the Ministry for Housing and Town Planning (1919–1926) in Prussia, shaping public housing policy including the principles of lay-out and development. He was an authority on city planning and housing, editor of *Die Form*, and author of the book *The Victory of the New Building Style*, among many other works.
In 1926, he published *Städtebau und Wohnungswesen in the Vereinigten Staaten*, a homage to American planning. Behrendt immigrated to the US in 1934 to teach at Dartmouth College through the help of his friend Lewis Mumford. In 1937, he became a Professor of City Planning & Housing at the University at Buffalo, SUNY, and returned to Dartmouth College in 1941.

Julius Berndt *(Kloster, Breslau 1832—New Ulm, Minnesota 1916), Brown County, Minnesota*
Julius Berndt was the architect, surveyor and superintendent of the monument to Hermann at New Ulm, Brown County, Minnesota. He attended a poly-technical school at Breslau and was involved in the Revolution of 1848, with his sympathies with the revolutionists. In 1854, the first large group of German settlers from the Chicago Land Society arrived in Brown County to found the town of Neu Ulm. Berndt arrived in the US in 1852 and readily found employment in Chicago, having received an excellent education in Breslau in civil engineering and architecture, and he was a skilled draftsman. In 1852 he became associated with the Chicago Landverein which had for its main object the founding of a German colony. He was Secretary of the German Land Association, and in 1857 he came to New Ulm. In response to anti-German sentiment, he co-founded the Society of the Sons of Hermann, one of the strongest and most popular German societies in the US. During his residence in Neu Ulm, he was engaged as architect, contractor and surveyor, until his retirement in 1899. He had superintended the erection of many of the most important buildings in the county, including the Grand Hotel. In 1897, he realised a replica of the Hermann Monument: he conceived the idea that a monument should be erected in Neu Ulm to the memory of Hermann the Cherusker, similar to the monument in Lippe Detmold, near the Teutoburger Wald; he prepared the plans and practically without funds started the building process.

Adolf Ludwig Cluss *(Heilbronn, 1825—Washington D.C., 1905), Washington, D.C.*
Cluss became one of the most important, influential and prolific architects and engineers in Washington, D.C. in the late 19th century, responsible for the design of numerous schools and other notable public buildings in the capital. Several of his buildings are still standing today. He was also City Engineer and a Building Inspector for the Board of Public Works. The failure of the 1848 German Revolution led him to leave Germany for the US in the same year, and settled in Washington, D.C. in 1849. In 1862 he started his private architectural practice with another German immigrant, Josef Wildrich von Kammerhueber (the firm exited until 1868). Red brick was Cluss's

favourite building material; that, and his early communist sympathies, led some to dub him the "Red Architect", though in later life he became a confirmed Republican. Cluss retired from his private practice in 1889, having built almost 90 buildings, including at least eleven schools, as well as markets, government buildings, museums, residences and churches.

Julius S. Ender *(Korningsberg, 1851—Chicago, 1906), Chicago*
Julius Sigismund Ender was born in Korningsberg and immigrated to the United States in 1870. By 1875, Ender was practicing architecture in Chicago, where he became a naturalised citizen in the same year. Ender was one of three architects—the others being Frederick Baumann and James Willett—who served as architects to the Chicago Board of Education in 1882. Ender designed the new North Division High School at Wells and Wendell streets, which was one of the schools the Board had determined were needed to accommodate the growing population of students (see image). He designed a three-story Romanesque structure with a rusticated stone base, red brick load-bearing walls, and an ornate cornice; the school opened in 1883. He continued to practice architecture in Chicago until his death in 1906. Other 19th century German immigrant architects in Chicago included Frederick Dinkelberg, Richard Schmidt and Karl Martin Vitzthum.

Ulrich J. Franzen *(Duesseldorf, 1921—Santa Fe, 2012), New York City and Santa Fe*
Franzen immigrated as a boy with his family to the United States in 1936. After studying at Harvard Graduate School of Design in the mid-1940s when Walter Gropius was its chair of architecture, Franzen became part of a cohort that would disseminate the Modernist vocabulary of the Bauhaus founder in the US during the post-World War II boom period. He obtained a Master's degree in 1950. By 1951, he was working for I.M. Pei in New York City. In 1955, he left Pei and formed his own firm, Ulrich Franzen & Associates. He is mainly known for his "fortress like" muscular Brutalist buildings, such as Alley Theatre in Houston. His work specialised in educational, corporate and elegant residential commissions. By the 1960s, Franzen had also become the guiding spirit of the Architectural League of New York, where he was president from 1966 to 1968 and subsequently acted in an unofficial capacity as its godfather; mentoring younger architects such as James Stewart Polshek. Franzen was generous with his time as educator and a frequent lecturer; he served as a visiting professor at a number of universities, including Harvard, Yale, and Columbia.

James Ingo Freed *(Essen, 1930—New York, 2005), New York City*
Freed was born in Germany to a German-Jewish family during the Weimar Republic. In 1939, his family immigrated (hiding on a train) via France to the US and settled in Chicago, where he studied architecture at the Illinois Institute of Technology (graduating in 1953). Freed first worked for a year in Chicago with Ludwig Mies van der Rohe. In 1956, he began working with

I.M. Pei in New York at the firm eventually known as Pei Cobb Freed & Partners. In the late 1970s, he was a member of the *Chicago Seven*, a group which emerged in opposition to the doctrinal application of modernism, as represented particularly in Chicago by the followers of Mies van der Rohe. From 1975 to 1978, Freed was dean of the School of Architecture at the IIT. He also taught at Cooper Union, Cornell University, the Rhode Island School of Design, Columbia University and Yale University. He worked on major US public buildings and museums, including the Javits Convention Center in New York City, the San Francisco Main Public Library and the US Air Force Memorial in Arlington, Virginia. He designed several major buildings in Washington, D.C., including the US Holocaust Memorial Museum. He worked with I.M. Pei on the design of the Kips Bay Plaza project in New York City. In 1988, he was elected into the National Academy of Design and in 1995, Freed was awarded the National Medal of Arts.

Albert Frey *(Zurich, 1903—Palm Springs, 1998), Palm Springs*
Albert Frey was a Swiss-born architect who established a regional style of modernist architecture centered on Palm Springs in California, which came to be known as "desert modernism". With a name synonymous with Palm Springs and "modernist utopia in the desert" (Koenig), Frey is inseparable from the desert landscape and the awe it inspires. Since 1964, the soaring crest of the Tramway Gas Station (now Palm Springs Visitors Center) with its butterfly roof has served as both an iconic welcome sign and a beacon of modern design to every car that turns off Interstate 10 to enter town. Born in Zurich, Frey received his architecture diploma in 1924 from the Institute of Technology in Winterthur. There Frey trained in traditional building construction and received technical instruction rather than design instruction. Prior to receiving his diploma, Frey apprenticed with a local architect in Zurich. In the mid-1920s he became aware of the Dutch De Stijl movement, the German Bauhaus, and the modernism movement developing in Brussels. All would prove to be significant influences to Frey's later work. From 1925 through 1928, Frey worked on various architectural projects in Belgium, and in 1928, he secured a position in the Paris atelier of Swiss architects Le Corbusier and Pierre Jeanneret. Frey was one of two full-time employees of the atelier and co-workers included Josep Lluis Sert and Charlotte Perriand; during this time he worked on the Villa Savoye project (arguably the most important house of the 20th century). In 1929, Frey left the atelier to take up work in the United States, but continued to maintain a friendship with Le Corbusier for many years. From 1930 to 1935, Frey had a partnership with Lawrence Kocher in New York (the managing editor of *Architectural Record*). In 1932 he meets Rudolph Schindler, Richard Neutra and Frank Lloyd Wright. One of their commissions was an office building for Kocher's brother in Palm Springs; this project introduced Frey to the Californian desert, which was to become his home and the backdrop for most of his subsequent work. In 1935 he moves to Palm Springs. At the end of World War II, Palm Springs' population almost tripled and the city experienced a building boom. Known as an escape for the Hollywood elite and a winter haven for east coast industrialists, Palm Springs emerged in the post-war years as a resort community and Frey's buildings helped establish Palm Springs as a progressive desert mecca for innovative modern architecture during the 1950s to 1970s. Like fellow Californian luminary John Lautner, he produced designs for the spectrum of architectural commissions, from bespoke custom homes to institutional and public buildings, most of which are still in use today.

Hermann J. Gaul *(Cologne, 1869—Chicago, 1949), Chicago*
Gaul came to the US in 1899 and settled in Chicago. After apprenticing for a time with noted architects Adler & Sullivan, he established an architectural firm under his own name in 1902. During his long and distinguished career, he designed many landmark buildings for Roman Catholic clients, including the Chicago Diocese, throughout the Midwest: he also designed a number of Catholic churches, schools, convents and rectories in Missouri, Illinois and Indiana (see image). Generations of German craftspeople, designers and parishioners made St. Michael's Roman Catholic Church a Romanesque monument with a Bavarian Baroque interior, and Gaul was in charge of the 1913 remodelling of the church. In the early 1930s, Gaul's son Michael F. Gaul (1913—1996) joined his father's firm, known as Hermann J. Gaul & Son, and carried on the practice after his father's retirement in 1948. Several of Gaul's buildings have been placed on the US National Register of Historic Places.

Sigfried Giedion *(Prague, 1888—Zurich, 1968), Cambridge and Boston; Zurich*
Swiss architectural historian Sigfried Giedion had an ambiguous relationship with the US. He spent much of his successful teaching, research and publishing career at Harvard and at MIT. Paradoxically, he consolidated his reputation as one of the most influential architectural historians of the 20th century in America, and his extended stays in the US offered him a laboratory to propel his scholarship, e.g. through his friendship with philosopher Marshall McLuhan and historian Lewis Mumford. While in the US, he was able to write his two most well-known books, "Space, Time and Architecture: The Growth of a New Tradition" (1941) and "Mechanization Takes Command: A Contribution to Anonymous History" (1948), when he taught at Harvard GSD between 1938 and 1945. These two books are an important analysis and critique of American material culture. World War II kept Giedion in America though he, unlike many other German-speaking European intellectuals, returned home to Zurich in 1946 to take up a teaching position at the Federal Institute of Technology (ETH) as professor of art and architecture history. Being a friend of Walter Gropius and Le Corbusier was decisive for him to occupy the post of General Secretary of the Congrès Internationaux d'Architecture Moderne (CIAM), for which he served until the group dissolved in 1956.

Ferdinand Gottlieb *(Berlin, 1919—New York, 2007), Greenburgh, New York*
After escaping from Nazi Germany in 1934, he immigrated to New York in 1937. After the war, he attended Columbia University School of Architecture, graduating 1953. Before opening his own practice, he was associated with Morris Ketchum, a leading New York architect who was a pioneer in shopping centre design. From 1961 to 2007, he headed his own firm, Ferdinand Gottlieb & Associates, based in Dobbs Ferry, New York. He is perhaps best known for his interior design of the original Rizzoli Bookstore at Fifth Avenue in New York City. In addition to a substantial number of private residences (see image), Gottlieb

also designed several large commercial projects in the New York area. An early leader in the advancement of graduate real estate education in the United States, Gottlieb taught classes as an adjunct professor at the New York University Real Estate Institute, now known as the NYU Schack Institute of Real Estate, starting in 1967.

 **Walter Gropius** *(Berlin, 1883—Boston, 1969), Cambridge and Boston, MA* Widely regarded as one of the pioneers of modernist architecture, he is the founder of the Bauhaus school in Weimar and Dessau. Architecture was in the family: Walter Gropius was born to wealthy Berlin parents; his great-uncle Martin Gropius (1824—1880) was a prominent Berlin architect who studied at the Preussische Bauakademie in Berlin and went on to form one of the largest architectural firms in Berlin. From 1904 to 1907, Walter Gropius studied architecture at the Technical University of Berlin (and briefly at the Technical University of Munich); from 1908 to 1910, he was an assistant to Peter Behrens, where he met his future partner Adolf Meyer, as well as Mies van der Rohe and Le Corbusier. Gropius and Meyer left the studio of Peter Behrens in June 1910 to establish their own office in Potsdam. Despite Meyer's no doubt crucial role in the firm, Gropius described him as "merely the office manager". Fagus Factory established Gropius's career. In 1919 he was appointed Director of the Grand Ducal Art School and Arts and Crafts School at Weimar, which he merged and reorganised under the name of the Staatliches Bauhaus. In 1925, the Bauhaus moved to Dessau to its new campus designed by Gropius. In 1928 Gropius left the Bauhaus to resume private practice in Berlin, and he built the Dammerstock Siedlung in Karlsruhe. In 1930, he directed the Deutscher Werkbund Exhibition at the Paris Salon; and in 1931 he became Vice-President of the International Congress for Modern Architecture (CIAM). Gropius is the eminent figure in the Bauhaus story: the founder, creator of the ideology, its first director, and the architect of its iconic campus buildings in Dessau. Gropius is remembered as inventor of a new form of art, architecture and design education that influenced schools worldwide. In 1934, he immigrated to London, where he worked in partnership with Maxwell Fry. In 1937 he im-migrated to the USA: there, he was Professor in the Department of Architecture at Harvard University, and 1938 to 1952 the Chair (head) of the Graduate School of Design at Harvard University in Cambridge, Massachusetts. German art historian Nikolaus Pevsner published *Pioneers of the Modern Movement: From William Morris to Walter Gropius* in English in 1936, a book which further cemented Gropius's reputation as pioneer. Architecturally, Gropius was influenced by Schinkel and Behrens. From 1937 to 1940 he was in partnership with Marcel Breuer in Boston. In 1945 he founded *The Architects Collaborative* (TAC) in Boston. As director of the Bauhaus and as head of the GSD, Gropius exerted a major influence on the development of modern architecture and design education. His works were mostly executed in collaboration with other architects, which allowed him to be more productive and active in many areas. With the help of his Harvard students and colleagues, especially Martin Wagner (Berlin's former city planning director during the Weimar Republic), Gropius's approach to urban design played a key part in shaping the post-war American urban landscape. Joseph Hudnut, dean of the Graduate School of Design, who first had brought Gropius there in 1937, became a fierce opponent of Gropius's urban plans and ideas for the modern city.

Victor D. Gruen *(Vienna, Austria, 1903—New York, 1980), New York City*
Victor Gruen, born Viktor David Grünbaum was an Austrian-born architect best known as a pioneer in the design of shopping malls. An advocate of prioritising pedestrians over cars in urban cores, he was the designer of the first outdoor pedestrian mall in the United States. He studied architecture at the Vienna Academy of Fine Arts and worked for Peter Behrens in Berlin, before opening his own architectural practice in 1933 in Vienna. His firm specialised in remodelling of shops and apartments. When Germany annexed Austria in 1938, he immigrated to the US. He landed "with an architect's degree, eight dollars and no English" in New York, where he changed his name from Grünbaum to Gruen and started to work as a draftsman. In 1941, he moved to Los Angeles and remarried. In 1951, he established the architectural firm Victor Gruen Associates, which was soon to become one of the major planning offices of that time. He designed the first suburban open-air shopping facility called Northland Mall near Detroit, in 1954. After the success of this project, he designed his best-known work, the Southdale Mall (1956) in Edina, Minnesota; it was the first enclosed shopping mall in the country. Because he invented the typology of the modern mall, he was often referred to as "the most influential architect of the 20th century." Until the mid-1970s, his office designed over fifty shopping malls. In the 1960s, Gruen designed a new district in Beirut, Lebanon. In 1968, he returned to Vienna, where he engaged in the gradual transformation of the inner city into a pedestrian zone, of which only some parts have been implemented. Gruen's book *The Heart of our Cities: The Urban Crisis, Diagnosis and Cure* was a big influence on Walt Disney's city planning ambitions.

Erwin Hauer *(Vienna, 1926—Branford, CT, 2017), New Haven, Connecticut*
Hauer was an Austrian-born designer and sculptor who studied first at Vienna's Academy of Applied Arts and later under Josef Albers at Yale University. Hauer was an early proponent of modular constructivism known for his minimalist, repetitive works and light-diffusing wall designs. Erwin Hauer was a professor at the Yale University's School of Art, where he taught from 1957 until 1990. He began in 1950 to explore modular sculptures featuring infinite continuous surfaces; some of these structures lent themselves to architectural usage as room dividers and perforated architectural screen walls, which he called "Continua". Inspired first by Henry Moore, and later the Constructivist sculptor Naum Gabo, Hauer cast his most popular series from molds in concrete, gypsum and acrylic resin using processes he developed while living in Vienna. Hauer developed these technologies to manufacture the walls and installed several such walls in churches in Vienna. As a result, he was awarded a Fulbright scholarship and came to the US in 1955 for graduate studies at the Rhode Island School of Design. In 1957 he was invited by Josef Albers to join the faculty of Yale University, where he taught until 1990.

Werner Hegemann *(Mannheim, 1881—New York, 1936), New York*
Werner Hegemann was an internationally known city planner, architecture critic, and author. A leading German intellectual during the Weimar Republic, his criticism of Hitler and the Nazi party forced him to leave Germany with his family in 1933. He fled via Switzerland to the US, where he died prematurely in New York City in 1936. In 1933, Hegemann was invited to teach urban planning at The New School for Social Research in New York City. He began lecturing at the New School and organised assistance for intellectuals and scholars detained by the Nazis. In 1935 he worked as a lecturer at Columbia University, where he taught seminars on housing. Due to his early death, Hegemann left a great number of publications but few built examples. Hegemann studied in Berlin, Paris and Philadelphia, and completed a doctorate in 1908 at the University of Munich. He spent early formative years (1904-1905 and 1909-1910) and a considerable part of his career (1913-1921 and 1933-1936) in the United States. In 1910 and 1911, he directed the City Planning Exhibitions in Berlin and Duesseldorf, contributing to the theoretical formation of the new discipline of city planning. He played an important role in the early development of city planning as a profession. In 1916, he established an urban planning practice in Milwaukee, Wisconsin; after eight years in the US, lecturing at the University of Michigan and working on urban projects, he returned in 1921 to Berlin. In 1930, he wrote the seminal book "Das steinerne Berlin", which combines historical and architectural criticism. Hegemann's early years in the United States made him an intermediary between architects and city planners throughout Europe and the US.

Ernest Helfensteller and Wiliam Albert Hirsch *(no dates available), St. Louis, Missouri*
Hirsch & Helfensteller Architects was founded in 1903 in St. Louis, Missouri and operated until 1940. The firm's partners included Ernest Helfensteller, William Albert Hirsch and, from 1907 on, Jesse Watson. No further biographic details are available. The firm quickly gained prominence with its 1912 design of the Moolah Temple in St. Louis, designed by Helfensteller who gave the building "a Moorish feel with a brick facade, winding staircases, vaulted ceilings and ornate, boldly colored tiles." In 1907, William Albert Hirsch designed the Liederkranz Club of St. Louis, a typical German-American social club founded in 1870. It was considered the most exclusive social club among German-Americans in St. Louis. The large building combined the facilities of both a social club and a Saengerbund (choral society), with game rooms, a Rathskeller (guild hall), dining areas, bowling alleys, lounging and reading rooms, private parlours and meeting halls, concert and dancing hall, dressing rooms, rehearsal hall, and a musical library. The Liederkranz was the club for the more affluent German-Americans who wished to retain ties with the gemütliche (homey) community and preserve the rich tradition of German music. However, prohibition hurt the club's membership, making the building sale in 1920 necessary. The building was demolished in 1963 (See: image of the Liederkranz building).

Ludwig Hilberseimer *(Karlsruhe, 1885—Chicago, 1967), Chicago*
From 1906 to 1911, Hilberseimer studied architecture in Karlsruhe under Friedrich Ostendorf and then moved to Berlin to work as an architect and urban planner. In 1927, he wrote the essay "Großstadt-architektur" and participated in the Weißenhof Siedlung housing estate in Stuttgart (masterplan by Mies van der Rohe). He taught during the last years at the Bauhaus in Dessau and Berlin: in 1929, Hilberseimer was hired by Hannes Meyer to teach at the Bauhaus, but in July 1933 was identified by the Gestapo (Geheime Staatspolizei, the Nazi's Secret State Police) as problematically left-wing. At the Bauhaus, he developed studies concerning town construction for the decentralization of large cities. Against the background of the economic and political fall of the Weimar Republik, he developed a universal adaptable planning system ("The new town centre", 1944), which planned a gradual dissolution of major cities and a complete penetration of landscape and settlement. With climate change, some of these ideas of renaturing cities are now again very relevant. He fled Germany for America in 1938, following Mies van der Rohe to work with him at the IIT School of Architecture in Chicago, where he was heading from 1955 the department of city planning at IIT. Later, Hilberseimer became director of the city of Chicago's planning office. His project "The New City" (1944) explored his concept of the decentralized city and the integration of agriculture and transportation in regional planning. Hilberseimer's mature planning theories derived spatial order from principles of industrial economy and a commitment to spatial order as an expression of social order (in contrast to the history of regional planning based in geological determinism, as advocated by Patrick Geddes and Ian McHarg). In 1944, he organized the exhibition "The City: Organism and Artifact" and published his first English-language book on planning, "The New City: Principles of Planning". He worked with students on self-commissioned research projects that focused on the re-planning of Chicago: these projects proposed the reordering of Chicago's urban fabric with a distributed network of public parks and gardens and restructuring into small, walkable units imagined as neighbourhood enclaves, insulating residents from automobile traffic. Despite his decades-long campaign for Chicago's re-planning, he ultimately had little impact on the form of the city. Hilberseimer taught hundreds of students at the IIT, authored dozens of publications, and conceived of his most significant professional projects. Yet, in spite of these three decades of work in and on Chicago, much of the relationship between his planning proposals and the urban history of his adopted hometown is still widely underresearched.

Helmut Jahn *(Nuremberg, 1940—present), Chicago*
Jahn is a Chicago-based German-American architect known for his flamboyant designs, such as the Sony Center on the Potsdamer Platz in Berlin; the Messeturm in Frankfurt a.M.; the One Liberty Place in Philadelphia, Pennsylvania; and the international airport in Bangkok, Thailand. Jahn came to Chicago in 1966 as a young architecture graduate to study under Ludwig Mies van der Rohe at the IIT. While Mies had recently retired from his chair at the architecture school and was plagued by health problems, his teachings and architectural ideals were still very much alive and consistently taught at the IIT School. Before immigrating to the US, Jahn received his diploma in architecture in 1965 from the Technical University in Munich;

important and influential architects such as August Thiersch und Theodor Fischer had taught at TU-Munich in the early 20th century, and they instilled the need to design for human scale and urban context, while honouring local craft traditions and materials. Walter Gropius was probably the school's most famous alumnus. Jahn's German architecture diploma was equivalent to a Master's degree in the US, so there was no real need for him to finish the three-year course of study he was enrolled in at IIT. One of his professors, Gene Summers, recognised Jahn's talent and ended up hiring him. Summers had been Mies van der Rohe's right-hand man for many years and had recently joined the Chicago architecture firm of C.F. Murphy as lead designer. Helmut Jahn joined C.F. Murphy Associates in 1967 and enjoyed a steadily successful career within the firm. In his early years at C. F. Murphy, Jahn continued to follow the direction of the late Mies van der Rohe for a while, before embracing commercial postmodernism and high-tech. Jahn took sole control of the practice in 1981, renaming the firm Murphy/Jahn. He also served as a visiting professor at both Harvard (1981) and Yale (1983). In 2012, the global practice was retitled JAHN, with offices in Chicago, Berlin, Doha and Shanghai.

Albert Kahn *(Prussia, 1869—Detroit, 1942), Detroit*
Albert Kahn was the foremost American industrial architect of his time. He immigrated with his family to Detroit in 1881, and following his studies, he worked in the office of George Mason until 1895. He founded the firm Albert Kahn Associates in 1896 in Detroit, which existed until his death in 1942. He made himself quickly a name using new construction systems of reinforced concrete for large-span factory buildings, plants and large manufacturing complexes for a booming industry, including Ford Motor Company, Packard, etc. In 1917, he became the official architect for the Aircraft Construction Division of the U.S. Army. From 1928 to 1931, he built factories for the Soviet Union's first five-year plan. Albert Kahn is probably the most important industrial architect of the 20th century. With his factory for the Ford T models, a large-scale architecture designed for mass production, he found himself at the beginning of modern industrial architecture. His buildings are characterised by a desire for simplicity, streamlining and economy, aimed at facilitating speed, efficiency and adaptability.

Otto Karl Kleemann *(Posen, Prussia, 1855—Portland, 1936), Portland, Oregon*
Kleemann was born in Ostrowo, Prussia, and attended a technical school at Holzminden. He moved to the US in 1871, making his way to San Francisco via Panama. He was unacquainted with the language and customs of the American people and at first it was difficult to get steady work, but later he was employed by several architects and spent nine years in California. He moved to Portland in 1880 and became a draftsman at Clark & Upton before joining the German architect Justus Krumbein. In 1882, he established his own architectural practice in Portland and his work included the design for Hotel Arminius, St. Patrick's Roman Catholic Church and Rectory, and the monastery in Mt. Angel. He went on to do important work for different Catholic organisations, although not Catholic himself. He was president of the Consolidation of German Speaking Societies of Oregon, a member of the German Aid Society and a member of the Masonic fraternity.

Edmund R. Krause *(Thorn, 1859—Chicago, 1935), Chicago, Illinois*
Krause studied architecture in Germany and came to the US in 1880 at the age of 21. He began his architectural practice in Chicago in 1885, where he was a sole practitioner in Edgewater. He was mainly an architect of hotels, warehouses and large apartment buildings, as well as the Majestic Building and Theatre at Monroe Street in the Loop (1906) in French Renaissance style with a richly-detailed terracotta facade, and large brick-and-stone mansions in a Romanesque style in Chicago's Lincoln Park.

Udo Kultermann *(Stettin, 1927—New York, 2013), St. Louis, Missouri*
Kultermann taught Architectural History and Theory at Washington University in St. Loius for nearly 30 years and is the author of numerous books on contemporary architecture in Africa and the Middle East. He was the author of more than 35 books. He studied art history and German literature at the University of Greifswald, earned a doctorate from the University of Muenster in 1953, and served as the director of the City Art Museum in Leverkusen before immigrating to the US in 1967.

Detlef Lienau *(Uetersen, Holstein, 1818—New York City, 1887), New York City*
With the failure of the German Revolution, Lienau immigrated to the United States in 1848. In the mid-19th century, Lienau was one of a relatively small group of trained architects, and they brought with them to the New World the traditions of the Old. He is credited with having introduced the French style to American building construction, notably the mansard roof and all its decorative flourishes. Educated at L'Ecole des Beaux-Arts in Paris, he designed virtually every type of structure—from cottages to mansions, townhouses, apartment houses, hotels, tenements, banks, stores, churches, schools, libraries, offices, factories, railroad stations and a museum. In Paris, he had studied under Henri Labrouste in the Beaux-Arts tradition. Lienau was recognised as one of the most creative and technically proficient architects of the period, and he was one of the 29 founding members of the American Institute of Architects (AIA). But Lienau differed from his colleagues in one important aspect: moulded by the North German environment, and by years of study in Paris, Lienau had a point of view more international than theirs—a rarity in an age of ardent nationalism. Thus, a fusion of traditions enabled him to adapt quickly to life in America and deal successfully with the demands of an increasingly eclectic age. Other German architects, including Henry Hardenbergh and Paul Johannes Pelz worked in Lienau's office. His son August became a partner, designing mostly residential structures after taking over his father's practice in 1887. His drawings and archive is at the Avery Library of Architecture and Fine Arts at Columbia University.

Dirk Lohan *(Rathenow, Havelland, 1938—present), Chicago*
Lohan continues the family tradition: his grandfather was Ludwig Mies van der Rohe. He left his native Germany to begin his architectural studies at the Illinois Institute of Technology under the tutelage of his grandfather. He returned to Germany and finished his studies in architecture and planning at the TU-Munich in 1962. When Mr. Lohan returned to Chicago permanently, he worked from 1962 to 1969 closely with Mies on such projects as the New National Gallery in Berlin, the IBM office tower in Chicago and The Toronto Dominion Centre. He currently works with Floyd Anderson as Lohan & Anderson, mainly in Illinois but also internationally with hotels in São Paulo und Mumbai. He established Lohan& Anderson with the philosophy that successful architecture must respond not only to economic constraints but also to the larger social and physical conditions. Throughout his career, Mr. Lohan "aims to humanise the traditional modernism of the fifties and sixties by infusing variety and texture to enrich each building design." Dirk Lohan currently serves on the Board of the IIT and the Board of Overseers of the College of Architecture at IIT.

Erich Mendelsohn *(East Prussia, 1887—San Francisco, 1953), San Francisco*
Mendelsohn studied architecture at the Technical Universities in Berlin and in Munich (like Gropius), where he met and befriended the expressionist painters of the artists' group Der Blaue Reiter and graduated in 1912. Known for his expressionistic architecture of the Einsteinturm (Potsdam, 1917—1920), the Mossehaus office building (Berlin, 1923), the Schocken Department Store (Stuttgart, 1928) and the hat factory in Luckenwalde (1923); his dynamic functionalism helped Mendelsohn to an early success. In 1924, along with Ludwig Mies van der Rohe and Walter Gropius, he was one of the founders of the progressive architectural group known as Der Ring. Mendelsohn fled in 1933 from Berlin to London (one year before Gropius and Breuer), and practiced in the UK, in short partnership with Serge Chermayeff (until 1936), where they built the De La Warr Pavilion in Bexhill-on-Sea (1934). In 1941, he came (via London and Jerusalem/Palestine) first to New York; and in 1945 to San Francisco, where he settled with family and taught at the University of California at Berkeley (although never appointed to a property faculty position due to the politics at UC Berkeley). Until the end of World War II, his activities were limited by his immigration status to lectures and publications. In 1945, he became an American citizen and established his practice in San Francisco. From then until his death in 1953, he undertook various projects, mostly synagogues for Jewish communities. In his second career in the US, he never again achieved the prominence as designer at the centre of the avant-garde, a role which he enjoyed in Berlin pre-1933.

Detlef Mertins *(Stuttgart, 1954—Philadelphia, 2011), Toronto; Philadelphia*
A professor at the universities of Pennsylvania, Columbia, Harvard, Princeton and Toronto, Dr. Mertins was a prominent architectural historian, educator, architect and writer. Born in Stuttgart, he immigrated with his parents to Canada in 1960. After completing a Ph.D. at Princeton University, he started teaching at the University of Toronto in 1985. From 2003 to 2008, he was Chair of the department of architecture at the University of Pennsylvania.

Ludwig Mies van der Rohe *(Aachen, Germany 1886—Chicago, 1969), Chicago*
Widely regarded as one of the pioneering masters of modernist architecture, Ludwig Mies van der Rohe (or simply "Mies") taught at the Bauhaus school in Dessau and Berlin. Born into a family of stonemasons, young and ambitious Ludwig Mies moved in 1905 from the provincial city of Aachen to the German capital Berlin. In 1905 to 1907, Mies designed furniture in the office of Bruno Paul in Berlin, before working as assistant to Peter Behrens (1908—1911).
At Behrens's atelier, he met other young architects, including Walter Gropius, Adolf Meyer and Le Corbusier. In 1911, Mies established his own practice in Berlin, which lasted until his departure to the US in 1937. In 1926, Mies was the first Vice-President of the Deutscher Werkbnd, and in 1927 became director and master planner of the Werkbund Exposition at Stuttgart Weissenhof. During this time, he presented the first cantilever steel chair. In 1929, he was director of the German Section at the International Exposition in Barcelona, which enabled him to design the famous Barcelona Pavilion (one of the key buildings of 20th century architecture). From 1930—1933 he was director of the Bauhaus, first in Dessau and then in Berlin. The Nazi regime stymied Mies' architectural practice in Berlin and he received few commissions throughout the 1930s. Frustrated by the political changes and unhappy about the closure of the Bauhaus, he left Germany reluctantly at the end of 1937 and immigrated to the US, as he saw his opportunity for any future commissions vanish. He accepted a residential commission in Wyoming and then settled in Chicago, taking up an offer to head the department of architecture of the newly established Illinois Institute of Technology (IIT) in Chicago in 1938. In Chicago, he became director and professor of the Department of Architecture, at the newly established IIT, formerly the Armour Institute of Technology. He stayed as director of IIT's school of architecture until 1958. Here, he was able to introduce a new kind of architectural education and programme, later known as *Second Chicago School*, which became very influential in the following decades in North America and Europe. He also became campus architect for the university and built a series of high-rise towers in Chicago and New York. Architecturally, he was most influenced by Schinkel and Behrens. Two houses designed by Mies are modern icons: Villa Tugendhat in Brno (1928—1930) and Farnsworth House, a weekend retreat outside Chicago (1946—1951).

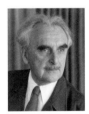

Richard Neutra *(Vienna, 1892—Wuppertal, Germany, 1970), Los Angeles*
Richard Joseph Neutra was a Jewish Austrian architect active in Southern California and considered among the most prominent and important modernist architects. Neutra studied at the Vienna University of Technology (1910 to 1918) and also attended the private architecture school of Adolf Loos. After World War I Neutra worked first in Switzerland, and in 1921 he joined the office of Erich Mendelsohn in Berlin. Neutra moved to the US by 1923 and became a Naturalised citizen in 1929. In 1927 he published *Wie Baut Amerika?* ("How America Builds"), an overview of new American architecture. Neutra worked briefly for Frank Lloyd Wright in Chicago before accepting an invitation from his friend and university companion Rudolph Schindler to work and live communally in Schindler's house in Los Angeles. Neutra's first work in Los Angeles was in landscape architecture, where he provided the design for the garden of Schindler's Lovell beach house (1922–1925). Schindler and

Neutra collaborated on an entry for the League of Nations competition of 1926–1927, and Neutra subsequently developed his own practice. He went on to design numerous buildings embodying the International Style and became celebrated for rigorously geometric but airy structures that symbolized a West Coast variation on the mid-century modern residence (such as the residence for Edgar J. Kaufmann in Palm Springs, 1946). In the early 1930s, Neutra's Los Angeles practice trained several young architects who went on to independent success, including Harwell H. Harris (who later became dean of the school at the University of Texas at Austin) and Raphael Soriano. In 1932, Neutra was included in the seminal MoMA exhibition on modern architecture, curated by Henry-Russell Hitchcock and Philip Johnson. In 1949 Neutra formed a partnership with Robert E. Alexander that lasted until 1958, which finally gave him the opportunity to design larger commercial and institutional buildings, such as the new US Embassy in Karachi. In 1965 Neutra formed a partnership with his son Dion Neutra. Between 1960 and 1970, Neutra created eight villas in Europe, stressing an open, multifunctional plan for living spaces that are flexible, adaptable and easily modified for any type of life or event.

Cornelia Hahn Oberlander *(Muehlheim, 1921—present), Philadelphia and Vancouver, British Columbia*
In 1938, Oberlander fled with her sister and mother to the UK, and in 1939 immigrated to the US. In 1944, she received a BA from Smith College and was one of the very first women to be admitted to the Harvard GSD. In 1947, she was among the first class of women to graduate from Harvard with a degree in landscape architecture. Although based in Vancouver, much of her career was in the US. She began work with Louis Kahn and Oscar Stonorov in Philadelphia and then with landscape architect Dan Kiley in Vermont before moving to Canada. The early years of her career were dedicated to designing landscapes for low-income housing projects and playgrounds, the most famous is the Canadian Government Pavilion, Children's Creative Centre play area for Expo 67 in Montreal. Her first playground, for a 1951 public housing project for architect Louis Kahn, included a vegetable garden and a fruit tree. She founded her firm, Cornelia Hahn Oberlander Landscape Architects, in 1953 when she moved to Vancouver. In the same year, she married Peter Oberlander, who held a Ph.D. in regional planning from Harvard. Peter Oberlander was Canada's first professor of Urban and Regional Planning, and he died in 2008. During her long career, Oberlander has contributed to the designs of numerous high-profile buildings in both Canada and the United States, including the National Gallery of Canada, and the Canadian Chancery in Washington, D.C.

Paul Johannes Pelz *(Waldenburg, Silesia, 1841—1918, Washington, D.C.), Washington, D.C.*
Pelz is best known as the main architect of the Library of Congress in Washington, D.C. His father was a politician, elected as a representative of Silesia to the Frankfurt Parliament in 1848. Subsequent political repression led him to immigrate to the US in 1851, while the rest of the family temporarily stayed in Breslau, where Paul studied architecture. In 1858, Paul joined his

father in New York City and served there as apprentice to architect Detlef Lienau. In 1864, he was employed as chief draftsman by Jewish architect Henry Fernbach, where he worked on New York's Central Synagogue. In 1866, Pelz moved to Washington D.C., where he first worked as a civil engineer. In 1873, Pelz partnered with John Smithmeyer; and their proposal for the Library of Congress won the competition. However, the difficulties experienced on the Library of Congress project, with many delays from congressional dithering, eventually strained their collaboration. In 1888, Pelz became the lead architect for the Library of Congress and Smithmeyer was dismissed; Pelz in turn was dismissed in 1892 and succeeded by Edward Pearce Casey. Pelz had the main role in the design of the building and the execution of its exterior, while Smithmeyer was instrumental in securing the commission, and Casey supervised most of the interior finishing. Pelz went on to design churches, public buildings, private houses and commercial buildings, and participated in key debates of the time on Washington's urban design. At the 1900 AIA Convention he presented a plan for the remodelling of the National Mall, which was a key source of the McMillan Plan the following year. Like other architects of his time, Pelz mastered a range of architectural styles and was willing to switch across them depending on program and client's taste.

Brigitte Peterhans *(born Brigitte Schlaich, in Sulz am Neckar, 1928—present), Chicago*
Brigitte Peterhans is a German-American architect and sister of the internationally known structural engineer Joerg Schlaich. She received a Master in Architecture degree in 1960 from the University of Stuttgart. Encouraged by Myron Goldsmith, she studied at the IIT in Chicago as a Fulbright Fellow (1956-57), where she received a second Master of Architecture in 1962. In 1957, she married the Bauhaus teacher and photographer Walter Peterhans, who taught at this time at the IIT. As a student she was hired in 1958 by Skidmore Owings and Merrill (SOM, at that time the largest architectural firm in the United States), where she remained involved in projects, on and off for thirty-three years. In 1973, she was made an associate at SOM, and an associate partner in 1979. She retired in 1990. German photographer **Walter Peterhans** (Frankfurt a.M., 1897—Stetten, 1960) was from 1929 to 1933 a Bauhaus teacher and course leader of photography. Invited by Mies van der Rohe, he immigrated to Chicago in 1938 to teach the "visual training" course to architecture students at the IIT. He was instrumental in working with Mies on the new curriculum at IIT. The four-semester course was so successful, it survived Peterhans by over forty years.

Johann A. Roebling *(Prussia, 1806—New York, 1869), Brooklyn Heights, New York*
Roebling was an architect and civil engineer with a fascination for wire rope suspension bridges, and he is best known for the construction of the Brooklyn Bridge in New York. After studying science in Erfurt, he enrolled in 1824 at the Preussische Bauakademie in Berlin. In 1831, he bought land with his brother in Pennsylvania and they immigrated to the US to establish a German settlement. He first conducted surveys for railway lines and new canals, but soon returned to bridge construction and established a company for steel wire and cable

production. He constructed several large-span railway suspension bridges in Canada, Pittsburgh and Ohio – before he started work on Brooklyn Bridge spanning the East River in New York (the world's longest suspension bridge at the time it was finished).

Peter Roesch *(Leipzig, 1929—Chicago, 2018), Chicago*
Roesch came to the Illinois Institute of Technology in Chicago in 1952 to study with Mies van der Rohe, which set the course for the rest of his life. He later taught at IIT for about 35 years, until he retired in 2013. His initial studies in Germany had taught him the components of buildings, from bricklaying to carpentry. In 1945, at the end of World War II, believing his future was limited in post-war East Germany, he left Leipzig to study in Hamburg. From there, he qualified under the Fulbright program to come as a refugee to the US. Mies became his mentor and Roesch was one of his last students at the IIT. After two years of studies in Chicago, Roesch returned for a short time to Germany to help with post-war rebuilding efforts, but in 1957 returned to Chicago to work for SOM. There, he met James Hammond, and in the early 1960s, the two formed the partnership Hammond & Roesch. They designed a range of clean modern buildings similar to Crown Hall. The design studios at IIT taught by Roesch were committed to advancing the ideals of the Bauhaus philosophy that good design could better society. Affordable housing was a frequent topic, and he would say "Good design should be for everybody". In a 2005 interview he recalled the power of Mies's silent scrutiny and how it exposed one's flaws: when he showed Mies some of his designs, "he did not say one word for twenty minutes. It forced me to look at my own work, and I found all the mistakes—everything became clear."

Sigrid Lorenzen Rupp *(Bremerhaven, 1943—Palo Alto, 2004), Palo Alto, California*
In 1953, she emigrated from Germany to Oakland, California, with her family at the age of 10. She studied architecture at the University of California, Berkeley, graduating in 1966; and received a California Architecture License in 1971. She worked for various firms in the San Francisco Bay Area before establishing her own practice, SLR Architects, in 1976 (which she led until 1998). She specialised in technical and industrial facilities and provided designs for early tech companies in Silicon Valley, including Apple, Claris, IBM and Sun Microsystems; she designed Stanford University's Storey House and Press Building, and completed projects for San Jose State University and United Airlines. Rupp was an advocate of women's rights and a member of the Organization of Women Architects (OWA), the Union Internationale des Femmes Architectes (UIFA). She noted "It seemed that the time for gender differences should be long over." She was the chairperson of the City of Palo Alto Architectural Review Board, director of the AIA Santa Clara chapter, and director of California Women in Environmental Design. Of her career, she said, "I'd like to be remembered for dissenting when everyone else thought it easier to go with the grain even when the grain was wrong. I'd like to be remembered for being a competent architect who did competent work, and someone who told good stories."

Frederick C. Sauer *(Heidelberg, 1860—Pennsylvania, 1942), Pittsburgh, Pennsylvania*
Sauer worked as a stonemason, bricklayer and carpenter while studying at the Technical School in Wittenberg, before studying architecture at Stuttgart University. He moved to Pittsburgh in 1880, where he established an office in 1884; he also established the Aspinwall-Delafield Land Company in 1904, and built about a dozen Catholic churches in the area. His most notable work is St. Stanislaus Kostka Church (1891) in Pittsburgh. After remodelling his chicken coop in an eccentric mode from 1928 to 1930, he gradually transformed a wooded hillside into an architectural fantasy, a bizarre collection of buildings: a complex of castlesque buildings and landscape features in an Art Nouveau style that gradually took shape, and was progressively added to by Sauer until his death in 1942.

Emil Schacht *(Schleswig-Holstein, 1854—Portland, 1926), Portland, Oregon*
Schacht was a prominent architect in Portland and his work was prolific from the 1890s until World War I, when he produced a large number of commercial buildings, including factories and warehouses as well as residential projects, hotels and theatres. He is known for his craftsman architecture style homes and was a founding member of the 1902 Portland Association of Architects. In 1909, his practice Emil Schacht & Son designed the Wheeldon Apartments, a 5-story brick Tudor Revival building in Downtown Portland; and in 1904 the neo-classical Astoria's City Hall; and the North Pacific Brewery.

Rudolph Schindler *(Vienna, 1887—Los Angeles, 1953), Los Angeles*
Rudolph (Rudolf) Schindler was a Jewish-Austrian architect active in Los Angeles and considered among the most prominent and important modernist architects. He was five years older than his lifelong friend and rival Richard Neutra; they met at university. Their careers would parallel each other: both would immigrate to Los Angeles, for a short time living together, and both were recognised as important early modernists creating new styles suited to the Californian climate; sometimes, both would even work for the same clients. Schindler studied at the Vienna University of Technology before attending the Vienna Academy of Fine Arts (or "Wagnerschule") graduating in 1911 with a degree in architecture. His teachers included Otto Wagner and Adolf Loos. In 1914, Schindler moved to the US, first to Chicago, then to Los Angeles (where Neutra would join him in 1923). Between 1919 and 1931, Schindler worked on and off for Frank Lloyd Wright, who spent much of his time in Japan. During this time, fractures started to appear in the Schindler-Wright relationship with disputes over whose work was whose, and Schindler complained of being underpaid and exploited. Schindler was not included in the highly influential 1932 International Style exhibition at the MoMA, while Richard Neutra was and incorrectly, was credited as "the Austrian who worked on the Imperial Hotel with Wright." Although Schindler worked with some of the foremost practitioners, his ability to work with concrete successfully within tight budgets have placed him as one of the most inventive mavericks of 20th century modernism. Reyner Banham wrote that he designed "as if there had never been houses before."

Don Paul Schlegel *(1926—Albuquerque, 2019), Albuquerque, New Mexico*
The inaugural chairman of the University of New Mexico's Department of
Architecture, and later dean of the School of Architecture and Planning, Don
Schlegel died in 2019 in Albuquerque. He studied at the University of Cincinnati
and at the Massachusetts Institute of Technology (MIT) under Buckminster
Fuller. Schlegel arrived in Albuquerque (New Mexico) in 1954, and at home
he and his family kept the German traditions alive. His student Antoine
Predock recalls (2019) that "Don Schlegel was a transformative figure, the foundation for the
formation of the UNM School of Architecture and Planning, and his insight and vision drove
the destiny of the School. His 40-year leadership not only helped to guide the school and its
programs forward, but also helped shape the profession and our faculty and students'
careers." His daughter said her father once told her, "There was a point in his life that he
knew he would not be a famous architect, which was his dream; so he took all his knowledge
and his wisdom, all his energy, and turned it to teaching and became a dedicated professor
of architecture. He knew that being a professor was really his calling. He touched so many
lives as a professor who brought students along in their formative years as they became
architects, colleagues and friends" (2019).

August Gottlieb Schoenborn *(Suhl, 1827—Washington, D.C., 1902),
Washington, D.C.*
Schoenborn is best known as the designer of the US Capitol dome in
Washington, D.C. In 1843, he enrolled at the Technical Institute and School
of Art in Erfurt, where he studied architecture. After completing his studies,
he immigrated to the US in 1849 and first settled in Wisconsin; two years
later, he moved to Washington, D.C. where he found a position as a draftsman
with Thomas Walter, the architect of the Capitol. With only a small-scale model and some
very rough drawings to work from, Schoenborn produced highly detailed architectural plans
for the US Capitol. Walter did not initially believe that Schoenborn had done the work himself
but was quickly satisfied when he found out that Schoenborn was a trained architect. President
Millard Fillmore was highly impressed with the work and often visited him in the architectural
offices at the Capitol. Schoenborn made two important additions to the US Capitol building:
when the Capitol Library burned down in 1851, it was replaced with an iron library designed
by Schoenborn. He also made the original drawings for the new iron dome of the Capitol.
During the American Civil War in 1861-62, Schoenborn worked as a surveyor, mapmaker and
architect of numerous military barracks, hospitals and offices for the US Army. He spent the
post-war years in Washington, D.C., designing numerous public buildings.

Helmut C. Schulitz *(Bublitz, Pommern, 1936—present), Los Angeles and
Braunschweig*
In the late 1960s, Helmut Schulitz enrolled in graduate studies at the University
of California in Los Angeles, after completing his studies at the Technical
University of Munich. He had done work on prefabricated building systems for
the Bavarian government before coming to California. In 1969 (until 1982)

he was appointed to a teaching position at UCLA, where he set up the Team for Experimental Systems and Techniques (TEST), a research group to develop an "open" building process which would use a wide range of industrial products and components readily available on the warehouse shelf and from various manufacturers. Influenced by Charles Eames's Case Study House, the first TEST experimental steel building was a prototype house built in 1976–1977: a hillside house above Los Angeles, defined by architectural critics as "high tech", and praised for its innovation and a rigorous approach to detailing. Perched on a steep cliff lot that many thought to be unbuildable, the house served as both daily residence for Schulitz and his family and prototype for a new process of design and construction. The construction system maximized the use of pre-finished industrial components to minimise labour time and reduce material costs. After 16 years in Los Angeles, Schulitz returned in 1983 to Germany to take up a teaching position Professor at the Institut für Baukonstruktion und Industriebau at the TU Braunschweig (until 2002). The practice Schulitz Architects was founded in 1975, and transferred to Braunschweig in 1983. Schulitz is the co-author of a number of relevant books including the *Steel Construction Manual* and *Stahlbau Atlas*. His son Marc Schulitz is a faculty member at Cal Poly Pomona.

Werner Seligmann *(Osnabrück, 1930—Syracuse, New York, 1998), Syracuse, New York*
Seligman was a prominent educator, architect and urban designer. His live was split between Germany, Switzerland and the US. His family was Jewish and they were arrested in 1936 by the Nazis to spend the latter part of the war in a concentration camp. In 1945, he was picked up by American troops and in 1949 sent to the US to live with relatives in upstate New York, a short distance from Cornell University. Seligmann received his bachelor from Cornell in 1954 and became a naturalised citizen in 1955. He first taught at the University of Texas at Austin from 1956 to 1958, where he became part of a small group of faculty later nicknamed "The Texas Rangers," including: Colin Rowe, Werner Seligmann, Robert Slutzky, John Hejduk, Bernhard Hoesli and others. After this group was dismissed from Austin, Seligmann returned to Germany, where he pursued graduate studies at the Technische Hochschule in Braunschweig, from 1958 to 1959, and taught as Assistant at the ETH in Zürich, from 1959 to 1961. He returned to the US in 1961, where he was until 1974 a Professor of Architecture at Cornell University, and from 1974 to 1976 at the GSD, Harvard University. From 1976 to 1990, he was Dean at Syracuse University School of Architecture, and from 1990 to 1993 he returned as Professor of Architecture to the ETH Zurich. He also held a number of visiting positions, such as at Yale and the University of Virginia. He was named a Distinguished Professor in 1998 and awarded the Topaz Award in Architectural Education jointly from the ACSA and the AIA. Throughout his teaching career, he maintained a practice, Werner Seligmann & Associates, which he founded in 1961 in Cortland, New York. His work on housing prototypes for the New York State Urban Development Corp. in the 1970s established his reputation, especially the "Ithaca Scattered Site" housing project, which was modelled after the low-rise high-density Halen estate by Swiss architects Atelier 5.

Oscar Gregory Stonorov *(Frankfurt a. M., 1905—Emmet County, MI 1970), Philadelphia*

Oscar G. Stonorov was a modernist architect, sculptor and architectural writer who immigrated to the United States in 1929, first to New York, before settling in Philadelphia. He studied architecture in Italy at the University of Florence (1924-25), and at the University of Zurich (1925–1928), Switzerland, and in 1928 worked in the office of André Lurçat in Paris. In these years, Stonorov researched and co-edited with Willy Boesiger the publication of the work of Swiss architect Le Corbusier, covering the period 1910 to 1929 (published in 1929). In 1940, Stonorov worked with Louis Kahn on the design of housing developments in Pennsylvania; a formal office partnership between Oscar Stonorov and Louis Kahn began in February 1942 and ended in March 1947, and produced fifty-four known projects. In 1943, Stonorov co-wrote with Kahn *Why City Planning Is Your Responsibility*, and in 1944: *You and Your Neighborhood ... A Primer for Neighborhood Planning*. Between 1950 and 1954, Philadelphia architect and future Pritzker Prize winner Robert Venturi (who later worked directly with Kahn) worked in the office of Stonorov. In 1957, he established the partnership of Stonorov & Haws; he tragically died in a plane crash in 1970.

Wilhelm Viggo von Moltke *(Kreisau, Silesia, 1911—Boston, 1987), Philadelphia and Cambridge, MA*

Part of an aristocratic family (his father, Helmuth Graf von Moltke was a General and led the German Army from 1906 to 1914), Viggo ("Willo") von Moltke received an architectural degree from the Technische Hochschule in Berlin-Charlottenburg in 1937, and in the same year immigrated to the UK, due to his political opposition to the Nazi government. His oldest brother, Helmuth James von Moltke, a member of the German resistance (and founder of the Kreisau Circle), was executed by the Nazis in January 1945. Viggo spent the late 1930s working as an architect at various offices in London and Stockholm, and in 1940, left Europe for the United States. During his first year in America he worked for short periods in New York with Alvar Aalto, and in Philadelphia with Oscar Stonorov & Louis Kahn. Stonorov, like von Moltke, was an immigrant from Germany and had already made a name for himself as modernist architect and partner of Louis Kahn. In Stonorov & Kahn's office, von Moltke met Peter Blake, who became an influential architectural critic and a lifelong friend. In 1941, he won the first prize in the design competition for the new Museum of Modern Art. He received a second degree from Harvard's GSD in 1942, studying with Walter Gropius and Martin Wagner. At Black Mountain College in North Carolina, he met Josef and Anni Albers and other Bauhaus refugees. In the following years, he became an influential architect and urban planner, working as the chief designer on projects in Philadelphia and at the MIT. Between 1948 and 1953 he worked for SOM and Eero Saarinen in New York. In 1953, he returned to Philadelphia and obtained a leading position in the city's planning commission, with Edmund Bacon, until 1961. After he left Philadelphia, von Moltke took a position as chief designer for the Guayana project at the Joint Center for Urban Studies of MIT and Harvard University: the project assisted the government of Venezuela in the development of a new city in the Guayana region. According to Donald Appleyard (1976), "The project was not a success, but a lesson in a promising approach to urban design that involved future residents in the process." In 1964, he returned to Harvard's GSD, where he held a professorship and became director of the urban design programme, until 1977.

Konrad Wachsmann *(Frankfurt a.d.Oder 1901—Los Angeles, 1980), Chicago and Los Angeles*
Wachsmann is notable for his contribution to the mass production of prefabricated building components and as pioneer in industrial construction. Originally apprenticed as a cabinetmaker, he studied 1920 to 1925 at the Academy of Arts in Berlin under the Expressionist architect Hans Poelzig, and at the Academy of Arts in Dresden. In 1926, he became chief architect for a manufacturer of timber buildings. He designed a summer house for Albert Einstein, one of his lifelong friends, in Caputh, close to Potsdam. He received the Prix de Rome from the German Academy in Rome in 1932. In 1938, he first immigrated to Paris and in 1941 to the US, where he began a collaboration with Walter Gropius: they developed the "Packaged House System," a design for a prefabricated modular timber panel house which could be constructed in less than nine hours (the collaboration ended in 1948). Before the end of World War II, he also developed a mobile aircraft hangar and later designed aircraft hangars for the U.S. Air Force in the 1960s. Wachsmann taught at the IIT in Chicago from 1949 to 1964 (on invitation by Mies), and later at the School of Architecture at the University of Southern California (USC) in Los Angeles, from 1964 to 1979. At USC, he was director of the Building Research Division and chairman of the graduate school in the department of architecture. Among his written works is *The Turning Point of Building* (1959; Eng. trans. 1961), in which he made a point of insisting that technology and art were inseparable. Ikea, the Swedish furniture giant, started in the 1940s with standardised flat-pack furniture for middle-income families, inspired by the work of Gropius and Wachsmann.

Martin Wagner *(Koenigsberg ,1885—Cambridge, 1957), Boston*
Martin Wagner was a German architect, city planner and author, best known as the driving force behind the construction of modernist mass housing projects in Berlin. Wagner was educated at the Technical University Berlin and worked as draftsman in the office of Hermann Muthesius, before he was appointed the City Building Commissioner for Berlin-Schöneberg, in 1918.
He served as the chief city planner (Planning Director) of Berlin from 1925 to 1933, and most of Berlin's modernist housing estates were constructed under his leadership (including Bruno Taut's Hufeisensiedlung). In 1924 he founded the building society GEHAG, which was responsible for seventy percent of Berlin's new housing built between 1924 and 1933, amounting to many thousands of residential units. Wagner was more planner than designer-architect. His role was to lead the large-scale housing effort to standardise building technology, rationalise construction, and organise industrial suppliers and labour unions. In 1929, he published *Städtebauliche Probleme in amerikanischen Städten und ihre Rückwirkung auf den deutschen Städtebau*, a comparison between planning in Germany and the US. As socialist, when the Nazis came to power in 1933, Wagner fell under increasing pressure and

was expelled from the Deutscher Werkbund. From 1933 to 1938, he was in Turkey in exile, where he worked with Bruno Taut on the city plan for Ankara. In 1938, he moved to the US (by invitation of Gropius) and took a position to teach city planning at the Harvard GSD, where he taught until 1951. His immigration to the US was assisted by his friend Walter Gropius and in 1944, he became an American citizen. However, by 1940, his relationship with Gropius was strained, and he complained of Gropius abandoning the underlying social principles of modernism, and practicing modernism only as a style (similar critique was expressed by Joseph Hudnut, dean at the GSD). In 1944, Wagner produced a new city plan for Boston, which called for a restructuring of the downtown area, but it remained unbuilt.

Rudolf Wittkower *(Berlin, 1901—New York City, 1971), New York City and London*
Wittkower was not an architect, but an influential architectural historian. In 1933, he fled with his wife from Berlin to London because they were both Jewish. He had first an academic career in the UK, before immigrating to the US. His most significant book is *Architectural Principles in the Age of Humanism* (1949), discussing the work of Alberti, Palladio, Bernini and Michelangelo, studying the mathematical proportions of their buildings. From 1934 to 1956, he taught at the Warburg Institute, University of London, and in 1949 was appointed professor at the Slade School of Fine Arts, London. In 1956, he moved to the United States to take up an appointment at Columbia University in New York, where he was chair of the Department of Art History and Archaeology until 1969. Wittkower's writing was very influential for the thinking of a large number of architects and historians, such as for Colin Rowe.

Paul Zucker *(Berlin, 1888—New York, 1971),* New York City
Architect, art historian and educator Paul Zucker was forced to flee Nazi Germany and arrived in New York in 1937. He was, since 1938, Professor of History of Architecture and Art and The Cooper Union in New York City. Before immigrating to the US, Zucker had studied architecture and art history in Berlin and Munich; after obtaining his doctorate at the Technische Hochschule Berlin (in 1913), he taught courses in architecture and city planning from 1916 to 1935, first at the Prussian State Academy for the Arts, then at the Lessing Hochschule in Berlin, where he was Dean from 1930 to 1935. Until 1933, Zucker enjoyed a high reputation in Berlin's intellectual circles. Before coming to the United States, he headed his own architectural firm in Berlin and designed numerous office buildings, banks, stores and country houses.

PART II
Consolidation of the Modernist Approach in US Architectural Education

1. Leaving Germany, Embracing New Challenges: First to the UK, then Coming to America

In 1933, when the National Socialist Party came into power in Germany, they forced many Bauhaus masters and artists into exile. As a consequence, the Bauhaus teaching principles began to spread worldwide, especially to the US. Adolf Hitler came to power in March 1933, which was the beginning of Nazi Germany (1933–1945), a period when US universities offered teaching jobs to immigrating intellectuals and took in numerous refugees.

We can identify three waves of US immigration in the 20th century: first in the 1930s, the group of German-born architects and educators fleeing Nazi Germany into exile (including the Bauhaus refugees Gropius, Mies, Hilberseimer, Albers, Zucker and others); the second wave in the 1940s, after World War II, to escape poverty in war-demolished Europe (including Erich Mendelsohn and Konrad Wachsmann); and a third, smaller wave in the 1970s (including Werner Seligmann, Peter Roesch and Helmut Jahn), attracted by the construction boom and scale of opportunities available in the US. All three waves of immigrants influenced US architectural education in their own ways.

In 1934, Walter Gropius and his family left Nazi Germany for Britain, relocating to London. Gropius fled to the UK with the help of British architect Maxwell Fry. The Bauhaus teachers Breuer and Moholy-Nagy (Mies stayed in Berlin until 1937) also decided to first go to the UK. But they were soon disappointed about the limited opportunities and subsequently left the UK to move on to the US.

Once he arrived in London, Gropius entered into a partnership with Maxwell Fry, who had graduated from Liverpool University in 1923. In the year they arrived in the UK, Walter Gropius, Erich Mendelsohn and Serge Chermayeff gave lectures and participated in critiquing student work at the University of Liverpool, facilitated by Maxwell Fry. By this time students at the school had already adopted a modernist style, even though the teaching techniques were still based on the Beaux-Arts model. Student works throughout Britain often displayed modernist principles, but this was not clearly reflected in the curriculum. Only in the 1940s, Bauhaus-inspired courses became the norm in the US and British schools, and the Bauhaus began to be perceived as a more systematic form of training.

The progressive Bauhaus teachers' first hope was to build a future in the UK. However, soon after arrival in 1934 they struggled to get important commissions. They failed to find significant work in the UK, where they encountered British reservation, scepticism and conservatism.

Britain rejected their progressive design thinking; in addition, negative comments about Germany and anti-German sentiments that had begun to appear in Britain in the 1870s deepened during World War I, creating an unfavourable atmosphere.

Their concepts were ahead of their time, and it appears that they arrived fifteen years too early in the UK, a country that was still anti-modernist and simply not ready for radical new ideas; this situation would only change after 1951, with the Festival of Britain in London. In fact, in the 1960s, London would emerge as one of the intellectual centres of progressive architectural thinking, with groups like Archigram and new talents such as James Stirling, Ernö Goldfinger and Team 4, and the AA School as a hub of innovation. But at the time when Gropius, Breuer, Mendelsohn and Chermayeff arrived, it was still stuck in conservative conditions. Owen Hatherley (2019) notes, "There was an enormous hostility in Britain to the Bauhaus and what it stood for. Bauhaus just wasn't British. The US universities were much more enthusiastic for their ideas than Oxford and Cambridge." Britain in the 1930s was still an anti-modernist backwater and it took a progressive architect like Berthold Lubetkin (1901—1990), a Soviet émigré and modernist architect, many years in London to build a modest career.

So, for a number of reasons, the UK did not offer the same opportunities to revive the Bauhaus pedagogy as the United States did, and it is in the US that the legacy of the Bauhaus is most evident. Heathcote (2019) notes, "There has been much discussion recently about exactly how much influence the émigrés from the Bauhaus actually exerted during their brief sojourn in England in the mid-1930s. Certainly Walter Gropius, Marcel Breuer and László Moholy-Nagy struggled to get work at the scale they might have expected–but, then again, they were only here for a few years and architecture takes time. Were they rejected by a conservative professional clique, fearful for its own work (in the midst of the worst downturn of the 20th century)? Was it an apprehensiveness about the new Modernism, a seemingly politicised (and therefore very un-English) architecture? The USA, for which many 'Bauhauslers' left, was a different story: a country of immigrants."

In 1904, the German critic and architect Hermann Muthesius published his admiring romantic study of English domestic architecture, *Das Englische Haus*. Its three volumes provide a romantic and retrospective record of the revival of English domestic architecture during the latter part of the 19th century. It suited the anti-modernist British attitude, which found expression in numerous ways, including in Evelyn Waugh's portrayal of a German Bauhaus architect (supposedly Gropius), called Professor Silenus, in the novel *Decline and Fall* (1928): there is sneering at a supposed Germanic perfectionism, a cool, rational, detached view of architecture as a mechanistic rather than an emotional endeavour. Many of the UK architects cultivated anti-urban sentiments, with Ebenezer Howard's study of garden cities (1902) being highly popular.

Gropius's stay in London was disappointing professionally, but it proved a fertile period for his theoretical, creative and academic development and good preparation for what was to come. In 1937, Gropius was appointed as professor at Harvard University in Cambridge, Massachusetts, and just a year later he became director of its Department of Architecture.

However, in many ways it's surprising that British society was not more open to foreigners, since British modernism was not much later shaped by immigrants: among many others, there was Berthold Lubetkin, Ernö Goldfinger, Walter Segal, Nikolaus Pevsner (who formalised and catalogued the history of British architecture into a coherent canon), Joseph Rykwert (who introduced genuine intellectual enquiry into architectural academia) and others.

Gropius's Position at Harvard University

The story that follows is a well-documented narrative: the dean of Harvard University's Graduate School of Design (GSD), Joseph Hudnut, visited Walter Gropius in London in 1937 and subsequently offered him a job at the GSD. Inspired by Gropius's innovative approach to arts and design teaching, Hudnut tasked him to reorganise Harvard's traditional design curriculum. Gropius accepted and moved to the United States in late 1937 and took up the position along with fellow émigré and former student, Marcel Breuer. In 1938 Gropius became chair of the Department of Architecture at Harvard University's newly established GSD and taught there until 1952. (In the same year, in 1938, Mies was appointed as head of the School of Architecture at the Armour Institute, later IIT).

Gropius was Harvard's first modernist architect, and he began his tenure by immediately reforming the school's curriculum. Gropius was interested in strengthening the links between the school and industry, as he did eighteen years earlier at the Bauhaus. As the founding director of the Bauhaus, he brought an immense reputation to the job and provided extraordinary strategic leadership and vision for the new GSD.

Shortly after his arrival, Gropius built a house for himself and his family in Lincoln, Massachusetts; now known as Gropius House, this building was hugely influential in introducing international modernism to North America. The Lincoln House was a typical cool Bauhaus-style house and was soon known as a port of call for European refugees. In 1945, eight years after his arrival and when he became a US citizen, Gropius co-founded the Architects' Collaborative (TAC) in Boston with a new generation of young American architects. Under the democratising influence of American universities, Gropius became an advocate of public discourse, participation and collaboration. Building upon the teamwork-based ethos he had fostered at the Bauhaus, TAC went on to become one of the most respected post-war architectural practices of the United States. It went bankrupt in 1995 after many major projects it was planning in the Middle East were cancelled.

The two schools, the experimental Bauhaus and the traditional Harvard, couldn't have been more different. Before Gropius's arrival, Harvard architecture students learned design by sketching plaster casts of ornamental fragments from historical buildings. Gropius rejected this traditional model of education based on copying the past—what he called "endlessly reviving revivals"—and assigned his students to design solutions for real sites as part of a team of diverse professionals including engineers and city planners, as architects do in the real world (Durth and Penth, 2019).

Soon after his arrival, Gropius presented his manifesto *Suggestions for the Curriculum of an Architect's Training at Harvard* (1938). His confident written doctrine added to its intellectual appeal. Despite the reputation of the Bauhaus, its importance to architectural education owes more to the version of it that Gropius promoted than to the Bauhaus itself. While this manifesto largely reinvented his experience at the Bauhaus, it became the pedagogical programme for the modern paradigm of US architectural education. Goddard (2019) notes that the main thrust was towards the scientific and technological and away from the premise that "design vocabulary grew from the orders, measured drawings, courses in history and ornament, archaeological projects, and grand-tour sketchbooks." Gropius suggested avoiding "intimidation and imitation" by delaying the study of history to the third year, which encapsulates his criticism of Beaux-Arts methods. His 1938 manifesto integrated what he presented as the Bauhaus educational model into the American university system. The text of his presentation was first published in the cultural magazine Twice a Year (1939), but it was available earlier in May 1937 as an interview with him entitled "Architecture at Harvard University" in the US journal *Architectural Record*.[5]

Kentgens-Craig (2018) notes that at this time, "nowhere did the artistic and intellectual heritage of the Bauhaus find ground as fertile as in America". However, there was also criticism and resistance from some old-guard American colleagues, who argued that "the modernism of the Bauhaus did not grow from the social and historical context of the US but was instead imported and alien". They rejected the Bauhaus mainly on pedagogical grounds, while the politics of the time certainly played a part as well.

At Harvard, the Bauhaus model was able to evolve into something new in the fertile soil of an established, well-funded elite university, where the atmosphere was liberal, forward-looking and unconstrained. Many of Gropius's students went on to become leading and highly regraded American modernists, graduating into the booming post-war era, including I.M. Pei, Fumihiko Maki, Harry Seidler, Philip Johnson, Edward Barnes and Paul Rudolph, among others (see Images 8 and 9).

MacCarthy recalls that Gropius never lost the sense of his European past and German origin (2019, 8). Even far away from Germany through his years in exile, Gropius would frequently speak about the architecture of Berlin. In 1944 Gropius became a naturalised citizen of the United States and over the next two decades continued his architectural output, receiving numerous accolades, including the election into the National Academy of Design and the AIA Gold Medal. With TAC, he was able to realise a number of buildings in the final stage of his activity, including the Interbau apartment block in Berlin (1957), American Embassy in Athens (1956), PanAm Tower in New York (1963) and a new housing district in Berlin named after him. Gropiusstadt (1960) was composed of 16,000 homes using prefabricated concrete technology, which created a monotonous, banal version of modernism. Gropius died in Boston, Massachusetts in 1969. Although Gropius is remembered for championing architectural mass production techniques and as a key figure in introducing modernist architecture to the US, his most lasting achievements were as an educator and school administrator.

Architectural history describes Walter Gropius as a man of extraordinary charisma, often as flamboyant, sharp and sophisticated. Under his leadership, Harvard University's Department of Architecture evolved as a hotbed of new ideas, and numerous avant-garde European architects became involved as faculty. Gropius had a wide international network, was able to gain and exercise increasing influence in the US, and was always interested in bringing other European architects to Harvard. Besides Marcel Breuer, he helped at least three other European talents: Sert, Giedion and Chermayeff.

Spanish architect Josep Lluís Sert (1902–1983) worked since 1939 in exile in New York City, before he was appointed at Harvard in 1953. He was the last president of the International Congresses of Modern Architecture (CIAM) and dean of the GSD (from 1953 to 1969), replacing both Hudnut and Gropius. Sert not only took over Dean Hudnut's position but also Gropius's role as head of the architecture department. Sert hired a number of Gropius's close allies to teach at the GSD, among them Siegfrid Giedion, Serge Chermayeff and Naum Gabo, continuing the Bauhaus legacy and making urban design his greatest priority. Sert founded the discipline of urban design and introduced the world's first programme in urban design at the GSD.

Another European who joined the GSD was the Swiss architectural historian Siegfried Giedion (1893—1968). He wrote his two most well-known books, *Space, Time and Architecture: The Growth of a New Tradition* (1941) and *Mechanization Takes Command: A Contribution to Anonymous History* (1948) while he taught at Harvard, between 1938 and 1945. Both books are seen as an important analysis of American material culture. World War II kept Giedion in America, though he, unlike many other German-speaking European intellectuals, returned home to Zurich in 1946 to take up a teaching position at the Federal Institute of Technology (ETH) as professor of art and architecture history. Serge Chermayeff (1900—1996) was a Russian-born British architect, industrial designer, writer, previous partner of Erich Mendelsohn, and co-founder of the American Society of Planners and Architects. In 1940 Chermayeff immigrated to the US, and in 1946 was recommended by Gropius to become the president of the Institute of Design (ID) in Chicago. He oversaw the Institute's merger with the IIT before ultimately stepping down in 1951. After teaching at MIT for a year, he also served under Dean Sert as a professor at the Harvard GSD from 1953 to 1962.

Image 8: Walter Gropius and Ludwig Mies
van der Rohe in the US, around 1940.
Both men shared an admiration for the neoclassical
work of German architect Karl Friedrich Schinkel

Image 9: Walter Gropius with GSD students, 1946

2. Gropius's Power Struggles at the GSD at Harvard

The German immigrants fled Nazi Germany in the 1930s and took on minority status in their new country, in hopes of a better future politically than in their homeland. Because of their professional ambition and focus on success, these kinds of "minorities" are more likely to do well, easily adapting to a different culture and language in the new country. All the time, the German immigrants were (and are still today) a minority group, which created an interesting condition for them through adapting to a new cultural identity where creation became a matter of a permanent debate and daily adjustment.

Gropius and Mies were both already in their early fifties (and at the peak of their careers) when they arrived in the US. The architects arrived as middle-aged European intellectuals with a mature vision for architecture and for shaping the contemporary city. The planning principles and intellectual commitments that underpinned their thinking were formed in the context of the first half of their lives, and for most of the time, they remained remarkably consistent throughout their later careers on both sides of the Atlantic, which also reveals their capacity for adaptation.

Gropius and Mies arrived just at the right time in emerging superpower America to advance and modernise architectural practice, especially in the field of low-cost housing, and to influence architectural education. The US was just coming out of the great Depression and, as Pearlman notes, "Americans were willing to consider new, and even 'foreign' ideas to solve the housing problem" (2007, 156). Housing ideas of other immigrants beforehand were often rejected as "foreign to American practice and principles of living", but now there was a change in tone.

The student numbers at Harvard University increased after World War II, and the GSD needed several more instructors. This gave Gropius the opportunity to bring in allies and to hire—in the Bauhaus tradition of "students becoming teachers"—several master's graduates to fill the vacant positions. Not everybody was supportive of his decisions. Some American colleagues accused him of trying to place as many other Germans as possible in important university positions all over the country. Tensions and even resistance to the import of educational innovation in a recipient country is not uncommon. Gropius's experience of hostility at the GSD and his long, ten-year power struggle with Dean Hudnut is an example for this; some American colleagues asked Gropius to provide educational experiences that were more grounded in the cultural realities of the United States.

However, there was enough optimism and positive development for Gropius and Mies to embrace their new lives in the US, and they were fascinated by the possibilities they found in their new home country. During this time, the US was led by an open-minded pragmatism and a willingness to try out new ideas. Gropius noted in 1968, "I have found throughout my life that words and, particularly, theories not tested by experience, can be much more harmful than deeds. When I came to the USA in 1937, I enjoyed the tendency among Americans to go straight to the practical test of every newborn idea, instead of snipping off every new shoot by excessive and premature debate over its possible value, a bad habit that frustrates so many efforts in Europe" (as cited in Herdeg, 1983, 84).

Joseph Hudnut (1886–1968) was an American architect, educator and scholar who was the first dean of Harvard's GSD. After heading the architecture schools at the University of Virginia and at Columbia University, Hudnut created the GSD in 1936 and led the school until 1953, one year after Gropius resigned. The newly created GSD was unique as it brought together architecture, landscape architecture and planning into one school. From the beginning, Hudnut gave the school its modern pedagogical direction, and he continued to oversee its curriculum and staffing for the next seventeen years.

In the following year, Dean Hudnut strategically recruited Gropius, Martin Wagner and Marcel Breuer to the faculty. With the two Germans (Gropius and Wagner) as part of the GSD, the social aspects of housing quickly became a central concern throughout the school. Hudnut knew of the positive influence that the German planner Werner Hegemann and the British architect Raymond Unwin had in New York, where they turned the focus at Columbia University's School of Architecture on housing, and he was concerned that Harvard would lag behind its New York rival (in 1917, Hudnut had briefly worked in New York as assistant of Werner Hegemann). From 1938 on, Gropius and Wagner taught courses on low-cost mass housing and student housing, exploring the possibilities that prefabrication and systems thinking might offer to large apartment buildings (Pearlman, 2007, 165). Gropius and Wagner's prime concern was in the economic factors of housing with issues of utility, standardisation, flexibility and prefabrication methods. During this time, Gropius worked also with Konrad Wachsmann on the design of a flexible "packaged house", a demountable construction system using timber panels to demonstrate the efficiency of modern architecture. Gropius frequently used his interest in prefabrication systems as part of the studio assignments in his design studios. At Harvard, he aimed to bring students' projects closer to real-world situations and what he called "the real problems of society, teaching teamwork and methods rather than skills". His solution was to involve the three GSD departments in the educational projects: architecture, city planning and landscape architecture. It was this collaboration (not between the arts and crafts, as at the Bauhaus, but between landscape and planning) that achieved international acclaim (see Images 10 and 12).

With the help of his students and Martin Wagner, Gropius's approach to urban design played a key part in shaping the post-war American landscape. Although originally an admirer of Gropius's work and theories, Hudnut came to clash with him over the direction of modern architecture and planning, and over the pedagogical direction of the GSD. From around 1943, Hudnut took issue with the direction in which Gropius's teaching seemed to be moving, claiming that Gropius was losing his interest in social responsibility, and instead overemphasised technology and formal aspects. Hudnut became a fierce opponent of Gropius's urban planning ideas for the modern city. At Harvard (as at the Bauhaus), Gropius's social aspirations still informed his teaching and thinking in very significant ways; however, some historians (such as Karen Koehler) have questioned whether Gropius–after immigrating to the US–changed and turned away from his original social goals to purely aesthetic ones.

Hudnut did not agree that the economic factor should play such an important role in the design of dwellings, which led to his open criticism of Gropius's work on prefabrication and "standardised urbanism". Hudnut publicly accused Gropius of turning towards formalism and a preoccupation with the economic and technical aspects of architecture. Hudnut and Gropius had never shared much common ideas of the city, and when this growing rift between the two leaders over the issue of post-war city rebuilding and housing escalated, it brought an end to their friendship.

Martin Wagner had similar concerns. In 1938, Wagner moved to the US (by invitation of Gropius) and took a position to teach city planning at the GSD, where he taught until 1951. His immigration to the US was assisted by Gropius, and in 1944, he became an American citizen. However, by 1940, his relationship with Gropius started to become strained when he complained of Gropius abandoning the underlying social principles of modernism and practicing modernism only as a style (not dissimilar to the criticism that was expressed by Joseph Hudnut earlier). In addition, Gropus and Hudnut had different thoughts on the first-year course at the GSD, which Gropius always wanted to be modelled after the Bauhaus's famous *Vorkurs*, which, he argued, served as the successful backbone of the Bauhaus model.

A New Foundation Course Based on the Vorkurs, and a Partial Success
By the time Gropius came to America, at the age of fifty-four, he was an established architect, and his contribution to modern architecture and design education was internationally known and had already been enormous. For most of the time, Hudnut was in the shadow of Gropius, whose influence and reputation quickly grew. At Harvard, he was instrumental in installing an educated group of designers who were beginning to transform the culture and pedagogy of the school, including former Bauhaus teachers Marcel Breuer, Walter Peterhans and Herbert Bayer. In his first article published in the US, Gropius lamented the "stagnating academism" and the lack of cohesive instruction in architecture, design and the arts in the American educational system (in *Education toward Creative Design*, 1937, 21): new to the US system, he suggested that an experimental school be set up, similar to the Bauhaus model, to generate an appropriate interdisciplinary and fully integrated curriculum in art, design and architecture, focusing on broad based skills of producing spatial forms. In the book *Scope of Total Architecture* (1962), Gropius wrote extensively on the topic of the education of architects and designers and on his conception of the Bauhaus idea. However, soon after arriving

at Harvard, Gropius quickly recognised that he would need to be patient with reforming the curriculum and the introduction of any pedagogical changes, given the stubbornness of the old guard of teachers and alumni. With the beginning of World War II, everything had to be put on hold, so by the mid-1940s, Gropius was eager to move forward with the changes he saw as necessary.

As at the Bauhaus, Gropius wanted all first-year GSD students to take a preliminary foundation course of basic design for six or twelve months, before pursuing any studies in their chosen fields, to "establish a universal language of form-making appropriate to the new machine age and accessible to all people, regardless of their nationality or social status" (Gropius, as cited in Pearlman, 2007, 203). He started a re-examination and modification of the *Vorkurs* to fit the situation at the GSD. But Hudnut rejected the idea of the basic design course and Gropius's suggestion to hire Josef Albers to teach it. While Gropius finally won the power struggle to introduce a preliminary course (entitled Design Fundamentals), he could not persuade Hudnut to hire Josef Albers. Instead, Albers joined Yale University in New Haven to head the department of design (see Image 17). Gropius tasked Richard Filipowski with the development of the new Design Fundamentals course, which was directly modelled on the *Vorkurs* and which remains a cornerstone of GSD's design pedagogy to this day. In the end, Design Fundamentals proved to be very popular with students and converted many of them to Gropius's way of thinking.

Richard Filipowski (1923-2008) was a designer, sculptor, painter, filmmaker and educator born in Poland. As a child he moved with his family to Ontario, Canada. He studied under Laszlo Moholy-Nagy at the Institute of Design (formerly the New Bauhaus) in Chicago from 1942 to 1946 and taught there after graduating. Filipowski quickly developed an abstract and amazingly consistent visual language of his own, and he was the only student Moholy-Nagy called upon to join the GSD faculty in 1950, where he taught alongside Gropius and Breuer. Gropius immediately realised his potential to organise and teach Design Fundamentals at the GSD, and recruited him to serve as professor of visual design from 1950 to 1952, before Filipowski left to join MIT.

The animosity and sometimes even hostility against Gropius was more than the usual envy between architecture professors; it was often permeated with the scent of antisemitism– even though Gropius himself was not Jewish–as modernism, like Bolshevism, was perceived as a Jewish movement, designed to purge the West of its traditions. In these years of internal power struggles at the school, Gropius became increasingly absorbed with the responsibilities of his position as head of the department and his architectural practice TAC. Gropius eventually retired from the Harvard position in 1952, having left his mark on the US education of architects. To the displeasure of Hudnut, Serge Chermayeff, then head of the ID, wrote: "The GSD, under the leadership of Professor Gropius, has set the standard in architectural education which is being emulated by schools everywhere. Everything that the GSD has achieved is identified directly with Gropius himself" (1952).

Gropius is rightly credited with the huge achievement of setting up the Bauhaus and recruiting and gathering such a variously talented body of teachers in Weimar and Dessau, all artistic egos with strong opinions, including Paul Klee (Mies's favourite painter), Wassily Kandinsky, Josef Albers, Oskar Schlemmer, Marcel Breuer, Laszlo Moholy-Nagy and others. Gropius always viewed argument and discussion as part of creativity itself, and argument and debate as intrinsic to creativity. Unusually for someone in his position in the 1920s and 1930s, Gropius encouraged women's artistic endeavours and sought equal rights for female teachers and students.

However, later at the GSD, what was possible was much more limited: the opportunities to recruit the most talented people to GSD's Department of Architecture, the possibilities to turn the curriculum into a continuation of the Bauhaus's experimental ambition, were often blocked and presented a constant struggle. Too many uninformed people had to be consulted and involved and were required to approve. The former Bauhaus director and his followers were in a minority, and the GSD would continue to run essentially on established lines.

While the Bauhaus masters were quickly settling into their new teaching positions in Cambridge and Chicago, there was never a heroic or continuous line of developments; the ruptures and contradictions within Gropius and Mies's work following immigration reveals their struggles to continue an influential role in US exile. For Gropius at Harvard and Mies at the IIT, the integration of Bauhaus pedagogy in US curricula proved to be more complicated than expected. The pedagogical Bauhaus component that was easiest and therefore most frequently integrated in US curricula was the Bauhaus *Vorkurs* as taught in Weimar and Dessau by Johannes Itten, Josef Albers and Lazlo Moholy-Nagy. It was this preliminary design course that was built as a foundation course around design fundamentals, geometric abstraction, problem solving and the use of different materials that gave students the basic methods of design.

Influencing Black Mountain College and Cranbrook Academy of Art
The *Vorkurs* course became the foundation course at numerous US schools of architecture and is still in use at many schools today. In 1933, Josef and Anni Albers (who went directly from Berlin to the US) were the first to import the Vorkurs to the US: at Black Mountain College in North Carolina, it was enthusiastically adopted by the students. Kentgens-Craig (2018) comments on the success of the *Vorkurs* at US schools: "While the institution and idea Bauhaus as a whole could not be transplanted, even if members of the original faculty were at hand, specific programs, structures and courses could."

The Black Mountain College (1933–1957) was a unique, experimental school that lasted for 24 years in a remote area of the Appalachian Mountains in North Carolina. Much like at the Bauhaus, the arts played a central role in the academic curriculum: drawing, academic theory, crafts and experimental theatre, music and dance. At the end, the pedagogical Bauhaus concept found its most pure continuation in North Carolina, not in the education of architects, but in the education of artists. Bauhaus artists Josef and Anni Albers imported the pedagogy to Black Mountain College and succeeded in doing what Gropius and Mies could not fully succeed in: they created a new arts school on the pedagogical principles of the Bauhaus and John Dewey, while Gropius and Mies were not in the position due to the numerous constraints they found themselves in and the compromises they had to make to achieve even small changes at a time.

The pedagogy taught at the Black Mountain College was a combination of the Bauhaus ideas and the pedagogical concepts of John Dewey (1859—1952). Dewey was a progressive American education reformer and psychologist whose ideas have been influential in education and social reform. He was a proponent of hands-on learning, problem-based learning and learning through active inquiry, which went well along with the Bauhaus pedagogy. Regarded as one of the most prominent American scholars in the first half of the 20th century, Dewey is known for considering the two fundamental elements—schools and civil society—to be major topics needing attention to encourage experimental intelligence and plurality. He had very specific notions regarding how education should take place within the classroom, arguing that education and learning are social and interactive processes, and thus that the college itself was seen as a social institution. He argued that students thrive in an environment where they are allowed to experience and interact with the curriculum, and all students should have the opportunity to take part in their own learning. Dewey also suggested that the purpose of education should not revolve around the acquisition of a pre-determined rigid set of skills, but rather be about the active realisation of one's full potential and the ability to use those skills for the greater good.

Cranbrook Academy of Art, founded in 1932 in Bloomfield (Michigan), is another US art school that was – to some extend – modelled after the Bauhaus. It is sometimes called the "Scandinavian Bauhaus" through the influence of Finnish architect Eero Saarinen, whose father Eliel oversaw the school and its curriculum based on modernist principles. He also designed the school buildings. Saarinen devoted the last decades of his life to Cranbrook, from 1926 until his death in 1950. He integrated important parts of the Bauhaus design theories, where all learning was self-directed under the guidance and supervision of the respective artist-in-residence (Master). Similar to the Bauhaus school, Cranbrook was conceived to be an institution where artists could live, learn and share in ideas and expertise. Under Saarinen's direction, and not dissimilar to Gropius's programme, the school focused on the importance of craft and art in the age of the machine. Disciplines taught at the school ranged from weaving to metalwork with the goal of creating a more complete sense of material and structure. Cranbrook imbued its students with a sense of experimentation, exploration and collaboration. It was part artists' colony, part school and part design laboratory, devoted to individual expression and partially modeled after the Bauhaus, where students pursued independent study under the guidance of masters in their field. Cranbrook is ''not an art school in the ordinary sense,'' Saarinen noted, "but 'a working place for creative art. The leading idea is to have artists of the highest ability live at Cranbrook and execute their work there." The school influenced emerging designers who studied there, including Ralph Rapson, Charles and Ray Eames, Florence Knoll, Harry Bertoia and Harry Weese.

In "The Cranbrook Vision" (1984), architecture critic Paul Goldberger compares Cranbrook Academy of Art with the Bauhaus; he notes:

> "Both institutions, Cranbrook and the Bauhaus, were created to encourage new achievements in 20th-century design, and both were created in the hope of breaking down barriers between various design disciplines. In each case, the founders hoped that their school would bring about new connections between art and life, and would make design quality accessible to a wider

number of people. But the histories of the two institutions belie the similar intentions. The Bauhaus was always troubled by politics, both internally in the form of friction between practitioners of different disciplines, and externally in the form of pressure from the German government, which considered the school to be left wing. Ultimately, the Nazis forced the Bauhaus to close in 1933, and its leading lights, among them Ludwig Mies van der Rohe, Walter Gropius, Josef Albers and Marcel Breuer, scattered. Cranbrook's past was more tranquil, at least superficially. With Saarinen secure in the president's chair and Booth's generous financial backing, the school seemed in the 1930's and 1940's, an idyllic place. [...] Surely the most important distinction between the schools was in terms of ideology. While the Bauhaus made certain claims toward ideological freedom, in reality there was never much diversity; the Bauhaus's greatness was in its almost evangelical sense of itself as an academy for the sleek modern forms of the International Style. And its real legacy is not in its teaching methods, but in the important International Style work it produced–the tubular steel chairs of Marcel Breuer, the headquarters building at Dessau by Walter Gropius, and so on. But there was no real Cranbrook style to serve as an American equivalent of the Bauhaus style. Eliel Saainen's architecture was itself relatively non-ideological; it was a gentle and inventive mix of modernism and tradition, lavish in its detail and craftsmanship, and never quite the same from one building to the next. [...] There was no party line at Cranbrook, no single way to do things, as there so clearly was at the Bauhaus. For while the Bauhaus itself did not prosper, its style did, and the glass-and-steel buildings and sleek objects encouraged by the Bauhaus became unquestionably the dominant style of modern design in the United States in the 1950's and 1960's." (Goldberger, 1984)

Image 10: Konrad Wachsmann (right) and Walter Gropius at the assembly of a "packaged house" for General Panel Corp., around 1942. Both prefabrication enthusiasts partnered with the building industry to develop an inexpensive, standardised panel system for off-site manufactured houses consisting of a complete kit of components, a flexible kit of parts, which would be easily assembled on site, as the "synthesis between art and technology". They shared the belief that elegant design could be made affordable for the masses.

Image 11: Walter and Ise Gropius with Harry Seidler at the Rose House in Sydney, May 1954. (Photo by Max Dupain, courtesy of the NSW State Library)

Image 12: Walter Gropius with supporter-turned-rival, Dean Joseph Hudnut, 1942, in Chicago

3. The Lasting Legacy of Mies van der Rohe at the IIT in Chicago

By the time Adolf Hitler came to power, Ludwig Mies van der Rohe was one of the three most celebrated architects in Germany. He had established his reputation in Europe during the late 1920s, in large part due to two iconic buildings–the German Pavilion for the Barcelona International Exposition of 1929, and the Tugendhat House in Brno. Both buildings utilised open plans, fluid spaces with freestanding walls, transparency and asymmetry. Both were noble pavilions perfect in proportion, exquisite (and expensive) in materials, with subtle classical references. From 1930 to 1933, Mies was the last director of the faltering Bauhaus, until the school was finally closed by the Nazis. What followed was a period of struggle to find commissions and, at the end of 1937, Mies immigrated to the United States, where he had accepted a teaching position in Chicago. Hitler's rise to power in 1933 effectively ended Mies's career in Germany. The Nazis were adamantly anti-modernist and their adjective for modern art was *entartete* ("degenerated") art. Under the Nazis, he could not find work, his architectural views were systematically ridiculed by the Nazi state, and his career had been thwarted at every turn by party functionaries. Mies's main source of income from 1933 to 1937 came not from architecture—he built almost nothing during this period—but from sales of his furniture.

Mies was aplotical, and there is some debate if he ever was a Nazi sympathiser. Between 1933 and 1937, Mies submitted several competition proposals to state-organised design competitions, but his proposals were never selected. His biographer, Franz Schulze notes, "Mies's own attitude was a conflicted patchwork of indifference toward national politics in general, hostility toward Nazi philistinism in particular, dedication to architectural principle, and desire to build regardless of who asked him." Schulze goes on to observe that Mies was apolitical and just wanted to build; he was, after all, "a man who within eight years' time had designed a monument to Communist martyrs, a throne for a Spanish king, a pavilion for a moderately socialist government, and another for a militantly right-wing totalitarian state." (Schulze and Windhorst, 1985).

At the end of 1937, Mies finally decided to immigrate to the US to take up the position as head of the Department of Architecture at the Armour Institute of Technology (later renamed the Illinois Institute of Technology, or IIT), in Chicago from 1938 on. There, he was able to partially introduce an architectural education approach loosely based on the Bauhaus curriculum, later known as the Second Chicago School (or "New Bauhaus"). With the ambition of making it the premier school in the country, his teaching at the IIT became influential in the following decades. One of the benefits of taking this position was that Mies would be commissioned to design the new buildings and master plan for the IIT campus, including the S.R. Crown Hall, which was built from 1952 to 1956 to serve as the building for IIT's new School of Architecture. By 1939, Mies had been asked to draw up a master plan for the institute's 100-acre campus, and he eventually designed nineteen buildings on campus.

In 1944, in the same year as Gropius, Mies became an American citizen, completing the final severance from his native Germany. His thirty years as a practicing American architect and twenty years as head at IIT reflect an approach towards achieving his goal of a new architecture for the 20th century: an architecture of "universal" spaces with clearly arranged structural frameworks of steel and glass. In the US, Mies found plenty of corporate clients willing to realise ideas that had seemed impossible while practicing in Germany, such as the high-rise towers at Lake Shore Drive in Chicago and Seagram Building in New York. Striving for simplicity, Mies's architectural language became an accepted mode of building for American educational institutions and large corporations, and some of his distinguished students went on to become leading American modernist architects, including Gene Summers, Myron Goldsmith, George Schipporeit, Bertrand Goldberg and partners at the firms SOM and Murphy/Jahn.

Most of these former students adopted the "Miesian style", which became popular as developers were easy converts of the architectural simplicity, given that it could mean lower costs. Unfortunately, few architects practicing in the Miesian style matched the sophisticated refinement and finesse of Mies's design idiom, and a large number of misunderstood, low-quality copies emerged everywhere. More often than not, their building copies would turn out uninspiring compared to the subtle qualities of scale, proportion and massing found in Mies's original work. Despite the failings of the works of some of his followers, the Miesian style further proliferated and could soon be found in every state throughout the United States and around the world.

It is noteworthy that Mies's former students Goldberg and Schipporeit should become the architects of the most interesting residential high-rise structures in a post-Miesian Chicago: Marina Towers (1963–1967, by Bertrand Goldberg) and Lake Point Tower (1965–1968, by John Heinrich and George Schipporeit) gave up the Miesian dogma of the minimal rectangular box and created an independent new vision of vertical living with designs of equally enduring significance.

Under Mies's leadership, the architecture department had evolved a code of discipline and morality that was as strict as any governing a religious order. "God is in the details," Mies said of his rigorously designed pavilions of steel and glass. Mies, like Gropius, played a significant role as an educator, believing his architectural language could be learned and applied to design any type of modern building. It was significantly easier for Mies to set up a new educational model at the IIT based on the Bauhaus compared to Gropius's experiences at the GSD. He replaced the traditional and outdated École des Beaux-Arts curriculum with a three-step curriculum, beginning with crafts of drawing and construction, leading to planning skills, and finishing with theory of architecture. He worked personally and intensively on prototype solutions and then allowed his students, both in school and in his office, to develop derivative solutions for specific projects under his guidance. Today, some part of Mies's curriculum is still in use in the first and second-year programme, including the precise drafting of brick construction details, so unpopular with aspiring student architects. Some parts of his achievements in creating a teachable architecture language that can be used to express the modern technological era still survive (Lambert, 2001; Mertins, 2014).

Similar to Gropius's appointment of Bauhaus masters at Harvard, Mies was keen to recruit Ludwig Hilberseimer to the IIT. Ludwig Karl Hilberseimer (1885–1967) was a German urban planner and architect who taught during the last years at the Bauhaus in Dessau. In 1929, Hilberseimer was hired by Hannes Meyer to join the Bauhaus, but in July 1933 was identified by the Gestapo (Geheime Staatspolizei, the Nazi secret state police) as problematically left-wing. He fled Germany for America in 1938, following Mies to the IIT, where he was heading the Department of Urban Planning. We can assume that Mies was glad about this, as he could rely on an ally from previous years and a loyal supporter of his new direction at the IIT. Later, Hilberseimer also became director of Chicago's city planning office. Mies always believed that teachers of architecture should be currently involved in practice. While at the IIT, Mies kept practicing and designed numerous large-scale projects, leading a busy practice, while Hilberseimer dedicated his time at the IIT to theoretical research and teaching of radical concepts of urban planning, such as the Decentralized City project, with a strong interest in cost-effective mass housing.

4. Teaching Mies: the Miesian Step-By-Step Approach to Learning

The Armour Institute of Technology, one of IIT's predecessor institutions, was founded in 1890, just as Chicago was emerging as a centre for progressive architectural thought. Architects like Burnham and Root, Adler and Sullivan, and William Le Baron Jenney were transforming practice and developing a design vocabulary that emphasised structure and function over ornamentation. This generation of architects founded what became known as the first Chicago School of architecture. Mies founded the next. In 1936, when Earl Reed resigned as director of the Department of Architecture at Armour Institute, the school engaged Chicago's architectural leaders in the search for a new director. The search committee, headed by John Holabird, recruited Mies to Chicago. Mies's first task was to rationalise the architecture curriculum.

The curriculum that Mies established at the IIT was not a pure Bauhaus-style curriculum, as the situation was too different and he thought that "this would not work under altogether different conditions" (Lambert, 2001, 180). When Mies arrived in 1938, he missed the interdisciplinary context with the artists he was used to from the Bauhaus (working alongside with visionaries like Kandinsky or Itten). He found that there were hardly any workshops for prototyping designs, and the school had no permanent building; the S.R. Crown Hall on the IIT campus, designed in 1952, was only completed in 1956. Mies insisted on a back-to-basics approach: he argued that architecture students must first learn to draw, then gain thorough knowledge of the features and use of materials, and finally master the fundamental principles of design and construction. During these early years, Mies held classes in space provided by the Art Institute of Chicago. Mies developed a new curriculum that he thought was more suitable to the American context, with urban planning incorporated as a modular part into the architecture curriculum and students working on real projects and sites in Chicago. Mies introduced the extensive use of the study of typologies, a research method largely used by Hilberseimer, with a final written research thesis as capstone project to be produced by the graduate students.

In answer to a query from the art historian Nikolaus Pevsner, then an editor of *Architectural Review*, about Mies's method for teaching design, Mies explained that he taught students "first to build with wood, then stone, then brick and, finally, with concrete and steel". In *Architectural Review* (1950), on education, Mies offered the following unelaborated description: "An architectural curriculum is a means of training and education. It is not an end in itself but depends on and serves a philosophy. [...] At the IIT we are concerned among other things
> with the idea of structure, structure as an architectural concept. [...] We are for this reason concerned with the right use of materials, clear construction, and its proper expression. Since a building is a work to be done, and not a notion to be understood, we believe that a method of work, a way of doing, should be the essence of all architectural education" (as cited in Swenson and Chang, 1980).

Between 1938 and 1941, Mies developed IIT's architecture curriculum with the help of others, namely Walter Peterhans and Ludwig Hilberseimer, and they kept refining it into the 1950s. The studio was a place of solving building problems. Former student Harrington wrote about Mies's educational programme:
> "The curriculum was defined in terms of means (materials), purpose (building types) and planning and creating (mechanistic and idealistic principles). The first year taught basic drafting or graphic literacy, the second year, simple short span wood and masonry construction, the third year, mid-span steel and concrete structures, fourth year, long span structures and space problems and fifth year, a complete building project. Two additional subjects, planning

and visual training complemented the studio. Planning, as conceived by Ludwig Hilberseimer, was the logical distribution of program elements relative to human behaviour and environmental considerations. Taught by Walter Peterhans, visual training practiced aesthetic discipline. Planning and visual training provided a parallel and fundamentally related set of practices" (Harrington, 1986).

There were no stand-alone courses in materials or methods; these subjects were integrated into studio teaching, which consisted of a well-defined series of problems to be solved, as opposed to the exploratory design exercise format of architectural education today. Wetzel (2008) notes that "studio teaching at IIT today maintains a direct link to the intentions set forth in Mies's inaugural address of 1938 and curriculum of 1941. The 1941 curriculum comprised a five-year undergraduate education in architecture with graduate coursework reserved for the development of individual expertise." She notes that "the program grew from a department of less than 50 students before WW II to a fairly stable 125 students in 1958 when Mies left IIT. The intimate teaching under Mies's direction allowed for the singularity of a common philosophy"(2008). However, as the school grew in size, this singularity of a common teaching philosophy was no longer possible.

The linear step-by-step approach could also not be continued beyond Mies's departure. With Mies absent and enrolment at IIT's school of architecture increasing to four hundred students by 1978, and eight hundred by 2006, the singularity of approach could no longer be sustained, opening up the educational experience from a linear approach to a more broadly accepted integration of design and technology and a multiplicity of different approaches.

In 1940, Armour Institute and Lewis Institute merged to form Illinois Institute of Technology. Armour Institute's original seven-acre campus could not accommodate the combined schools' needs, and Mies was asked to develop plans for a new, expanded 120-acre campus. Not since Thomas Jefferson's University of Virginia (1819) had an American campus been the work of a single architect. Mies's original proposal called for a more traditional layout of several large buildings grouped around an open space, but in his final masterplan he embraced Chicago's rectilinear street grid and designed two symmetrically balanced groups of buildings. The academic buildings stood in sharp contrast to the patrician campuses of the past. They embodied 20th century methods and materials: steel and concrete frames with curtain walls of glass and brick. The sleek urbanism of the new campus was a reflection of the university's technological focus. Mies's buildings are harmonious in proportion and set a new aesthetic standard for campus architecture in the US. His designs have so pervaded our definition of architecture that it is difficult to imagine how revolutionary the campus was when it was first built.

If there is a central focus on campus, it is the S.R. Crown Hall, which Mies designed with tectonic logic as a grand pavilion raised on a podium, placed on a "floating" platform. Crown Hall was reported to be Mies's favourite building on campus. Once completed, it became the new building of the architecture school, offering only one central, large, open and column-free classroom space wrapped by curtain walls. Mies's idea was to provide a single large room for the school's three hundred students so that no student would be lonely or isolated from others who may be further or less advanced in the course. Its roof is suspended from four plate girders that rest on exterior columns and leave the large clear-span interior space free of supports, following his concept of the open "universal space". Mies understood the concept of the "open plan" as a further development of Le Corbusier's earlier "free plan". However, once the number of students grew, the concept of one single universal space soon proved to be problematic, and numerous students complained about the noise and distractions (see Images 13, 14 and 15).

Mies is quoted in an oft-repeated phrase that "architecture is the will of an epoch translated into space" (Schulze and Windhorst, 1985). His architecture has been described as being expressive of the Industrial Age. In 1956, famed architect Eero Saarinen spoke at the inauguration of S.R. Crown Hall and lauded Mies as Chicago's third great architect, placing him in the prestigious lineage of Louis Sullivan and Frank Lloyd Wright. "Great architecture is both universal and individual," Saarinen said, "The universality comes because there is an architecture expressive of its time. But the individuality comes as the expression of one man's unique combination of faith and honesty and devotion and belief in architecture."

Mies tended to emulate the formal clarity and simplicity of neoclassicism, seeking to embody in his own architecture the balanced proportions of Karl Friedrich Schinkel. This rationality was cause for much criticism, especially after his death in 1969. Like many modernists, he believed that architecture was more than mere building, and that it was called upon to express the ethos of a culture—what he called "the spirit of the age." Hochman (1989) stresses the idealistic elements in Mies's work; she argues that the formal vocabulary of neoclassical public architecture also helped to furnish Hitler and Speer (as well as Mussolini and others) with their idea of architectural grandeur. Indeed, one source of inspiration for German modernism in its formative stages was the neoclassical tradition of Schinkel. But there were also other, equally important, sources, for instance, the new Dutch housing developments, early 20th-century American concrete industrial buildings, and the geometrical abstractions of the De Stijl movement.

One could say that Mies's buildings combined simple and carefully considered structural solutions with formal and material beauty. A formal language evolves over time, and Mies developed and refined his stringent yet elegantly simple vocabulary of pure geometric form, from the Barcelona Pavilion to Farnsworth House to Crown Hall. At first, his vocabulary appeared to be based on a minimalist approach, using a very limited palette of materials. However, his building designs were also highly formal reinterpretations of classical language: in each there is a move towards a rigid set of formal rules and the use of simple structural elements to create an ordered composition, with an independent column grid and a floating roof above, which he called "Free Plan" or "Open Plan" space. The neutral, autonomous and indefinite Cartesian grid, where the uninterrupted glass enclosure was used to dissolve the separation between inside and outside, referred to precedents by Schinkel and Behrens: this rigorous and abstract grid is the beginning and end of Mies's architecture, "the degree zero of architectural thought" (Michael Hayes).

The austere aesthetic, expressed in his much-publicised steel-and-glass skyscrapers of the 1950s in Chicago and New York, had come to symbolise post-war American affluence and even democratic values. Mies went on to design some of the nation's most recognisable buildings, including the Lake Shore Drive Apartments (1949) in Chicago and the Seagram Building (1954) in Manhattan. His high-rise buildings are characterised by their grid-like, exposed steel-frame exterior and curtain wall façade construction creating a precise, sharp rectangular form (usually using a 5 x 5 feet façade grid). At Seagram, a formal plaza creates a podium and serves as entry platform, with the ground floor of the building set back behind a series of steel columns, creating a visual effect of the building "floating" above its site. The 26-floor apartment buildings at Chicago's Lake Shore Drive (1949—1951), an elegant composition of four minimalist glass-and-steel apartment towers, came about because a barely thirty-year-old Chicago real estate developer, Herbert Greenwald, wanted to build the finest architecture using modern technology. Walter Gropius told him that Mies was his man.

The commission for Seagram Building was more competitive. Among the architects that were already rejected during the extensive selection process for the project were Eero Saarinen, Marcel Breuer, Walter Gropius, Louis Kahn, Paul Rudolph, I.M. Pei and Le Corbusier. Philip Johnson was influential in New York and helped to establish Mies's name as an eminent 20th century architect; in turn, Johnson asked to be involved and named as collaborator on the Seagram Building. While this "partnership" was far from equal, Mies needed Johnson, as he was not licensed as an architect in New York and Johnson had a way to deal with Phyllis Lambert, the client's daughter, who was a young architect involved in the selection of the designer for the tower. This was important, as Mies very much wanted to build a high-rise tower in New York City for some time. Johnson's involvement with the Seagram high-rise tower allowed him to claim a role in the design that went beyond his actual contribution of the interior design of the Four Seasons restaurant and lobby. Mies was asked if it bothered him that Johnson was taking credit for Seagram. "Not especially," Mies replied. "What would bother me would be Johnson claiming that I was chiefly responsible for one of his buildings" (as recalled by his former IIT student, Peter Roesch).

Once completed, Seagram Building created the architectural concept and model for numerous other 1960s New York skyscrapers: set back from the traffic lanes on Park Avenue, the tower was one of the first to have a public plaza out front for pedestrians and office workers to gather and mingle. Seagram was a new prototype for the urban office, and this immaculately proportioned high-rise block was endlessly imitated across the US and beyond. But even the most skilled of practices were unable to match its structural clarity and delivered only disappointing imitations.

Both Gropius and Mies had a strong interest in construction technology, especially in standardised modular grid systems for construction in steel or concrete and in prefabricated building components. The American construction industry in the 1940s was not yet well advanced, but from the 1950s on, the standardisation of prefabricated building components could be implemented to scale. For better or for worse, the Bauhaus émigrés made an enormous and lasting impact on the American cityscape and the way architecture is taught in the US. To understand why the Bauhaus philosophy and design approach took such a strong hold on North America, it is important to remember their character and ambition: both Europeans devoted a great deal of their time and effort to reforming the architecture programmes at Harvard and IIT; both had charismatic convincing personalities, outstanding leadership skills and strong work ethics; and they knew how to inspire younger people wanting to become architects. Austrian-American architect Friedrich St. Florian (a classmate of Raimund Abraham) arrived in the US in 1961 and visited Mies at the IIT in the same year. He recalls that "when I visited him at the IIT, Mies still held the Chair of the department and I felt like a pilgrim. His office was wide open, there were no doors. When I spoke with him, he was very curious to get news from Germany."

Both never lost interest in what was happening in their home country after the war, and both would build in Berlin in the 1960s. Mies was able, just before his death, to design the New National Gallery in Berlin: in 1968, for the opening of this temple to modern art, Mies gloriously returned to Berlin where he was celebrated as "Modern Schinkel". After twenty years as the director of architecture at IIT, Mies resigned in 1958 at the age of seventy-two. In 1959, the Royal Institute of British Architects awarded him its Gold Medal, and the following year he received the AIA Gold Medal, the highest award given by the AIA. President Lyndon Johnson presented Mies with the Presidential Medal of Freedom in 1963. In 1966 Mies began suffering from cancer of the oesophagus, and he died three years later in his adoptive hometown, Chicago.

After the Second World War, Gropius was also invited to realise several large buildings in Berlin. Beside Gropius, the 1957 International Building Exhibition (Interbau) involved a large number of internationally recognised architects, including Alvar Aalto, Egon Eiermann, Arne Jacobsen, Vasily Luckhardt, Oscar Niemeyer, Sep Ruf, Max Taut and Le Corbusier. The Interbau featured two high-profile contributions by US architectural firms: the "Gropius House" by Gropius & TAC and the Kongresshalle (today Haus der Kulturen der Welt) by Hugh Stubbins. Stubbins formerly worked as Gropius's assistant in 1940 at Harvard University. Gropius designed the Interbau apartment block "Gropius Haus" with nine floors and 66 apartments, and the large Gropiusstadt housing estate, with around 18,000 apartments and construction starting from 1962. The museum Bauhaus Archive in Berlin's Tiergarten, which opened in 1979, also goes back to a design by Gropius, but he never saw it built; he died in Boston in 1969.

Image 13: Ludwig Mies van der Rohe with the model of S.R. Crown Hall, IIT, Chicago, 1956

Images 14 a and b: S.R. Crown Hall, the home of the School of Architecture on IIT campus in Chicago, designed 1952 by Ludwig Mies van der Rohe as part of a larger urban campus composition; the building's main entry and interior space (Photos by the author, 2020)

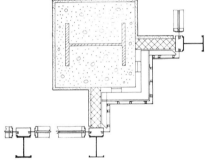

Image 15: Ludwig Mies van der Rohe on one of his tubular cantilever chairs, in Chicago in the 1960s

Image 16: The building corner of Seagram Tower, 1958, New York; by Ludwig Mies van der Rohe

Image 17: Josef Albers became head of the new art school, Black Mountain College in North Carolina; this school is seen by many as the successor closest to the Bauhaus idea

5. Critical Reflection on Gropius and Mies

Writing about the pioneers of modern architecture brings with it the risk that in hindsight one might glorify their narrative and actions. So much has been written about Gropius and Mies van der Rohe that texts have the tendency to over-glorify their contribution to 20th century architectural education. This study set out to assess and clarify if and how far the legacy of the Bauhaus is still relevant at today's US schools of architecture, by asking: What does the legacy of the immigrating Bauhaus teachers mean today? If and how do their educational contributions still resonate and are their contributions still relevant?

By the late 1960s, modernism was seen as intellectually bankrupt, and a search for new models of thinking was on the way to overcome the dead-end of the modernist paradigm and dogma. The dominance of mid-20th-century Bauhaus pedagogy was crumbling, and the hagiography of Gropius and Mies as saints or iconic leaders of modernism came into question. Their apparent lack of self-questioning has been mentioned by several writers and biographers. It is reported that both Gropius and Mies were charismatic and spoke with some authority and gravitas, although their English was limited (especially Mies's) and they maintained a strong German accent throughout their lives.

Peter Bosselmann (2020) offers the view that "there has always been a danger of glorifying Mies van der Rohe and Walter Gropius, and overlooking the contradictory nature in their work and teaching." Criticism of Gropius's contribution has been articulated by various writers, including Jill E. Pearlman and Peter Eisenman (interestingly, Eisenman worked briefly for Gropius from 1958 to 1959), who noted in a 2019 interview that "by then, Gropius was just another commercial architect and there was no ideology offered".

Hochman and others argue that towards the end of their careers, Gropius and Mies were rewriting history and creating their own legends and myths of their own beliefs, being increasingly disconnected from society. Some of the criticism argues that Gropius's contribution to 20th century architecture is overrated; that he could not sketch or draw as an architect (as opposed to Mies who loved to sketch and draw); and that he was too much concerned with marketing an image of himself, his influence and the Bauhaus. The Bauhaus was always a smallish elite phenomenon -- at its height, it just drew about 200 students – and despite its enormous influence, especially in the US, during its entire 14-year history the Bauhaus had only around 1,200 students and a full-time faculty of around thirty.

Gropius worked hard to uphold the heroic narrative, which did not always reflect reality. In alignment with this, Mendelsohn described the Bauhaus exhibition of 1923 as a "stage set for a Gropius performance." Pearlman (2007) argues that Gropius "did not affect the progress at the GSD alone" and, further, that the GSD was not merely an offshoot of the Bauhaus. It is also well documented that numerous people came to clash with Gropius within a short time (e.g., from Adolf Meyer to Marcel Breuer, Joseph Hudnut, Martin Wagner, and other colleagues, who first supported and at some point turned away from him); their relationship turned sour, most likely due to Gropius's larger-than-life ego, dogmatic attitude to architecture and authoritarian character. Collaboration was a running theme in the life of

Gropius, but he did not always have the means and patience to deliver on it.

In "Epitaph Exhibit of the Bauhaus", Martha Davidson wrote in a December 1938 review of the Bauhaus exhibition at the MoMA: "The integration of the main branches of art promised in the Manifesto of 1919 was clearly never achieved. Thus America, despite her evident admiration for the historic importance of the Bauhaus, must look forward—rather than backward to an ideology based on naked and unencumbered art—to a functioning rather than a functional relation between architect, sculptor and painter." Davidson criticised the Bauhaus for lacking the sense of unity and collaboration celebrated by many of its students.

The Fagus factory project was completed in 1913 and it established Gropius's early career. But he didn't like to share the success: despite Adolf Meyer's no doubt crucial role in the partnership, Gropius described him as "merely the office manager". Challenging the myths around Gropius as Bauhaus founder, Fiona MacCarthy's biography (2019) questions some long-held views of the architect. Tom Wolfe, in *From Bauhaus to Our House* (1981), was one of Gropius's sharpest critics, calling him "humourless" and his buildings "boring." By 1960, Gropius's reputation was on the wane, his post-war output suggesting that he was probably a better educator than architect—a man who had "overrun his prophecy". (MacCarthy, 2019)

In a similar way, sharp criticism of Mies has been published by respected scholars, including Elaine Hochman, Detlef Mertins and Franz Schulze, with Hochman noting that Mies could be "narrow-minded and self-absorbed". There is also scathing critique of his architecture: some of his glass buildings (such as the Farnsworth House) turned out to be impractical, as they would quickly overheat in summer, become uninhabitable due to their immense solar gain, and consequently not function without the support of a large air-conditioning back-up plant. In the 1960s and 70s, Mies was seen as the architect who represented cold technology and faceless bureaucracy. A growing problem were the numerous banal copies and poor imitations of his buildings by his followers, as these products were mostly of low architectural quality, lacking the refinement and exquisite selection of materials. At the IIT, another criticism was made: the habit of involving the most talented students to work in his private practice was seen by some an issue that created a conflict of interest, accusing him of giving the practice priority over his educational responsibilities.

Detlef Mertins discusses these unresolved contradictions in Mies's career, where he notes:
> "Spanning sixty years, two continents and two world wars, based first in Berlin and then in Chicago, Mies van der Rohe's career was a complex one, marked by discontinuities and struggles as much as continuities and success. He had been attacked by conservatives throughout his life, but beginning in the 1970s, a younger generation of progressive architects and critics sought to define themselves in opposition to him. He was called boring, anti-historical and authoritarian. Urbanists riled against the destruction of the traditional city and the endless proliferation of neutral glass boxes for which he seemed to stand" (Mertins, 2014).

In *Architects of Fortune: Mies van der Rohe and the Third Reich* (1989), Hochman reserves several generous parentheses for Gropius, whom she regards more highly than Mies; for example, she notes that "Gropius (who was personally kind and generous) saw architecture as serving people; Mies saw it as serving art" (Hochman). Was it just his quest for universal forms that seemed to serve art first? She goes on to describe, "his generally uncommunicative nature and his presence dominated, overpowered the space around him" (Hochman, 1989). It is reported that Mies could be radical and harsh in his attitude. Ambrose Richardson, a former IIT graduate, recalled Mies saying, "I have very little time to be for something. I have absolutely no time to be against anything" (cited in Schulze and Windhorst, 1985, 394). This principle applied equally to his professional work and to his lifelong aversion to politics, in Germany and in the US. Politically, Mies was passive and disinterested. His active energies were turned completely toward his art and away from practically all else. Hochman (1989) critically cites Mies's remark that clients should be treated as "children: humored, but given good architecture, not what they mistakenly thought they wanted." For Hochman, such sentiments are evidence of Mies's deplorable, self-serving and self-centred "arrogance".

Mies's architecture epitomises the ambitions, and failings, surely more than that of any other single architect. His buildings were regularly criticised in the press. The editor of the April 1953 issue of *House Beautiful* called Farnsworth House a "threat to the new America," saying the building was the icon of "a sinister group of International Stylists" that were trying "to force Americans to accept an architecture that was barren, grim, impoverished, impractical, uninhabitable, and destructive of individual possessions, as well as of individuals themselves." Mies was called the "high priest of curtain-wall modernism" (Wolfe, 1981), while Alex Beam coined the notion of "glass-box modernism" (2020).

Since his death in 1969, almost three dozen books about his life and work have been published. Franz Schulze's *Mies van der Rohe: A Critical Biography* (1985) received wide acclaim, with Paul Goldberger calling it "distinguished and eloquent." Schulze and Windhorst interviewed former employees working in Mies's office in Chicago, to find out that Mies exhibited a "stunning lack of generosity". One former associate recalled that "trivial mistakes by staff members were never forgotten or forgiven. [...] No matter what that person did for the rest of their life, Mies never really trusted them them [again]".

The story of Gropius and Mies is anything but simple, filled with the trauma of both world wars, the terror inflicted by the Nazis, and the obvious pressures associated with immigration in exile while becoming important architectural thinkers of the 20th century. There is also the question about their relationship to the new political forces in Germany. It is reported that Gropius was initially indifferent about the seizure of power by the Nazis, although the Nazis cut twice the budget for the Bauhaus. There was a hope that the functional aesthetic of the Bauhaus could become a means for this new regime to express itself, and in 1933, Gropius (as well as Mies) entered a competition for the new Reichsbank building in Berlin. Their proposals were not chosen and it soon became clear that there was little interest in modernism as the aesthetic language for this fascist regime.

On the relevance of the Bauhaus theory today, most educators interviewed for this book see it as a thing of the past that means little for them today. Instead, the urgency of climate change and the impact of the digital revolution are at the forefront of their concerns (see interviews in Appendix III). Bechthold notes that "while the fundamental approach of the Bauhaus remains relevant, the digital has shifted the focus and expanded with new opportunities". Heine thinks that "Gropius and Mies were some of the first global architects. But today we are faced with different challenges, especially environmentally, than in the mid-last century." As architectural education has moved on and expanded beyond the technical and formal focus of Gropius's and Mies's pedagogy, Steinmuller notes that "my German education in the 1990s was characterised by an outdated top-down model that I strongly reject."

It became obvious that modernism was not the revolution it pretended to be. By 1970, the long shadows once cast by Gropius and Mies over architectural education and US architecture had significantly shortened.

6. The Abstract Language of Space: Other Places, where the Bauhaus Pedagogy Blossomed

The aim of this study is to explore the important role that the Bauhaus—as idea and educational model—played in the formation of one of the most influential intellectual projects in 20th-century architectural history. Neil MacGregor wrote, "The Bauhaus reshaped the world. Our cities and houses today, our furniture and typography, are unthinkable without the functional elegance pioneered by the Bauhaus." At the end, who of the two men was more successful in importing the pedagogy and reshaping the school: was it Gropius at the GSD or Mies at the IIT? This is not an easy question to answer. It's always easier to reshape a younger school (like the IIT) that is known for nothing, rather than reforming a traditional Ivy League school that has been around a long time and therefore has plenty of traditions and politics to manoeuvre. The architecture programme at the IIT was tiny and there were few "old" faculty members to deal with compared to the much larger GSD. Gropius's role was also different: he was able to recruit a significant number of excellent European refugees to US universities, which had a broad impact. Mies, on the other hand, was able to focus on his own practice and to build significant projects—from high-rise towers to campus buildings—from his position at the IIT, which was at least equally important to him as the reshaping of the architecture curriculum. He knew that as long as he could hold on to an influential position as prominent teacher, he would continue to secure additional commissions.

However, both were not fully successful in their attempt to establish a "new Bauhaus" and continue the intellectual experiment that so abruptly ended in 1933 in Berlin. In the end, the most successful pedagogical import of Bauhaus ideas was by artists Josef and Anni Albers at the Black Mountain College in North Carolina, which was already mentioned earlier. The Albers were able to stay closest to the Bauhaus ideals and reconnect with the ethos of the "unfinished" Bauhaus project. There were also other schools of design and architecture that partially implemented a curriculum based on the Bauhaus, such as Pratt Institute in Brooklyn and the University of Texas at Austin.

The Texas Rangers at Austin, and Colin Rowe and Oswald Mathias Ungers at Cornell
The University of Texas, School of Architecture in Austin is of particular interest, as prominent educators including Werner Seligmann from Germany and Berhard Hoesli from Switzerland

were part of a movement called the "Texas Rangers." The Texas Rangers were a significant chapter in the history of post-war American architectural education. The term refers to a group of young architects who taught in Austin from 1951 to 1957. The group is known for the development of an innovative architecture curriculum that embodied numerous ideas from the Bauhaus and combined them with other concepts. It encouraged the development of a workable, useful body of theory derived from a continuous critique of significant works across history and cultures.

The movement that brought about the Texas Rangers began with the appointment of Harwell H. Harris (1903–1990) as the first dean of the Austin school (1952–1955). Harris had worked for Richard Neutra and assimilated European influences in his pedagogical thinking. He was impressed by the new approach to design championed by the Bauhaus and in particular by Josef Albers's teaching at Black Mountain College. He was able to recruit new faculty to Texas: modernist architects to teach at the Austin school whose approach to design and architecture was similar to the Bauhaus. Among those Harris succeeded in attracting to the school were Colin Rowe, John Hejduk, Robert Slutzky, Werner Seligmann and Berhard Hoesli (Caragonne, 1993; Varnelis, 1996). They were a group of architects and art historians who, within a few years, created a new curriculum for the newly founded School of Architecture. The Texas Rangers were by no means a unified group, and when they began their work in 1952, twenty years had passed since the "heroic" era of modern architecture (see Image 18).

Presenting a convincing model of formal architectural education based on the Bauhaus language of space, the Rangers had a substantial impact on the teaching of architecture in the US. Many of the projects contained within their studio curriculum are still assigned at architecture schools today. In the 1920s Bauhaus, the conception of "space" was formed: the language of space was developed by the artists Moholy-Nagy and Albers in their transdisciplinary *Vorkurs* course for first-year students rather than in the architecture studios. The Texas Rangers were interested in further developing this visual language and translating it into architecture. While retaining faith in modernism, they felt that although the system elaborated by Gropius would teach students to create buildings that would work functionally and structurally, it would fall short of rigorously addressing the real essence of architecture. In particular, the collaboration between Colin Rowe and Bernhard Hoesli provided the intellectual basis of the new curriculum, including Rowe's re-introduction of architectural history into design studio teaching.

"The purpose of architectural education," reads the manual in the official *Handbook of the School of Architecture of 1954*, "is not alone to train a student for professional occupation, but above all to stimulate his/her spiritual and intellectual growth, to develop his/her intellectual faculties and to enable them to grasp the meaning of architecture." The new curriculum of the school (derived from the Gestalt methods of Josef Albers), based on a memorandum drafted by Hoesli and Rowe, stressed exactly that: the possibility of teaching a process. The students would therefore have the possibility of knowing and understanding architecture as a discipline at large, with its own "intellectual content," where "grasping the meaning of architecture" meant to establish a research process of design by following a rigorous path within a frame of reference given by the teachers and their studio programme (Soletta, 2010).

In the end, the Texas Rangers had created an unprecedented teaching programme that was first based on the Bauhaus pedagogy and from there emerged further as a new pedagogical model that was ahead of its time and challenged the established pedagogies at other US schools of the time and the anti-intellectual tendencies of the pragmatic, regionalist American tradition. The new curriculum proposed that a workable, useful body of architectural theory could be derived from an analysis and critique of significant historical precedents of buildings and projects across history and cultures, leading to the development of the architectural idea in the design process.

Importance was given to the "architectural idea" as the *autonomous* and *unique* substance and catalyst of every architectural project and its content. Historical references and precedents, mainly introduced by historian Colin Rowe, were an important part of the design studio as a stimulus for students and their design process. Students were asked to choose: in their own design proposals, either they would agree and follow the presented precedence, or they would be going against the historical precedence. Brief yet powerful, their curriculum was considered as an alternative to the standard architectural education of the American schools at the time. While the curriculum evolved during those few years in Austin, it is in the dispersion of these ideas through the continuity and effort of the educators at other schools that one can identify its repercussions worldwide. However, in the conservative climate of 1950s Austin, the reaction to the Rangers' programme was negative, and by 1956 they all left to go their separate ways to spread their teaching methods both in the United States and back in Europe, achieving legendary status—Rowe at Cornell, Hejduk and Slutzky in New York, Hoesli and Seligmann at the ETH Zurich (Rowe, 1996).

British educator and architecture historian Colin Rowe (1920—1999) is a particularly interesting case. He was a student of art historian Rudolf Wittkower and, following his time in Austin, emerged as an influential teacher at Cornell University, where he taught from 1962 to 1990. In his view, by his time in Austin, modernism in architecture was already finished, and what was intended to be a revolution had failed. Rowe developed the theory that there is a strong conceptual relationship between modernity and tradition, using critical analysis in the comparison of the proportions of villas by Palladio with Le Corbusier's buildings as precedents. Rowe strongly favoured a formalist approach to architectural analysis, which was highly compelling to young architects who hoped to retrieve something of value from the declining modern movement. He was among the first to openly speak out about the failures of modernist urban planning and its destructive effects on the historic urban fabric. Colin Rowe became the inspiration for a generation of practising architects to consider history imaginatively, as an active component in their design process. His students included James Stirling, Peter Eisenman, Richard Meier and others.

In 1965, Colin Rowe invited the German architect Oswald Mathias Ungers (1926—2007) to teach at Cornell University as visiting professor. At this time, Ungers was a professor at the Technical University of Berlin, a position he held from 1963 to 1967, including serving briefly as the dean of the Faculty of Architecture, from 1965 to 1967. Ungers had studied in Karlsruhe under Egon Eiermann (1904—1970). Eiermann's unsentimental designs represented the ideas of post-war functionalism and shaped the image of the young Federal Republic of Germany over a period of more than two decades. Fascinated by the modern masters Gropius and Mies, and their dogmatic attitudes to architecture, Eiermann was able to successfully build on the tradition of the Werkbund and the Bauhaus. In 1968 Ungers moved to the United States, where he became the chair of the Department of Architecture at Cornell University in 1969. This was unusual at this time; there was mostly dialogue in architecture between the US and Italy and England, not between the US and Germany.

Ungers first visited Cornell in 1965 and again in 1967 as visiting professor, and in 1969 he was appointed chair of the deaprtment, serving until 1975. Ungers was also a visiting professor at Harvard University (in 1973 and 1978) and at the University of California, Los Angeles (1974—1975). After eight years in the US, Ungers returned to Germany in 1976, where his practice in Cologne became involved in numerous high-profile projects; he quickly emerged as a highly influential architect in Germany. His tenure at Cornell in the 1970s not only helped launch Cornell's architecture programme internationally but also served as a catalyst for Ungers's career. He identified with the ideas of postmodernism through academic publications and entries in design competitions that became internationally known. At Cornell, Ungers attracted a globally diverse mix of students who worked under his guidance to complete their masters' theses, as well as many international visiting faculty members, such as Joseph Paul Kleihues and Rem Koolhaas, and his former Berlin students Hans Kollhoff, Max Dudler and Christoph Maeckler (German architect J.P. Kleihues always suffered from being in the shadow of O.M. Ungers and internationally less recognized; although, it was Kleihues who built the Museum of Contemporary Art in Chicago, 1994-1996, an important urban contribution to the city by a German architect).

Ungers always stressed the importance of the concept of each project as "part of a larger cosmos, a larger order of form" (Ungers, 1978), which was part of his themes of transformation, typology and metamorphosis. While the relationship between Colin Rowe and Ungers deteriorated in the early 1970s, both shared an interest in refocusing the curriculum on issues of the city. Their common pedagogical goals allowed for a shared aspiration and rigour in promoting a theory of architecture that envisioned new methodologies and modes of thought of critical conditions for architecture. Both, Ungers's and Rowe's work was to establish new grounds for speculative production, based on extensive urban research and analysis, and processed through iterative adjustments of pedagogical frameworks. Studio and thesis projects became laboratories of larger methodological experiments, where publications and exhibitions were utilised as tools of analytical production. It is through the process of theory, research, analy-sis and speculation that the two seminal publications *Collage City* (1974) by Rowe and *Cities within the City* (1978) by Ungers became important manifestos to investigate new directions that were critical to the times, proposing an urban vision for a new collective.

The work led to the 1977 manifesto *The City in the City: Berlin, A Green Archipelago*, co-published with Ungers, Rem Koolhaas, Arthur Ovaska and Hans Kollhoff. The concept of the "Green Archipelago" was of particular interest, as it was the first intellectual model for a shrinking city. The publication is an urban manifesto about West-Berlin in the 1970s, a city in decline. In contrast to the reconstruction of the growing European cities that was popular at the time, they developed the idea of a polycentric urban landscape for Berlin that could cope with population shrinkage, long time before the focus of the urban planning discourse turned to the examination of crises, recessions and the phenomenon of demographic shrinking. It is probably the first ever reflection on a contemporary city with declining population, suggesting a city of many islands instead of one condensed centre.

Arthur Ovaska (1951—2018) was a critical part of these teaching and publishing activities. He studied architecture at Cornell from 1968 to 1974; his thesis advisors were Ungers and Rowe. From 1974 to 1978, he collaborated with Ungers in Ithaca and in Cologne on a number of international competitions, as well as on three landmark Cornell summer programmes: *The Urban Block* in Ithaca, and both *The Urban Villa* and *The Urban Garden* in Berlin. From 1978 to 1987, Ovaska worked in Berlin, where he co-founded the German-American office Kollhoff & Ovaska, with Hans Kollhoff, who he met at Cornell's graduate programme. Their office produced significant designs for Berlin's International Building Exposition, which was held from 1984 to 1987, including the housing project at Luisenplatz. Ovaska left Berlin in 1987 to accept a full-time academic position at Cornell, where he became director of undergraduate studies in 2005.

Jack Hoge notes about this critical period at Cornell that "if the decades of the '60s and '70s are recognised as a period when modernist ideals were questioned and the profession was infused with doubt and self-questioning, we find ourselves in a similar situation today, as architectural practice struggles again to identify its position within the multiplicity of aphasic spectacles and discord of heterogeneous complacencies." (Hoge, 2007) During this time, there was a unique stimulating atmosphere at Cornell prompted by the academic rivalry between historian Rowe and theorist and practicing architect Ungers. Challenges to the architectural establishment had already commenced in the 1968 Parisian student riots, but not everyone agreed that architecture or city planning should play a leading role in the reform of social problems or racial issues. The most outspoken and radical commitment to the disruptive aims of the 1969 student protests at Cornell came from Ungers in his role as department chair, speaking out in defense of a minority's right to protest; while Colin Rowe was unwilling to draw any connections between the racial issues affecting the US in 1969 and the future directions of contemporary design (See image 20).

Image 18: The "Texas Rangers" at the University of Texas at Austin, around 1955. The Texas Rangers were a significant chapter in the history of post-war American architectural education: a small group of faculty including Colin Rowe, Werner Seligmann, John Shaw, Robert Slutzky, John Hejduk, Lee Hirsche, Bernhard Hoesli, Lee Hodgen, Jerry Wells and W. Irving Phillips

Image 19: The novel *The Fountainhead* (1943, by Ayn Rand) was turned into a movie in 1949 with Gary Cooper in the role of the ambitious, arrogant modern architect Howard Roark, a modern architect (meant to be Frank Lloyd Wright) who resists the historicising decoration of his building.

Image 20: Oswald Mathias Ungers, then department chair at Cornell University (photo around 1974), with Fred Koetter, Werner Seligmann and others

7. The Bauhaus Pedagogy Reflected Back to Europe Through Hoesli at the ETH

Berhard Hoesli (1923–1984) was a German-Swiss architect and artist who grew up in Zurich, where he studied architecture at the ETH Zurich and graduated in 1944. In 1947, Hoesli moved to Paris to join architect Fernand Léger, and he was later accepted by Le Corbusier as an assistant. In 1948, he was sent by Le Corbusier to La Plata, Argentina, to supervise the construction of the Curutchet House. A year later, he was appointed to take charge of the Unité d'Habitation project in Marseille. Hoesli moved to the United States in 1951. He first joined the School of Architecture at the University of Texas at Austin as a professor of architecture. It was there where he teamed up with other young educators—British-born Colin Rowe, American John Hejduk and German Werner Seligmann, among others—to form the "Texas Rangers". In 1956, he returned to teach at the ETH Zurich. In 1959, which Hoesli hails as "the year Modern Architecture became teachable worldwide", many opinions on architectural instruction changed and ETH commenced to develop a new curriculum. It was the year of the death of Frank Lloyd Wright, and Hoesli felt a new era starting, marked by the freedom to discuss the process of design with students through a new pedagogy. His design problems, which "were so formulated that the student had to solve tasks within a given framework of requirements and achieve precise results" (as cited in Jansen et al, 1989) were still arranged by building types. The types of design exercises were created in order to instruct the students in a specific skill through their own self-discovery with trial and error.

At this time the design process at the ETH revolved strictly around different building typologies, but Hoesli believed—as he experienced through the adopted Bauhaus pedagogy and the new curriculum ideas in Austin, Texas—that the steps of a practical design process were more important than the mere function of different building types. After his US experience, Hoesli's leadership and persuasive skills were at their peak. He was able to formulate new course structures and effectively implement them with ease. Defending the modernist tradition, he saw the three main protagonists as Frank Lloyd Wright, Le Corbusier and Mies van der Rohe, using their buildings as a source of history and theory for his own teaching. Hoesli was also able to bring in important new people: in 1970, for example, when Aldo Rossi was asked to leave his university position in Italy because he was a member of the communist party, Hoesli invited him to teach at the ETH until 1972. Hoesli began the curriculum overhaul with the first-year basic design course, including skills in drawing as well as proportion, geometry, spatial organisation and material decision-making—all very similar to the Bauhaus *Vorkurs*. The ideas of the *Vorkurs* came full cycle, after having been introduced to the US, and then reflected back to the schools in Europe. It was a reverse flow and reflection of the concepts that had previously been imported to the US through the Bauhaus immigrants. For some time, Hoesli was an influential figure in reshaping the ETH architecture curriculum and in 1969, he was appointed chair of the architecture school. But the student body had changed; by then, the heroic modernism was passé, and his old methods of teaching reimported from Texas didn't seem to work with a sceptical new generation.

8. Consolidation of the Modernist Approach in 1950s US Architectural Education

The image of the Beaux-Arts traditionalist versus the modern "genius" was scorned in Ayn Rand's novel *The Fountainhead* (published in 1943) and in the popular 1949 film based on the novel: the central character is a modern architect, an individual hero fighting the established constraints of classical convention, lauding a modern "truth" in pure modern building. This was combined with a highly romanticised image of the struggling architect fighting the establishment that was associated with wealth and snobbery. The image became widely popular and *The Fountainhead* marked a decline in the public perception of the Beaux-Arts-trained architect (see Image 19).

From the mid-1950s on, we find a consolidation of the modernist approach to US architectural education. By then, German modernism and its interpretations in the US as a style and pedagogy were absorbed into the US architectural education and started to spread across the country. This era became synonymous with the triumph of the Bauhaus's modern architecture and design principles in architectural education. The modern movement had gained a lot of attention in the pre-war years, and it struck a chord with the booming post-war times. The modernist approach to architectural education was now consolidated.

Conferences and studies by the AIA provide interesting detail on the development of architectural education, providing a reference point for the changes in the way architects were educated. Turpin Bannister's review of the AIA "Report for the Commission for the Survey of Education and Registration", published in 1954 as "The Architect at Mid-Century", marked a turning point. In the UK, similar conferences were held, and the RIBA report "The Architect and His Office" (1962) and the subsequent Layton report "The Practical Training of Architects" (1962) examined the British context with similar conclusions. The separation between design and construction had been a central part of contention for a long time. In Britain, as early as in 1850, John Ruskin bemoaned the loss of craft skills as a consequence of the Industrial Revolution and reflected the concerns of the Arts and Crafts movement.

The remarkable 1954 report "The Architect at Mid-Century" offered a thorough study of the evolution of architectural education, making direct comparisons between the US and other nations' architectural educational models. The report ended by asking for reform. With the rejection of the Beaux-Arts principles, the thrust of modernist teaching was that there should be less focus on artistic ability and more on scientific knowledge, as well as a concentration on social and environmental concerns with an accompanying "influx of social scientists into architectural education". The report painted a rosy picture of opportunities created by the wonders of modern science and technology, with the optimistic post-war world providing abundant possibility for spreading the modern. The main thrust was that there should be less focus on artistic design ability and more on scientific evidence-based knowledge and social science.

In the 1950s, the US was characterised by optimism and a willingness to reinvent itself. It was clear to the architects in the US, and also increasingly to those in Europe, that the centre of the modernist project—and perhaps of Western cultural production—had shifted decisively across the Atlantic.

Goddard (2019) notes that educational methods associated with modernism were confirmed in Britain by the influential RIBA Conference on Architectural Education held in 1958 in Oxford. This became known simply as the "Oxford Conference"; it was a watershed event at which it was agreed that standards needed to be raised to match other professions, such as law and medicine. It is described by academic Christine Wall as "the final nail in the coffin for putting into practice ideas on craft and construction as a basis for architectural education." In 1959 the AIA, in conjunction with the Association of Collegiate Schools of Architecture (ACSA), also held a pivotal conference called "The Teaching of Architecture" in Wisconsin. There was strong support for the diagnostic Bauhaus approach taken at Harvard (Goddard, 2019, 86). The conference concluded that the Beaux-Arts approach was seen as having too many failures to make it applicable to the "realities of the 20th century". There was also debate about the role of technology in the curriculum, the difficulties faced in teaching technology, and the need for specialisation and research was agreed upon. This conference was followed in 1963 by a call from the AIA and ACSA for a deep reform in education.

Over the last hundred years, each country had to become "modern" in its own ways, and there is an incredible diversity and variety of modernity, different types of modernisms, with variations of modernity one can find in Finland, Yugoslavia, and Kenya and so on. Internationally, the modernist approach to the training of architects was further promoted at the Union Internationale des Architectes (UIA) Congress in Paris in 1965. General studies, technical education and design were discussed in three separate panel sessions. Modernism brought with it new materials and industrial processes which overrode interest in traditional materials and construction methods. There was a trust in tabula rasa, and it was believed that modern architecture could change or redeem society. Design technology, economics and social studies replaced the study of proportions, freehand drawing, modelling and history and theory.

However, in the late 1960s, with the collapse of functionalism, there was a sense of crisis in architectural education. The problems with architectural pedagogy were summed up in the 1967 "Princeton Report" prepared for the AIA by Robert Geddes, then dean of architecture at Princeton. The pivotal report identified architectural education in the US as "unable to prepare students for a successful career". Geddes argued that the basic structural problem with the profession was that "architectural education was training its students to be artistic geniuses instead of practical draftsmen and specialists in technology or social science-based knowledge". The Princeton Report was not alone: a contemporary survey of architectural educators by *Progressive Architecture* also found that architectural education was failing. As a response in the 1970s, most schools of architecture were introducing fundamental changes in their curricula and some architecture schools renamed themselves schools of environmental design (e.g., such as UC Berkeley) and moved away from the "art of space making" (in the spirit of Gropius and Mies) toward the social science of spaces and environmental concerns (Hejduk, 1971; Curtis, 1977).

9. The Banality of Modernism and the End of the Modernist Doctrine of Functionalism

While the Bauhaus legacy was highly relevant in transforming the American pedagogy and practice of architecture in the 1940s and 1950s, from mid-1960 on it had gradually lost its relevance. For decades after their deaths, numerous disciples and noted students continued the architectural language of Mies and Gropius, their ideas and working methods until new design theories came into play to replace them.

Since around 1970, theory and criticism started to play an increasingly important role in architectural pedagogy and the discipline as a whole. The Bauhaus concept of abstract modernism and rigid functionalism became the subject of sharp criticism by theorists including Jane Jacobs, Lewis Mumford, Robert Venturi, Ada Louise Huxtable and others. The crisis of modernism was based on the critique of its repetitive, monolithic and banal architecture that emerged everywhere, justified by the modernistic ideology and a misunderstanding of Le Corbusier's and Mies's architecture, but in fact was mostly built because it was cheap and fast to do so. Helmut Jahn remembers, "It wasn't Mies that got boring. It was the copiers that got boring... You got off an airplane in the 1970s, and you didn't know where you were as it all started to look the same" (Helmut Jahn in an interview in 1978).

The myriad Miesian knockoffs that at first glimpse looked like something of Mies's were problematic: these buildings lacked Mies's attention to detail and his sense of proportion.

Roger Kimball (1989) notes that "with the rise of postmodernism in the late '60s, it was only to be expected that Mies's style, like that of modernism itself, should suffer a sharp decline. What had once been hailed as aesthetically exacting and a model of artistic dedication was now dismissed as elitist and socially retrograde." Postmodernism, with its appreciation of and reference to history, started to change architecture; postmodernism claimed that it "revived the art of civic monumentality." (Johnson)

The debate on architecture in Germany was strongly influenced by Alexander Mischerlich's book *Die Unwirtlichkeit unserer Staedte. Thesen zur Stadt der Zukunft* [The Inhospitality of Our Cities. Theses on the City of the Future] (1965), in which he criticised the destruction of the existing urban fabric for the sake of low-quality developments of the post-war era, originally considered by many as a synonym for progress. A large number of new housing developments turned out to be disappointing, and the public became increasingly unhappy with modernism and started to mistrust the architects. When Robert Venturi's influential book "Complexity and Contradiction in Architecture" (1966) appeared, it was the first book on architectural theory published in the US for some time; it sharply questioned functionalism. Venturi called for an eclectic approach to design and an openness to the multiple influences of historical tradition and Pop Art, laying the foundation for postmodernism. Major postmodern buildings were designed, built and celebrated, such as Michael Graves's Portland Building in Portland, Oregon (1982), and the AT&T Tower (known today as the Sony Tower) by Philip Johnson in New York (1978–1984).

Collapsed Functionalism Gives Way to the Rise of Postmodernism
Modern architecture of the 1920s and 1930s was an architecture not only concerned with visual or aesthetic issues but also with a strong social agenda and reaction against the excess of historicism. But by the 1960s, the social programme was mostly lost. Beginning in the 1970s, a younger generation of progressive architects and critics sought to define themselves in opposition to the modern protagonists, especially against Gropius and Mies, who they called anti-historical. The educator and theorist Peter Eisenman was one of the earliest outspoken critics of functionalism (ironically, he worked for Walter Gropius in Boston in the late 1950s). He wrote in 1963, "The modern movement has identified itself with change and the ideas of change, indeed with the idea of a permanent revolution. It was a mode of speculation. There is an inherent danger in the absence of logical thought in this argument of the modern movement. Without theory, history becomes the dominant discipline, it even seizes to be possible to evaluate the significance of historical manifestations." One of Peter Eisenman's main contributions to the discussion was that architecture as a discipline could now be "detached from responding directly to a particular function". He realized that at the moment when architecture became reduced to a simple programme-driven, functional diagram, it became soulless. Eisenman argued that "if it has a theory, architecture can even be about itself." All this was refreshingly new and a break away from the strict dogma of the tired modernist doctrine of form follows function with its total disregard for history, culture and context.

The 1960s and '70s saw a large amount of banal architecture being built under the banner of modernism. Architecture's idealisation of technology and function was creating additional problems. The tide finally turned against the unrelenting form-based focus of the modernists. It was a time when the modernist agenda came under scrutiny and its principles were severely attacked by critics, such as Bruno Zevi, Robert Venturi and Denise Scott-Brown, Jane Jacobs, Christian Norberg-Schulz, Colin Rowe, Heinrich Klotz, Alexander Mischerlich, Tom Wolfe, and Charles Jencks. They criticised mainstream architecture's preoccupation with empty formalism, its indifference to history, its doctrinal application, and the rigid definition of modernism. At the same time, modernism seemed to be intellectually bankrupt: once there was a confidence in the modern movement of architecture that was expressed in numerous manifestos written in the 1920s and 1930s in form of self-confident architectural declarations (such as the ones by Gropius in 1919 and 1938), but the production of meaningful manifestos stopped around 1970, when there was no more need for ideological declarations. By 1970, many followers of Mies and Gropius abandoned their teaching of a strict set of formal rules, purist approach and idealistic concepts, because it erased historical traditions, was in conflict with the complexities of real life and could not adapt to the changing needs of everyday people.

Modernism anchored its social agenda in an ambitious public housing programme, and one of the central ideas of modernism was starting over anew—tabula rasa. Until then, housing was seen as the dominant strength of modernism. Le Corbusier, for example, was principally concerned with social housing, and his architecture was not intended to service preconceived ideas about what such habitation should be but to create new and as yet undetermined possibilities for living. However, the modernist realisations of these undetermined possibilities for habitation were increasingly considered failures. High-rise blocks of flats and housing estates like Pruitt-Igoe were routinely derided as "eyesores" for their non-human scale, visual monotony and crowdedness.

The demolition of the modernist public housing estate Pruitt-Igoe located in a depressed neighbourhood in St. Louis, Missouri was seen as a turning point. It was built in 1956, and the architect was Minoru Yamasaki, who was also the architect of the World Trade Center. The massive housing estate with 3,000 units was touted as the definitive model for public housing projects in the modern era, and it was identified with the modern movement as a whole. A multitude of social, economic and political forces contributed to its downfall: the failed estate management, segregation and high crime problems had become so problematic that only fifteen years after its construction, housing officials simply gave up, and the entire estate was emptied and subsequently demolished. In 1972, the federal government gave the St. Louis Housing Authority permission to begin bulldozing and demolishing the project, and by 1976 (only 15 years after its opening), all of the buildings were gone (see Image 21). Architectural historian and critic Charles Jencks described the demolition as "the day modern architecture officially died" (1977).

Postmodernism evolved in the late 1970s and reached the mainstream in the 1980s before falling again from favour in subsequent decades. Architects like Michael Graves, Robert Venturi and Denise Scott Brown and Charles Moore emerged as leading postmodern architects in the US in the 1980s. Internationally, James Stirling in London, Hans Hollein in Vienna and Arata Isozaki in Tokyo were seen as the "postmodern triumvirate".

Image 21: The spectacular failure of modernistic low-cost housing. The demolition of the modernist public housing estate Pruitt-Igoe in St. Louis, Missouri, between 1972 and 1976, was seen as a turning point: it was seen as the beginning of the collapse of modernism and the modern movement as a whole.

With the failure of large housing estates such as Pruitt-Igoe, the period of modernism was finally pronounced as finished. In 1978, Philip Johnson, one of the "inventors" of the international style, who proclaimed modernism in 1932, now declared the "death of modern architecture" (see Image 22). Johnson was one of the most influential figures of architecture in the US, not just as architect but also as curator and socialite.

As a consequence of all this, the dominance of mid-20th-century Bauhaus pedagogy lost in relevance. The hagiography of Gropius and Mies as iconic leaders of modernism came into question and the 1950s triumph of functionalism was finally over. A new era in architectural thinking was approaching, dominated for the next twenty years by postmodernism. In the early 1980s, US schools of architecture were entangled in long scholarly debates over modernity and postmodernity, with historians focusing primarily upon the rise of postmodernism as a new movement associated with eclectic historicism, irony and pastiche (Otero-Pailos, 2010). A new generation of postmodern theorists positioned themselves in the academy and in the debates over postmodernity, with publications such as Charles Jencks's *The Language of Postmodern Architecture* (1977), Hal Foster's *The Anti-Aesthetic: Essays on Postmodern Culture* (1983), Andreas Huyssen's "Mapping the Postmodern" in the New German Critique special issue "Modernity and Postmodernity" (1984), and Francois Lyotard's *The Postmodern Condition. A Report on Knowledge* (1984). Architects like Michael Graves, Charles Moore and Robert A.M. Stern, all influential educators and practicing architects, delivered the first US buildings for the new theory.

Joseph Bedford describes how "architecture was shifted away from the critique of the feared alienation of functionalist modern architecture that had defined the philosophical context behind postmodernism as a style, and towards a renewed embrace of modern architecture, now seen as an expression of the media conditions of the age; especially the emerging digital complexity, image saturation, and networks. A new theory ultimately worked to render postmodernity and modernity as virtually synonymous, thus bringing modern architecture into play once again in the early 1990s, in the new contemporary horizon of digital networks, advertising culture, flows and connectivity" (Bedford, 2020).

Rejecting the "high art" status of the international style, postmodernism drew also heavily on the writings by Jean-François Lyotard and Jean Baudrillard and was popularised by the work of cultural polemicists Charles Jencks and Robert Venturi. It embraced populism based on architectural aesthetics characterised by historicist motifs and bricolage, as argued by Venturi. Its underlying aims, scope and methods became subject to considerable debate (for example, Habermas, 1982). Hal Foster identified two distinct and opposing strains of thought behind postmodernism's claims: on the one hand, postmodernism was a reactionary movement in opposition to certainties that grounded modern architecture, and it challenged the idea that social progress was adjunct to rational design (e.g., that a building's form was relatable to function in a pre-determined way). On the other hand, postmodernism could be seen as a critical stance towards modernism that sought to reappraise its claims to truth and architectural meaning.

Roger Kimball argues that "with *Complexity and Contradiction in Architecture* (1966), Venturi helped set the stage for the campaign against Mies by castigating what he called the 'puritanically moral language of orthodox modern architecture'—the language of Gropius, Mies, Le Corbusier and other modernist pioneers. Where Mies's stringent aesthetic demonstrated that less really could be more, Venturi's anti-Miesian brief for architectural 'pluralism' dispensed with such encumbrances and insisted—in a mot that has become hardly less famous than the Miesian original—'Less is a bore'." (Kimball, 1989). The architectural critic and postmodernist impresario Jencks picked up where Venturi left off. In *Modern Movements in Architecture* (1973), his well-known and polemical survey of 20th-century architectural trends, Jencks argued that Mies's unwavering commitment to aesthetic purity was "reductive" and often resulted in an "inarticulate architecture."

With the fall of the Berlin Wall in November 1989 and the subsequent collapse of the Soviet Union, the 20th century is said to have ended and the 21st century began (as was noted by Francis Fukuyama and others). For the new century, Western liberal democracy was embraced as the global future, with a wave of optimism that followed in the 1990s which created the idea that as architect one could work anywhere in the world and encounter very similar conditions everywhere. This time of economic globalisation was a period when the world was urbanising at a staggering pace and investment in property became the driving force of many nations, moving from an industrial to a service and knowledge economy. One of the consequences was that architecture became a free enterprise and speculative activity, with the emergence of the "starchitecture" system and the posture of architectural extravaganza as a result of the economic boom and neoliberal capitalism. Cities were forced to compete with each other on a completely new scale, and a group of architects was chosen to help deliver these new urban icons. A model of rapid, instant urbanism was exported all over the world, operating along similar lines, from Singapore to Shanghai and Dubai. China emerged as the place were architects from everywhere could be involved in a new urban boom: in the last 30 years, China has built more skyscrapers than the US in the entire 20th century. The world supposedly opened up for a moment, just before many "new walls" were being built.

After forty years of separate political systems, economic conditions and architectural developments, the two opposing systems of West and East Germany were unified practically overnight. With the fall of the Berlin Wall, which had devided the city of Berlin from 1961 to 1989, and the subsequent reunification of East and West Germany in 1990, German architects found themselves suddenly very busy for the following decade. The centre of the architectural debate was the city of Berlin, which had been the macrocosm of the cultural, social and urban consequences of the separation. A building boom unfolded in the former area of East Germany. Anne-Catrin Schultz notes that "architecture after 1990, the year of the German re-unification, modelled a set of values aiming at progress, technical ability and optimism for a great future with architectural nostalgia for the past. The former East Germany underwent a comprehensive renewal, especially in the realm of infrastructure, civic, commercial and transportation buildings" (2020). The urban and architectural interventions played the role of creating a new German identity. Understandably, during this busy period at home, fewer architects were interested in immigrating to the US. In addition, the US schools appeared to be confused about the way forward and less interesting as a destination in a time when these schools were still heavily involved in debates on postmodernism (see Image 23).

Image 22: Architect Philip Johnson posing with a model of the AT&T Building (architects: Johnson & Burgee; today it's the Sony Building), in May 1978, proclaiming the end of the modern movement. Johnson was an influential figure, and this building remains his monument to the postmodern movement.

Image 23: The fall of the Berlin Wall on 9 November 1989 was a pivotal event in world history that marked the end of the Cold War. The fall of the inner-German border took place shortly afterwards and unfolded a large series of urban and architectural projects in Eastern German cities and Berlin. (Photo: courtesy Open Commons)

Appendix Part II
The Current Context

A Contemporary Overview: Short Biographies of 39 Educators Currently Active in the US

The following directory provides a list with short biographies of 39 educators. It is organised in an alphabetical order and illustrates the diversity of teachers. The list is most likely incomplete and the author included as many professors as he could identify. The compilation includes German-born educators as well as German-speaking Austrian and Swiss professors, due to their cultural similarities, background and shared German "Sprachraum" (there is a remarkable large number of young professors from Austria). The biographical information is based on the information publicly available online at the time of writing (2020); there are short biographies of around one hundred words for each educator. Some of the biographies have been edited slightly for clarity and brevity. There are currently estimated over fifty German-speaking educators appointed to influential US positions and active in shaping architectural education, influencing thousands of students as the next generation of future architects in this country, and many of them are listed and profiled here. The following Appendix III features six conversations (interviews) with selected professors of the group of currently active German-born architects. All of them have spent over a decade primarily involved in architectural education, making significant contributions to architectural education in the US and the wider Angle-Saxon context. The interviews examine the influence of these German educators on US architecture schools and education of architects today, and how early German-influenced pedagogies have changed and transitioned.

Map
The Locations of Currently Active German-born Professors at US Schools of Architecture

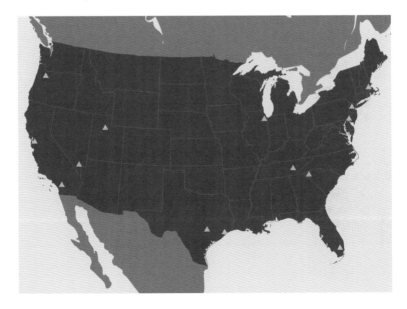

The Current Context – A Directory

Short biographies of German-speaking educators primarily involved in architectural education and based in North America (all texts are based on the online / publicly available information).

Ulrike Altenmueller-Lewis, *Philadelphia, Pennsylvania*
Former Program Director of architecture at Drexel University, which she joined in 2008, Dr. Altenmüller-Lewis was educated at the Bauhaus University in Weimar and at ETSAM in Madrid (Spain). She taught as lecturer at the Bauhaus University in Weimar (2002-2005), and moved to the US in 2005 to teach at the Washington Alexandria Architecture Center of Virginia Tech. From 2015-17, she was Co-Director of Drexel's Smart Initiatives Program.

Herwig Baumgartner, *Los Angeles, California*
Herwig Baumgartner, an Austrian native, is a licensed architect and co-founder of Los Angeles based practice Baumgartner +Uriu (B+U). He received his diploma in Music and New Media from the University of Music in Vienna and his M.Arch degree from the University of Applied Arts in Vienna. He is a professor for design and applied studies at SCI-Arc, the Southern California Institute of Architecture in Los Angeles, where he is the Applied Studies coordinator.

Gisela Baurmann, *Philadelphia and New York City*
Baurmann practices and teaches in Europe and the US. She is founding partner of Büro NY based in New York and Berlin. Baurmann has German citizenship, was born in Paris, and studied architecture at Columbia University, at the Architectural Association London and Technical University Berlin. She was a DAAD (German Academic Exchange Program) and Fulbright Scholar. She has taught architecture at multiple universities in the US and at the Technical University Berlin, where she coordinated the Department of Design and Building Design. She currently teaches at the Weitzman School of Design at the University of Pennsylvania.

Martin Bechthold, *Cambridge, Massachusetts*
Dr. Bechthold is Director of the Doctor of Design Studies Program and the Master in Design Engineering Program, and Kumagai Professor of Architectural Technology, at the Graduate School of Design at Harvard University. Since 2008, he has served as professor of architectural technology at the GSD. His current research investigates material and fabrication technology as a catalyst of innovation for design practice. Bechthold studied architecture at the Rheinisch-Westfaelische Technische Hochschule (RWTH) in Aachen, Germany, and holds a Doctor of Design degree from the GSD at Harvard University.

Peter Bosselmann, *UC Berkeley, California*
Bosselmann is a professor of the Graduate School in Architecture, City and Regional Planning, Landscape Architecture and Urban Design at the College of Environmental Design, University of California Berkeley. He graduated from Karlsruhe University in architecture in 1972, where he started his education under Egon Eiermann and completed his diploma with Gunnar Martinsson. He came to the US in

1974 (DAAD supported) to study architecture with Bill Mitchell at UCLA, later with Christopher Alexander at Berkeley and in Mexico until 1976. His first job was with Donald Appleyard until 1982. He joined the UC Berkeley CED faculty in 1983 to teach Urban Design and moved through the ranks, became full professor and Chair of Landscape Architecture and Environmental Planning. In 1995, he was a founding member of the Master of Urban Design Program at UC Berkeley and chaired the programme until 2016.

Markus Breitschmid, *Alexandria, Virginia*

Dr. Breitschmid received his education in Switzerland, the United States and Germany. He is a Swiss architectural theoretician and, since 2004, a professor of architecture at Virginia Polytech Institute and State University (Virginia Tech); where he is currently a professor at the Washington-Alexandria Architecture Center, a consortium of international schools of architecture. He has lived and worked in the USA since 1999, the year he obtained a Ph.D. from the Technical University Berlin.

Ralph Buehler, *Arlington, Virginia*

Dr. Buehler is an urbanist, Associate Professor and Chair of the Urban Affairs and Planning program at Virginia Tech University. His expertise is in sustainable urban transportation and he is the author of "City Cycling" (2012) a book about how to make cycling irresistible. He holds a Ph.D. (2008) and a Master's degree (2002) from Rutgers University, and a Master's degree (2003) from the University of Konstanz. Between 2012 and 2018, he served as chair of the Committee for Bicycle Transportation of the US Transportation Research Board.

Martin Despang, *Honolulu, Hawaii and Hannover*

Since 2000, Martin is founding principal of Despang Architekten based in Hannover, Germany. He has been a permanent resident in the US since 2007. From 2005 to 2010, he was a professor of architecture at the University of Nebraska, and from 2010 to 2012 at the University of Arizona. Since 2012, he is teaching at the University of Hawaii at Manoa. He holds a Master's degree (1994) from the University of Hannover.

Alexander Eisenschmidt, *Chicago, Illinois*

Dr. Eisenschmidt came to the US in 1999. He is an associate professor at the University of Illinois at Chicago (since 2008), and an architectural theorist and designer. He was curator of "City Works," a collaborative exhibition at the 13th International Architectural Biennale in Venice (2012), co-curator of the exhibition "Chicagoisms" at the Art Institute of Chicago (2014), and of the exhibition "Collective City" at the International Biennale on Urbanism in Shenzhen (2015). He is a founding partner of Studio Offshore and director of the Visionary Cities Project, a research-based platform devoted to the study of the contemporary city and speculations on new forms of urbanism. His recent book is entitled "The Good Metropolis". He holds degrees from the HTWK in Leipzig (1999) and Pratt Institute (2000); and a Ph.D. from the University of Pennsylvania (2008).

Dietmar Froehlich, *Houston, Texas*
Austrian architect Dietmar E. Froehlich is a professor of architecture and Associate Dean at the Gerald H. Hines College of Architecture & Design, at the University of Houston, Texas. He holds a master's degree from the Technical University Graz, and a Ph.D. from the University of Applied Arts in Vienna. His doctoral studies explored architecture's role in film.

Werner Goehner, *Ithaca, New York State*
Before joining Cornell University's Department of Architecture, Goehner was associate director of the Department of Comprehensive Urban Development at the University of Karlsruhe. At Cornell, he teaches design studios, served as associate dean and director of graduate studies, and directs Cornell's summer programs in Europe, South America, North Africa, Southeast Asia, and China. He studied at the Universität Karlsruhe, the École Nationale Supérieure des Beaux-Arts in Paris, and Cornell University.

Hansjoerg Goeritz, *Knoxville, Tennessee*
Goeritz is a practicing architect and educator at the College of Architecture and Design, at the University of Tennessee Knoxville (UTK). He was trained as a mason and studied at the Architectural Association School in London. In 1986 he founded Hansjocrg Goeritz Studio. He has been an educator since 1995, and a professor at the UTK since 2007. He has won numerous awards with his built work, including the Baukunst Award, Kunstpreis Berlin and the International Brick Award.

Esther Hagenlocher, *Eugene, Oregon*
Hagenlocher is an associate professor at the University of Oregon. She holds an M.Arch. degree from the Bartlett School of Architecture, University College London (1998), and a Dipl. Ing. degree in Interior Architecture from the State Academy of Art and Design in Stuttgart (1994). She is a certified cabinet maker, and her research focuses on the design of small spaces and exhibitions. She teaches interior architecture and furniture design studios, as well as courses and seminars on contemporary design and interior construction. Before becoming an academic, she practiced with Kauffmann Theilig Architects and with Matthias Schuler at Transsolar, Stuttgart.

Ulrike Heine, Clemson, *South Carolina*
Heine is an associate professor and assistant director of the School of Architecture at Clemson University in South Carolina. Since 2007 in the US, her approach to architecture in teaching and research is based on sustainability, in the way of applying simple natural laws in reaction to climatic conditions. She teaches architectural design as a process of integration. She graduated from the Brandenburg Technical University in Cottbus in 1999 and worked with Hascher Jehle Architekten in Berlin. Prior to coming to Clemson University, she spent three years teaching Design, Construction and Energy Responsible Planning at the Technical University of Berlin.

Barbara Hoidn, *Austin, Texas and Berlin*
Hoidn is the founding member of Hoidn Wang Partner (with Wilfried Wang), based in Berlin. In 1994, she joined the strategy department of the Senate Building Director of Berlin as head of the Architecture Workshop. In this position, she was responsible for the development of public urban design guidelines for central Berlin. Since 2002, she is a Visiting Associate Professor at the O'Neil Ford Chair at the School of Architecture, University of Texas at Austin. She has been teaching at the ETH Zurich, Rhode Island School of Design, and the GSD at Harvard University. She has also lectured at various other universities in Europe, the US, and Canada.

Anna Klingmann, *New York City, NY and Riyadh*
While she is frequently teaching in Saudi Arabia, Dr. Klingmann is based in New York and has taught at various US institutions. She is the founder and principal of Klingmann Architects and Brand Consultants, and author of the book *Brandscapes: Architecture in the Experience Economy*. Klingmann moved to New York City in 1984 and studied at the Parson's School of Design. She earned her architecture degrees from Pratt Institute (1994), the Architectural Association in London, and a Ph.D. from the Berlin University of the Arts (2006). She is currently the architecture department chair at Dar Al-Hekma University in Saudi Arabia; she has previously taught at Cornell and Columbia Universities.

Barbara Klinkhammer, *Philadelphia, Pennsylvania*
Klinkhammer is Dean of the College of Architecture and the Built Environment and Professor at Thomas Jefferson University in Philadelphia. She immigrated to the US in 1999, with architect husband Edgar Stach. She studied at RWTH University in Aachen and brings a deep understanding of the contemporary professional design world and a timely vision of the future of design education to her leadership role.

Daniel Koehler, *Austin, Texas*
Dr. Koehler is an assistant professor for architecture computation in the School of Architecture at the University of Texas at Austin. He teaches courses on architecture computation, urban form, mereological thinking and the design of distributive technologies at urban scale. Before joining UT Austin in 2019, he directed a research clusters at the UCL Bartlett School of Architecture in London, where he coordinated the theory module of the Urban Design Master's programme. He studied architecture at the University of Applied Arts in Vienna (2004-2008) and completed his Ph.D. at Innsbruck University (2015). He holds a B.Sc. Architecture degree from the University of Dortmund.

Julia Koerner, *Los Angeles and Salzburg*
Austrian-born Julia Koerner is currently an Assistant Adjunct Professor at UCLA's architecture and urban design program in Los Angeles. She is working at the convergence of architecture, product and fashion design, and in digital design for 3D-printing for the fashion and jewellery industry. Born in Salzburg, she received master's degrees in architecture from the University of Applied Arts in Vienna and the

Architectural Association in London. She is currently based between Los Angeles and Salzburg and has previously practiced in London and New York. Julia has been a faculty member at UCLA since 2012.

Ferda Kolatan, Brooklyn, *New York and Philadelphia, Pennsylvania*
Since 2016, Kolatan is an Associate Professor of Practice at the University of Pennsylvania. Born in Turkey, he grew up in Germany, received a Diploma in Architecture (Dipl.Ing, 1993) from the RWTH Aachen; and an M.Arch (1995) from Columbia University. He has lectured widely and taught design, fabrication and theory courses at institutions such as Columbia University, SCI-Arc, Pratt Institute, RWTH Aachen, Rensselaer Polytechnic Institute, Washington University, CCA, UCAM, University of British Columbia, and Cornell University. He is the co-founder and principal of SU11 Architecture + Design, an award-winning practice located in Brooklyn, founded in 1999.

Thomas Leeser, Brooklyn, *New York*
Leeser has been teaching architecture at nine different US universities: Columbia University, Cornell University, Harvard University, Pratt Institute, Illinois Institute of Technology, Rensselaer Polytechnic Institute, Parsons School of Design, The Cooper Union, and Princeton University. He prefers the freedom of not being permanent faculty of any particular school, but able to move between them for various short teaching assignments. He holds a master's degree from the Technical University of Darmstadt and founded Leeser Architecture in 1989; his practice has a commitment to innovation in museums, theatres and educational facilities.

Steffen Lehmann, *Las Vegas, Nevada and Sydney*
Dr. Lehmann has over 25 years of experience in senior roles in higher education leadership. He is past Director of UNLV School of Architecture in Las Vegas, where he is a tenured professor. In 1993, he became a licensed architect and founded his own design firm in Berlin. Prior to this he worked with Arata Isozaki in Tokyo and James Stirling in London. He has published twenty two books and numerous scholarly articles. He holds master's degrees from the Architectural Association School in London (1991), Mainz University of Applied Sciences (1988), and a Ph.D. in Architecture and Urbanism from the Technical University of Berlin (2003). He has been a full professor and chair of architecture programmes since 2003, and has led schools of architecture in Brisbane, Perth, and Las Vegas. He has established research institutes at UniSA in Adelaide and at the University of Portsmouth (UK).

Sandra Manninger, *Ann Arbor, Michigan*
Sandra is an Austrian registered architect and, since 2014, assistant professor of practice at the University of Michigan's Taubman College of Architecture and Urban Planning. She is principal of Del Campo Manninger Architects and SPAN Baukunst, a company she founded with Matias del Campo. Manniger began her studies at the Technical Institute for Educating and Experimenting in Building and Construction in Graz and completed a Master of Science in Architecture in 2003 at the Technical University in Vienna. She moved to the US in 2013.

Mark Mückenheim, *San Francisco, California*
Mark Mückenheim is a licensed architect in Germany and principal of MCKNHM Architects. Before establishing his own architecture practice in 2001, he worked and collaborated with different architecture firms in Germany, USA, and England. He received his Master of Architecture from Parsons School of Design, New York, and a Graduate Diploma in Architecture at the Bartlett School of Architecture, University College London. Before moving to the US, he taught for six years at the RWTH University in Aachen and as visiting professor at the TU Munich from 2009 to 2012. Since 2013, he is graduate director of the school of architecture at the Academy of Art University in San Francisco.

"I always said: no matter which architecture school you go to in the US, there is always a German professor."
— Mark Mueckenheim, 2020

Hajo Neis, *Portland, Oregon*
Dr. Neis is an associate professor of architecture at the University of Oregon. He came to the US in 1977. He holds a Ph.D. in Architecture from the University of California, Berkeley (1989), and a Master of City Planning (1980) and M.Arch (1979) from the University of California, Berkeley. He also holds a Dipl. Ing. degree in Architecture and Urban Design from the Technical University of Darmstadt, Germany (1976). He is director of the University of Oregon's architectural studies program in Portland, where he teaches design studios, courses and seminars. Prior to joining the UO faculty, Neis lectured throughout Germany and Japan and taught as an assistant professor at the UC Berkeley, and as a visiting professor at the Technical University of Dresden.

Sabine O'Hara, *Washington, D.C.*
Dr. O'Hara is currently the Director of Graduate Studies and the former Founding Dean of the College of Agriculture, Urban Sustainability and Environmental Sciences (CAUSES) at the University of the District of Columbia (UDC), in Washington, D.C. She earned a doctorate in environmental economics and a Master's degree in agricultural economics from the University of Göttingen. She is leading UDC's efforts to building a cutting edge model for urban agriculture that improves the quality of life and economic opportunity for urban populations. Sabine grew up in Kornwestheim (close to Stuttgart) and moved to the US in 1985.

Ute Poerschke, *University Park, Pennsylvania*
Dr. Poerschke is Stuckeman Professor of Advanced Design Studios at the Stuckeman School of Architecture and Landscape Architecture, College of Arts and Architecture at Penn State University in Pennsylvania. She teaches architectural design, technical systems integration and comprehensive studio. Prior to her tenure at Penn State, she taught design, construction and environmentally responsible architecture at the Technical Universities of Berlin and Munich (1999-2005) and completed her doctoral degree in architectural theory at the Technical University of Cottbus in 2005.

Christoph Reinhart, *Cambridge, Massachusetts*
Dr. Reinhart is a building scientist and architectural educator at MIT working in the field of sustainable building design and environmental modelling. At the Massachusetts Institute of Technology he is leading the Sustainable Design Lab (SDL), an interdisciplinary group that evaluates the environmental performance of buildings and neighbourhoods. He is also the head of technology company Solemma. Before joining MIT in 2012, Christoph led the sustainable design concentration at Harvard's Graduate School of Design. From 1997 to 2008, he worked as scientist at the National Research Council of Canada and the Fraunhofer Institute for Solar Energy Systems in Germany. He holds a doctorate in architecture from the Technical University of Karlsruhe.

Gernot Riether, *Newark, New Jersey*
Since 2016, the Austrian architect Gernot Riether has been director of the School of Architecture at the New Jersey Institute of Technology. He completed a Master's degree at the University of Innsbruck in 1998 and came to the US to continue his studies at Columbia University (1999-2000). From 2007 to 2012, he was Assistant Professor at the Georgia Institute of Technology, and at Kennesaw State University (2014-2016), before joining the NJIT.

Jörg Rügemer, *Salt Lake City, Utah*
Rügemer graduated with a Master's degree from the Southern California Institute of Architecture in Los Angeles, and a diploma from the University of Applied Sciences in Cologne. He is a licensed architect in Germany and has taught at the University of Karlsruhe, as well as Cottbus University of Technology, where he was the chair of Architectural Design and CAD. Other assignments included the Bremen University of Applied Sciences and Florida International University in Miami, where he served as the Director for Digital Design. Since 2006, he is at the University of Utah, where he teaches sustainable architecture and builds energy-efficient houses.

Goetz Schierle, *Los Angeles, California*
Dr. Schierle holds a Master's degree from Stuttgart University of Applied Sciences and a Ph.D. from the University of California Berkeley. He is a Fellow of the American Institute of Architects, founding Director of USC's Master of Building Science program and a professional architect. He lectures and publishes extensively on design for earthquake safety and tensile structures. Prior to joining USC in 1975, he taught at UC Berkeley and Stanford University. He is Executive Editor at *Journal of Steel Structure and Construction* and author of the book "Structure and Design".

Marc Schulitz, *Los Angeles and Braunschweig*
Marc Schulitz, NCARB, is a licensed architect in the US and in Germany, where he is a partner at Schulitz Architekten in Braunschweig. At Cal Poly Pomona, he is currently an Associate Professor and teaches structures classes and design studios. He received his professional degree from the ETH Zurich in 1999 and has worked as architect in Europe. He has previously taught at the Technical University of Brunswick.

Anne-Catrin Schultz, *Boston, Massachusetts*
Dr. Schultz is an Associate Professor at the Wentworth Institute of Technology's Department of Architecture, having joined in 2013. She is the author of four books and her scholarship on architecture in historic context and the work of Carlo Scarpa is informed by working at firms TGH and SOM in San Francisco, her post-doctoral research at the MIT, and one year at the University of Florence, Italy. She holds a Ph.D. in Architecture from the University of Stuttgart, has taught at the University of California at Berkeley, the California College of the Arts and at the Academy of Art University in San Francisco. Between 2011 and 2013, she was the Assistant Director of the School of Architecture of the Academy of Art University, building an online program.

Thomas Spiegelhalter, *Miami, Florida*
 Spiegelhalter is a professor at the Department of Architecture, in the College of Communication, Architecture + the Arts at the Florida International University (FIU), where he co-directs the Structural and Environmental Technologies SET Lab. Spiegelhalter is a registered architect and town planner and principal of Thomas Spiegelhalter Studio, since 1990. He teaches graduate sustainability and digital design studios, environmental systems and carbon-neutral building-city-infrastructure design courses at FIU. He came to the US in 1999. Prior to this (1992-1999) he was a Professor at the University of Applied Science in Leipzig.

Edgar Stach, *Philadelphia, Pennsylvania*
Dr. Stach is a professor at the College of Architecture and the Built Environment at Thomas Jefferson University in Philadelphia, where he holds a joint appointment with the Oak Ridge National Laboratories USA, Building Technologies Research and Integration Center. Before joining the faculty at Philadelphia University in 2012, he was teaching from 1999 to 2012 a professor at the University of Tennessee, College of Architecture and Design; and from 1995 to 1999 at the Bauhaus University Weimar in Germany. His current research focuses on advanced technologies for energy-efficiency.

Antje Steinmuller, *San Francisco, California*
Antje Steinmuller is the Chair of the Bachelor of Architecture program at California College of the Arts (CCA). Her research explores the role of designers at the intersection of citizen-led and city-regulated processes in the production of urban space. She is an Associate Professor and Associate Director of the Urban Works Agency, CCA's urban research lab. Prior to moving to the US, she worked with Braunfels Architekten and others. She earned her first architecture degree at the Technical University of Berlin (1998), and holds an M.Arch degree from the University of California, Berkeley (2002).

Katrin Terstegen, *Los Angeles, California*
Katrin Terstegen was previously a senior associate at the firm Johnston Marklee & Associates, and since 2014 works on her own, while teaching at Cal Poly Pomona in the Department of Architecture where she is an Assistant Professor since 2015. She studied architecture at the Technical University of Berlin (1994-2002) and studied in Barcelona and London (1997 and 1999). She immigrated to the US in 2002.

Geoffrey von Oeyen, *Los Angeles, California*
Prior to founding Geoffrey von Oeyen Design and von Oeyen Architects in Los Angeles (2011), Geoffrey was an Associate at Gehry Partners, from 2005 to 2011, where he played a key role in the design of several geometrically and technically complex projects, including the Foundation Louis Vuitton in Paris and the UTS Business School in Sydney. He received an M.Arch. degree from the GSD at Harvard University; and a Master of Philosophy degree from the University of Cambridge (UK). He graduated in Urban Studies at Stanford University. He teaches as an Assistant Professor of Practice at the University of Southern California (USC), School of Architecture.

Wilfried Wang, **Austin**, *Texas and Berlin*
He is currently the O'Neil Ford Centennial Professor in Architecture at the University of Texas at Austin. With Barbara Hoidn, he is founder of Hoidn Wang Partner in Berlin. Wang was born in Hamburg to a Chinese family, and studied architecture at the Bartlett School, University College London. Together with Richard Burdett, he was co-director of the 9H Gallery in London (1985-1990). He was director of the German Architecture Museum in Frankfurt a. M. (1995-2000). He taught at the Polytechnic of North London, University College London, ETH Zurich, Staedelschule, Harvard University's GSD, and at the University of Navarra. He received an honorary doctorate from the Royal Institute of Technology KTH, Stockholm, and is a member of the Academy of the Arts, Berlin.

"Most of what is taught in Germany as architecture today is done with the approach to technologically organise the required functional areas of space as defined by Hannes Meyer; there is very little artistic design being taught." — Wilfried Wang, 2020

PART III
Trans-Atlantic Engagements Today: German Educators Currently at US Schools of Architecture

1. Examining the Current Context: A Diversity of Pedagogical Positions

Being an architect in the US and in Germany poses significant differences. In the US, less energy-efficient construction standards and fully air-conditioned buildings are still acceptable; given the awareness of the threat of climate change, these kinds of outdated models have not been acceptable in Germany since the 1990s. Nevertheless, while in the US sustainable design principles are less established, the multicultural diversity of American cities and the convenience offered by amenities and ease of living are attractive to Germans.

Generally, European architects enjoy a reputation of being competent and well trained in the areas of technology, ecology, and sustainable design principles. Over the last decade there has been a withdrawal of German architects to the aspect of design, as is already widespread in the US. While a significant number of US architects are licensed and practicing in Germany, few German architects are licensed and working in the US. More recently, since 2000, several German and European firms have been able to establish dependences in the US, a trend that has been led by architects Stefan Behnisch, Werner Sobek, and the firm Graft. Similarly, some European offices, such as Grimshaw, Libeskind, BIG, Snoehetta, OMA and others, have been successful in the US market and have opened offices in New York. But overall, the US market remains relatively closed to European and German architects.

There are currently more than 115,000 licensed architects in the US (fewer than in Germany), where practicing architects have a higher average income than in Germany. These higher salaries do not necessarily apply in academia. The density of architects in the US is much lower than in Germany (according to 2007 data), with one architect per every 2,660 inhabitants in the US and one architect per every 850 inhabitants in Germany. Germany. In 2018, there were more than 131,000 licensed architects in Germany. In June 2020, the National Council of Architectural Registration Boards (NCARB) released its annual Survey of Architectural Registration Boards based on data collected from the architectural licensing boards throughout the United States. Based on this data, the number of architects licensed in the US has increased over the previous two years. The number of licensed architects rose to 116,242 in 2019, representing a 1 percent increase from 2018 and an increase of 10 percentage points compared to 2010.

One of the few things on which most architecture students in the US would probably agree is that the pathway to registration is too long, inflexible and increasingly expensive. In the US, becoming a licensed architect can easily take over twelve years (in Germany, the average is 8.5 years), and each state has its own licensing procedures and legislation. This means that

US programs are dauntingly long and, for many, prohibitively expensive. Although it's theoretically possible to achieve registration in eight years, the average time it takes in Europe or the UK is just under ten years.

The US has a credit-based system, rather than an emphasis on years spent at university, as we find in Europe. The EU directive on mutual recognition of professional qualifications (2016) stipulates that architectural training should comprise either five years of university-level training ("5 + 0" years) or not less than four years of study supplemented by a supervised professional traineeship of a minimum of two years ("4 + 2" years). The twenty-six EU member states recognise each other's professional qualifications, which allows for mobility of the workforce.

There are more than 3,700 public and private higher education institutions in the US, with 115 schools of architecture that offer some form of an accredited programme of studies. In 2020, in the US and Canada combined, more than 140 professional degree programmes in architecture were available, with around 6,000 faculty (full-time and part-time educators) educating more than 35,000 students in architecture. Architecture school programmes in the United States are accredited by the National Architectural Accrediting Board (NAAB), which standardises the education and training of US architects. NAAB is the only agency in the US that is authorised to accredit professional degree programmes in architecture. In 2019, reaching an all-time high number, 26,000 students were enrolled in the US in NAAB-accredited architecture programmes, with 51 percent being male, and 49 percent being female. Speaking of gender parity, 53 percent of new graduates were men and 47 percent women (NCARB, 2020).

Furthermore, in the US, the design training at schools of architecture is more intense than in Germany, with a focus on the architectural design studio, frequent meetings between professors and students (usually three times per week), and smaller class sizes. US universities also actively help students to find employment and commonly organise job fairs for graduates to meet employers.

In comparison: in Germany, there are 63 academic institutions offering studies in architecture, which include: 5 academies of art, 8 technical universities, 9 universities, and 40 universities of applied sciences (higher education is free in Germany). There are currently around 9,200 German students studying at US universities, and every year around 250 of them are enrolled in US architecture programmes.

While Germany saw a strong increase of the number of architecture students over the last decade, not so in the US: following the Great Recession (2008-2010), the overall number of architecture students in accredited US programmes has dropped by 6 percent between 2009 and 2017. There is also a decline of foreign students: while there was a steady increase of international students in North American architecture schools, from 5 percent in 2009 to 15 percent in 2015 (with about a third of them from China), by 2017, however, the number of foreign students has declined by 7 percent (it is likely that this figure will decline even further as foreign students face travel restrictions and visa issues due to US governments current stance toward immigration). At the same time, US universities have responded to the growing interest in design and have created more diverse degree offerings and specialisations (ACSA, 2020). While the gap in the number of male and female architecture students continues to close, in 2016 only around 36 percent of newly licensed architects in the US were female. Interestingly, women outperform men in the time it takes from the start of school to the earning of a license—11.8 years versus 12.6 years (NCARB, 2020).

The Scope of this Part

In Part II of this study, the focus shifted from broader trans-Atlantic and historical perspectives to a finer grained analysis of the influence of Gropius and Mies, and the social and cultural dimensions of their teaching and practice. Part III moves from these historical cases to the more recent contemporary context of architecture education. It aims to critically identify those aspects of architecture education that have become more essential in 21st century contemporary pedagogy. Bosselmann comments that "in Europe, much of the essential knowledge has found its way into European standards and regulations, while in the US—to the dismay of many—rules geared to protect the environment have been dismantled. I am also thinking about the skills we teach to improve social access, community building, equity, diversity and plurality. These are all aspects of an educational mission that builds respect for the larger public good" (in private conversation with the author, 2020).

While Part I and Part II demonstrated how the ideological underpinnings of the early 20th-century educators shaped American institutions and how the concept of early modernism was consolidated in the 1950s but came to an end in the 1970s, the question that is examined in Part III is whether these ideas still apply to the more recent history of architectural education and the group of German-trained educators. Most of them would have received a typical Bauhaus education at a German school of architecture. Until now little documentation has existed on German pedagogues teaching in the US. As architecture education is always in a state of transition, reflecting concurrent changes in the profession and society, it is helpful to better understand the contributions, ideas and strategies of contemporary educators. Considering the Gropius/Mies legacy, the final part of this book therefore examines the answers of six educators to key questions concerning the current context of US architecture schools today. German educators are a minority: around fifty or sixty are included in the group of faculty of more than one thousand full-time architectural educators currently working at US universities (around thirty of them are profiled in this study). However, this small group has a large impact.

The Bauhaus legacy has been interpreted in a wide variety of ways at the various schools, and much of the idea of bringing technology, industrial production, craftsmanship, science and design together as a unified concept remains timely. Today, besides Illinois Institute of Technology (IIT), only a few US architecture, art, and design schools remain committed to the Bauhaus's pioneering teaching methods. Adherents of the Bauhaus method include some faculty members at Pratt Institute in New York and the Art Institute of Chicago, amongst others. Harvard's Graduate School of Design (GSD) moved on and embraces a diversity of other pedagogical philosophies.

The arguments and discussions encountered in compiling this study prompted a closer look at education in the post-war years, with the aim of determining the most comprehensive method of teaching and learning in the study of architecture. The search for the most suitable teaching model is hundreds of years old, but one question we have not been able to answer conclusively is if we should educate architects as specialists or generalists. Consequently, the first four years of the bachelor's degree are typically general in nature, while graduate programmes in the MArch degree stream allow for self-directed specialisation in areas such as urbanism, sustainable design, healthcare design, and other areas. Different schools have different profiles, with a variety of specialisations.

There have been continual discussions, conferences, debates and curriculum workshops to try to define and capture how to best teach and learn about architecture. Therefore, rather than attempt to add to the already extensive scholarship on the lives and work of Gropius and Mies, or debates on pedagogy, the purpose of this book is to explore the current position of contemporary architectural education in the US regarding the Bauhaus legacy and to determine how far the early pedagogies have transitioned by examining the group of recent German-trained immigrants. While the historical cases of the last century, such as the Bauhaus, Gropius, Mies, Hilberseimer and Mendelsohn, have been comprehensively covered and an extremely rich body of scholarship on the subject already exists, the main contribution of this study lies in the discussions concerning the current context. The period of Gropius and Mies in America was the time of the American dream: rapid industrialisation, a post-war boom, trust in capitalism, and the beginning of the Cold War period—a political context that influenced their thoughts on architecture and the city. Therefore, some of the key questions for Part III and the interviews conducted included the following:

- How have early German-influenced pedagogies changed or transitioned, and what is their relevance to contemporary German-born educators today?
- How are more recent German-trained transplants influencing US schools today?

The experience of Gropius and Mies was closely intertwined with the condition of exile, as they were forced to become refugees. For half a century, the network of relationships between key educators was particularly strong between those who came from Germany, facilitated by the common language and a shared history of exile and struggle. However, contemporary educators are not in exile—they have voluntarily chosen to live and work in the US, and they see architecture as part of a globalised world. Hence, there is no strong network between German educators today. To work overseas, even globally, has become an accepted reality for many in education. They are used to working with colleagues from all kinds of backgrounds and nationalities, and many architects have followed the most exciting professional opportunities on offer, wherever these opportunities took them.

It is obvious that the rich and diverse account of German influences significantly contributes to the cultural, social and ethical currents that are shaping US architectural and design education today. It is an evaluation of these influences on US schools that highlights the imported excellence in education. Furthermore, the study celebrates the individual contributions German educators have made and continue to make to the vibrant North American educational scene through their design research, teaching and pedagogy.

So, what makes these German architects come to the US, and do they consider themselves German or American architects? Is national identity still relevant for them? What are the particular qualities they might bring to the education of architects in the US? What does the legacy of Gropius and Mies mean for them today? Are national attributes and identities, including preserving the cultural values of simplicity and efficiency, still relevant in a global interconnected society and profession? Which concepts do they import, and how do they assimilate to their new context and home country? How do they relate to American culture in general? How is national identity expressed in architecture—not just at the level of symbolism of government buildings or exhibition pavilions, but at the level of architectural teaching and design, such as in housing or workplace design? The interviews discussed in the sections that follow, and included in Appendix III, attempt to answer some of these questions.

2. Immigration and Positive Assimilation into American Society

The interviews with leading contemporary educators have shown that the link between German identity and architecture in general, and to pedagogy in particular, is seen as less relevant today. There is the view that "German-trained" is more relevant (character forming) than "German-born". Overall, national identity in relation to architectural education did not strongly resonate with the interviewees; none of them placed much importance on national identity. In this context, it is useful to acknowledge the differences between the educational traditions in the different German-related regions (e.g., between the TU Berlin and the TU Munich) and the different educational systems that exist in Austria, Switzerland, the Netherlands and Scandinavia.

In Part I we looked at the early emergence of the modern movement in Europe, which was pre-1914 mainly a non-German movement with the early avant-garde Dutch architects Berlage, Rietveld and Oud; Austrian architects Wagner, Olbrich and Loos; and Swiss architect Le Corbusier. Around 1914, the modern movement had arrived in Germany, and soon expanded to Northern Europe, where it was continued with leading architects in Finland (Eliel Saarinen and Alvar Aalto), Sweden (Gunnar Asplund, Sigurd Lewerentz and Sven Markelius) and Denmark (Arne Jacobsen, Kay Fisker and Jorn Utzon) — by the key protagonists of the early period of *Nordic Modernism*. Until then, it was the norm that architecture would lend itself to the creation of monuments and to the buildings that were necessary for the development of the nation's institutions of power: palaces, castles and churches. However, with modernism, there was a break from this norm: with the change of the role of the architect in society, the concern was now towards public housing and the infrastructure of a new social democracy (from libraries, to sanatorium, university buildings and railway stations).

A key part of the study are the conversations with the selected professors and colleagues. The detailed conversations with leading educators reveal more thoughts on this matter. Bechthold (2020) notes that "German-trained architects, no matter what their nationality is, bring a very solid education in the foundational building sciences and in building technologies to the US. [...] But German cultural values have softened and lost significance in this age of globally connected design cultures." When asked if there is something very specific about being German-born, Bosselmann notes that "undeniably there is, but there is a difference between being born into a culture and being educated within various cultures. There are subtle but distinct differences in the role that national identity plays in relation to architectural education; even within Germany, and more so among those who share German or related languages." Heine also believes that "the relationship between design and national identity is less relevant today." Klinkhammer offers the view that "buildings are expressions of their own time, reflecting political powers and systems, and cities are built expressions of their history, serving as witnesses of cultural identity" (2020).

Asked if national identity is relevant, Mueckenheim comments, "I do not consider national identity significant to me at all. Being born near the border of three countries and growing up in Europe's border-free Schengen Area [comprising 26 European countries], I see myself more as a European living in the US. However, I would say that there is definitely a Central European cultural imprint that is influencing how I approach architecture, teaching and re-search." Mueckenheim continues,

> "While there is nothing specific about German-born, there is something particular about being German-raised, at least in my generation and from my point of view. Through that, I have a strong aversion to nationalistic tendencies due to our country's history. If one deals decisively with the topic of globalisation and design, it becomes very apparent that there is a longing for a more distinct or regional cultural identity even in Germany. [...] I am concerned about this trend to recycle historical or national design attributes in an attempt to create what I consider a false value. This "retro-symbolism" is a dangerous development, especially as more and more societies seem to move into a post-factual era. It is in my mind an erroneous belief that a return to national identities is the answer in design, as it is similarly not an answer in politics."

He also states, "I do not think that Germans have a patent on efficiency or simplicity—many other cultures in the world appreciate these qualities. It is my hope that our global culture will continue to evolve without the advocacy of national ownership."

Steinmuller notes that "Charles Correa described identity as always evolving, based on cultural, social, economic, or political change. Wary of stereotypes, I consider national attributes and identities as continuously in flux. The German identity of Bauhaus educators–shaped by a world war and industrialisation–is not the German identity of today." Steinmuller adds, "Architects work increasingly globally today and were exposed to other cultures early on through travel and education, bridging more than one culture. In this context, it becomes more pressing to consider how architecture retains locally specific identity."

With globalisation, the 17th century concept of independent nation-states has become increasingly obsolete, and with it the idea of national identity. Until recently, the belief was that independent nation states could regulate things for themselves, but in a world full of interdependencies this is clearly no longer the case. Benjamin Barber, in the book "If Mayors Ruled the World" (2013), argues that democracy in its nation-state form is in a dilemma: climate change, migration, terrorism, poverty and pandemics all pose cross-border challenges that require global cooperation. He argues that we were trying to solve problems of the 21st century with a four hundred year old concept of nation states. "In times of globalisation, the nation state is no longer the appropriate scale to solve such challenges—the nations of the world seem paralysed as these problems are too complex, too interdependent, and too divisive for a single nation-state to solve." Indeed, the interconnectedness has become much stronger, due to an almost immediate information cycle. What happens in Wuhan, China, can result in consequences in New York; and what is going on in the Brazilian rainforest can change the climate in Spain. Because not one state alone can stop global warming or a pandemic, cooperation is increasingly needed. Barber's argument is that this makes the concept of nation-state and national identity less relevant. However, there is also a counter-trend (see, for example, Brexit in the UK; or forces in Catalonia fighting to preserve regional culture and language), where the nation state is regaining relevance, but it's still unclear if these trends will be sustainable.

The US is a Country Built on Immigration

It has been well established that the US is a nation of immigrants, and this continuous immigration has enhanced the country's cultural diversity, resilience and competitiveness. Throughout history, it has been immigrants that helped America become the great country it is and who made huge contributions to architecture, science, engineering and other fields. According to the National Science Foundation, more than 50 percent of postdocs and 28 percent of science and engineering faculty at US universities are immigrants. Of the Nobel Prizes in chemistry, medicine and physics awarded to Americans since 2000, 38 percent were awarded to immigrants to the US. It has been well documented that immigrants are often the hardest working people and that, despite their legal vulnerability, they still become major job creators and entrepreneurs themselves. It's important to acknowledge the massive contributions made and taxes paid by the recent arrivals. Some of the most ardent Americans you will ever encounter are people who were not born in the US, yet who believe wholeheartedly in the American Dream. However, it creates uncertainty when an immigrant's status in America is in question. This uncertainty causes stress and always the possibility that immigrants will leave and take their skills, talents and humanity elsewhere. The US's historic tolerance toward immigrants allowed for an influx of brilliant design thinkers from war-torn mid-century Europe. Many of our best architects and designers today were influenced and educated by first-generation immigrants from Germany, Austria, Switzerland and beyond.

Architects and designers grow and change because of their context and contact with other cultures, and in turn they influence others in those cultures. Again, Gropius and Mies are early examples of this reverse effect. But questions remain: how has integration into another culture changed the German-born educators' beliefs and interests? For instance, why are the technical aspects, such as building science, sustainable design and architectural engineering, the fields in which some German professors often seem to excel in their teaching and research pursuits? If this is true, their scientific and technical education at the Technische Hochschulen must have had an impact why buildings of high engineering quality and sustainability emerged as their areas of research.

Extensive scholarship exists on issues of design and national identity, discussing the complexity, historicity, and evolution of the relationship between design and nation building. For instance, Javier Gimeno-Martinez (2016) argues that the interrelationship between national identity and the distinctive characteristics of a nation's output and cultural production is closely connected with the demand and consumption of design products or building types by people within the country.

Cultural assimilation happens when an immigrant has spent time in another country and adopted the cultural values, language and societal beliefs of the new homeland. Americans have always been a heterogeneous population, a melting pot and diverse nation. Yet as Lalami (2017) notes, "One of this country's most cherished myths is the idea that, no matter where you come from, if you work hard, you can be successful. But these ideals have always been combined with a deep suspicion of newcomers. One reason that immigration is continuously debated in America is that there is no consensus on whether assimilation should be about national principles or national identity."

While traditional formations of the "national" seem increasingly inappropriate in an age of globalisation, cultural pluralism and diversity, design still plays some role in shaping, disputing and claiming the recognition of established and emerging identities. The Bauhaus teachers understood this and used these characteristics (often just stereotypes such as being orderly, austere or punctual) as a brand for a new type of thinking about architecture.

Heathcote also shares a positive view of the cultural contribution immigrants can make. He contends that "foreigners bring a different view of architecture, not necessarily as an extension of the genius loci, but rather as what it must always be—an amalgam of knowledge and impressions, half-remembered ideas and partially dreamt and interrupted dreams. Architecture can no longer be entirely of its place in a digitised world in which everything is accessible and instantly familiar, reduced to an image. Foreignness seeps in, just as it did with the Romans and the Renaissance" (Heathcote, 2019). Overall, the importance of nationality, place, or genius loci, seems to have lost its significance. Bechthold (2020) notes that "German cultural values have softened and lost significance in this age of globally connected design cultures" (see interview transcript in Appendix III).

This study argues that although the educators' position between two cultural spheres on both sides of the Atlantic creates discontinuities in their work, it also facilitates a mutual exchange between their European background and their North American peers and thereby helps to shape the development and reception of the educational projects on either side. Clearly, the influence of cultural models has impact in both directions.

While so far the emphasis has been on the reinterpretation of imported ideas and concepts into the US, international dialogue works both ways: reverse transference includes the reverse flow of cultural influences and ideas, affecting both cultures. Examples of this reverse flow of concepts are the *Amerikanismus* generated by travellers to North America upon returning to Germany and the curriculum reform Hoesli initiated at the ETH Zurich after his return from the US (for more on Amerikanismus, see also the Preface of this book by Alexander Eisenschmidt).

The export of American culture is one of the most influential forces in our interconnected world. Numerous scholars have written about the process of cultural assimilation of immigrants into American life, of adapting to the culture of another nation. Being assimilated into another culture is like being absorbed. The word assimilation has its roots in the Latin "simulare" meaning "to make similar." "Americanisation" is defined as the process of an immigrant to the United States becoming a person who shares American values, beliefs, and customs by assimilating into American society. Immigrants are expected, over an undefined period, to become similar to other Americans, a process metaphorically described as becoming part of the melting pot. This process typically involves more than just using the English language—it includes adjusting to culture and customs. Thus, the immigrants had to give up their own culture to assimilate into American society. The Bauhaus teachers were ready to do so: they became naturalised citizens of the US and finally severed from their native Germany, Gropius and Mies in 1944 and Erich Mendelsohn in 1945.

But how long does assimilation usually take? The experiences of European groups coming to the United States in the early 20th century suggest that full assimilation generally occurred within three generations, although no fixed timetable seems to govern completion of the process. It appears that this process happens much faster today, especially if the immigrant speaks good English. Assimilation of some professors of architecture would have happened within two generations. Prominent architecture educators Frederick Steiner, Karen van Lengen and Reinhold Martin, for example, all carry German family names but were born in the US, where they grew up as kids of immigrant families. They did not learn the German language at home, and they are fully American.

For young Germans growing up in the 1960s and '70s, America was a role model and a strong cultural influence, with music, art, pop culture and the flower power movement coming from the US. "Acculturation" is defined as cultural modification of an individual or group by adapting to or borrowing traits from another culture; for example, the acculturation of immigrants to American life is a merging of cultures. Contemporary German educators would have all experienced this form of acculturation in their formative years growing up in Germany.

The Germanic Values are Just Stereotypes

Three decades after the Berlin Wall fell, German society remains deeply divided over the question of what it means to be German. In general, one can say that the integration of East and West has in many ways been a success, although numerous people say that the West has "colonised" the East. It appears that unification did little to settle the neuralgic issue of "German identity". Katrin Bennhold (2019) writes that "the legacy of a divided history has left many feeling like strangers in their own land. Since 2015, Germany's effort to integrate more than a million asylum seekers welcomed by Chancellor Angela Merkel has been the most immediate challenge. In the decades since the wall fell, Germany's immigrant population has become the second largest in the world, behind the United States. One in four people now living in Germany has an immigrant background."

Mark Mueckenheim (2020) argues that "while there is nothing specific about [being] German-born, there is something particular about being German-raised and German-trained." In fact, one of the questions that repeatedly emerged during the interviews (see Appendix III) was, if there were any noticeable deeper cultural differences between Germans and Americans. The sense of humour is certainly different. It has been noted that a joke in Germany is no laughing matter. Germans are not a heterogenous group, as the various regions differ greatly. So what exactly are the cultural values that have influenced the educators in their formative years while they grew up in their home country?

The idea that Germans love discipline, rules, simplicity, and order has been a global stereotype for generations. In the recent article "What makes Germans so orderly?", Joe Baur (2020) notes that "for centuries, Germany has been synonymous with order." He goes on to describe "Germans strictly adhering to the rules in the name of preserving *Ordnung* (order). In fact, this proverbial saying is so well-ingrained in the German psyche that it has become a cultural cliché for Germans around the world, and a way of life and social conduct for them at home." But stereotypes aside, is Germany really more orderly than other nations? As with many things "German", the answer may go back to the reformer Martin Luther (1483–1546), a seminal figure in German culture (depicted in Image 24) who wrote, *"Ordnung muss sein unter den Leuten"* (literal: "There must be order among the people"). This characteristic also translates into architecture. Gropius's urban layouts for his new *Siedlungen* (housing estates) were not random, but based on balanced grids with few geometric distractions, expressing a clear and abstract new order.

Image 24: Portrait of protestant reformer Martin Luther (1529, by Lucas Cranach the Elder), a seminal figure in shaping German culture and values

Order is also considered a value on equal footing with punctuality, hard work and honesty, characteristics supposedly embedded within the fabric of German society. It seems that on the whole, German order is rather pragmatic, and Germans simply expect that systems and rules are in place to prevent the worst from happening (e.g., chaos). This sense of order is much more pragmatic and progressive than most people think. Yet from the hedonistic parties of the Weimar Republic, to the bottom-up movement that toppled the East German regime, to the techno temples in contemporary Berlin, there have been splashes of disorder. The city of Berlin is renowned as a tolerant laboratory of cultural experimentation, and people from around the world move there precisely to free themselves of rigid life plans and to be whoever and whatever they want without a judgmental glance. It seems that a lot of expressions, when put together, build a picture of a culture that is created by the diversity of its individuals.

German contemporary art has long been celebrated, with artists like Gerhard Richter, Georg Baselitz, Andreas Gursky, Sigmar Polke and Anselm Kiefer, who all represent confident artistic expression. Their art is usually either theory-heavy stringent conceptualism, or geometric compositions of abstract painting, or a brutally honest realism (of course, German artists do not have an exclusive on these forms of artistic expression; but it appears to be more common than at other places). Common subject matter includes the period of post-war reconstruction, with grim industrial landscapes, and the drama of East-West separation. It is sober, strategic and direct. Through their work, these artists have confronted issues of national identity, defeat and recovery, the burdens of history, and the responsibilities of art and design in society. In no other art forms is the Germanic character more present than in photography and cinematography. Bernd and Hilla Becher taught a generation of German photographers whose monumental deadpan view style and technical prowess (often showing industrial landscapes, using black-and-white photography with soft contrasts) convey both the ambiguities of the subject matter and the ambitions of the medium. Similar strategies can be found in the cinematography of filmmakers Wim Wenders and Werner Herzog. The work of the Duesseldorf School of photography, founded by the Bechers, expresses an enigmatic frontal look and minimal contrast that has become a synonym for German photography, combined with a sharp methodological approach. Baselitz commented about the experience of post-war Germany and the historical traumatic burden that "the pressure of being German really made us what we are. Without it, I don't know whether we would have succeeded as artists." The seriousness and heaviness of German art can also be detected in architecture (e.g., in the work of Hans Kollhoff or Max Dudler); it is in complete contrast to the consumer-oriented lightness and entertainment of American culture, and no doubt, these opposites have always attracted and fascinated each other.

Overall, it seems that the notion of national identity is now limited in its relevance to architecture; it appears overrated, and of little use today when it comes to the assessment of skills and qalifications attributed to different systems of architecture education. In the end, Germany—like any country—is more than just a few stereotypes or characteristics.

3. Why Teaching? On the Attractiveness of Being an Educator and a Writer

The academic freedom provided at US universities has always been highly attractive to educators from other countries. Today, most US universities welcome and encourage diversity among professors and seek to recruit and retain a diverse workforce with different backgrounds to ensure that their programmes offer students richly varied perspectives and approaches, and diverse ways of knowing and learning. It is widely acknowledged that such diversity and international experience contributes to a rich, stimulating learning environment—one that best prepares leaders in the making for the challenges and opportunities of tomorrow. Furthermore, US schools of architecture take a pluralistic approach to design by exploring it through a number of design cultures, for example, design through making, design as a catalyst and agent of social change, or design to explore emergent futures, often underpinned by a set of contextual themes.

Architecture is probably one of the most challenging disciplines, because if one wants to be very good at it, one has to succeed in very different fields at the same time. Most architects engage in the architecture profession simply through practice and, once they have completed their studies, lose the connection to academia as they focus all their efforts on a successful career as practicing architect. No doubt, practicing architects have influenced the history of architecture. So what about the architects dedicating their lifetime to teaching? Numerous educators work as theorists, critics and writers, and with an equally lasting impact on the history of architecture—just think of Adolf Behne, Nikolaus Pevsner, Colin Rowe, Sigfried Giedion, Reyner Banham and Manfredo Tafuri, to name a few. Teaching and theoretical, scholarly research has an enormous potential to change the world when combined with an understanding that published works and books can do as much to shape students or the future of a city as a lifetime of building.

An excellent example of this principle is German-born educator Detlef Mertins (1954–2011), who was a leading scholar of the history of modernism, particularly on the work of Mies van der Rohe, wrting about architecture. Mertins always asked students to make every effort to see new places and visit outstanding buildings as often as possible. His scholarly research and teaching at Pennsylvania, Toronto, Columbia, Harvard and Princeton Universities left a lasting legacy and impact, influencing the thinking of numerous younger architects who made it worthwhile for him to be an educator and researcher rather than a practicing architect. Like the theorist Manfredo Tafuri, Mertens chose to work theoretical rather than as practicing architect. Being an educator, fostering discovery and the production of new knowledge through research and scholarship, can be very rewarding intellectually and requires an immense time commitment.

Many architects are at home in both camps, as architects who combine practice with teaching. There is a long history of practicing architects who were committed to education, from Louis Kahn to Buckminster Fuller, Paul Rudolph and Hans Hollein—to name just a few. Numerous practitioners are involved in part-time teaching as drop-in adjunct faculty, such as New York-based and German-born architects Annabelle Selldorf, Kai-Uwe Bergmann (partner at BIG), Matthias Hollwich, Dieter Janssen and Markus Dochantschi. They all make important contributions as professors in practice to the education of the next generation of architects.

Peter Eisenman notes that "as an architect, you need to do three things: first, to read and think about architecture; second, to build; and, third, to teach architecture. It's all one thing!" (Cited from an online interview, 2017). Teaching and research are not in contradiction to practice, but ideally complementing it. Adolf Loos, Robert Venturi, O.M. Ungers and Aldo Rossi are the authors of relevant architectural books, who have done both: they were important educators, developed a theory and built significant works applying and testing their theory. It always seems that an architect is easier remembered in history through buildings. In 1989, when I worked with James Stirling, he told me, "If you don't build, nobody will care about what you think or your theory. People will only take your concepts serious when you have built them." Since then, I suppose this has changed and there is a place for the conceptual architect whose work is mainly theoretical. Books can have a longer lifespan than most buildings, which get changed or demolished after 30 years. Andrea Palladio's four books of architecture are probably more important to the world than the buildings he did.[6]

Chicago-based practicing architect Helmut Jahn has from time to time taught as a professor of practice. He introduced the term "archineering" for his technology-focused approach, which combines architecture with engineering. According to Jahn, the term broadens the scope of materials to be used (e.g., textile membranes) and employs scientific knowledge from physics, engineering, biology and ecological sciences. Instead of Louis Sullivan's famous dictum "form follows function", which had been the mantra for much of the modern movement in the 20th century, Jahn introduced the term "form follows force", which places the emphasis on structure rather than function. In an interview, Jahn described the difference of building in Germany and elsewhere like this: "The buildings in Germany are often more technically sophisticated because architects there work in a very high-tech industrialised country with the craftsmanship to build buildings. We're trying to transfer this to other locations and create a continuity that is not repetitive, but rather a language which is different than what other people do" (Kamin, 1998).

Another influential trans-Atlantic traveller, with a lifetime split between teaching and practice, between Vienna and New York, was Austrian-born architect and educator Raimund Abraham (1933–2010). He frequently articulated his European background and passion to engage in education. In an interview, Abraham explained his role as an educator (2001): "Teaching forces me to engage in a critical dialogue with somebody else and find a level of objectivity that allows me to have a fair critical argument. My role as a teacher is simply to clarify, although that's a bit simplistic. When I give a problem to the students, it's also my problem; I am trying to anticipate how I could solve that problem. And my joy is when the students come up with a solution I haven't thought of". Abraham arrived in the US in 1964, and for more than thirty years, he was a professor of architecture at the Cooper Union School of Art and Architecture in New York. Through his teaching he influenced generations of professional architects who remember his unusual teaching methods, architectural drawing style and visionary projects.

In a 2017 online lecture, the educator, writer, urbanist and architect Rem Koolhaas explained the interrelationship between his teaching and writing and the concepts he applies in practice, commenting that he always wants,

> "to maintain a degree of writing and teaching as an essential component of the profession. There are many reasons for that. One reason is, if you are a practicing architect, you are never alone and the work you do is almost always never your own work, but the work of a group, of collaboration and teamwork. Only when you write, you are really on your own. Only when you write, you take yourself full responsibility. Writing books and articles has ensured that I never lost my interests. When I became a teacher at the school where I studied myself, at the Architectural Association in London, it was a wonderful situation, because the separation between teachers and students was minimal and allowed for time to write. In other words, one could work very closely together on subjects rather than simply trying to transfer the knowledge of the teacher to a student. We were partners in developing languages and insights." (Koolhaas, 2017)

Koolhaas credits his successful career as a practicing architect to his acts of teaching and writing.

Similarly, the American architect and educator Steven Holl said in a 1999 interview,
> "today, I realise how important it is to write and teach, in addition to building. It's very important for an architect to be theoretically involved, and to be able to take a step back and take a longer view. I believe that I am a better practicing architect because I have taken time to teach and write, and to pull back instead of just building. The practice otherwise consumes you. Making buildings is incredibly complex and takes an enormous amount of time and energy. So if you don't take a distance and time to reflect, you can easily get dull as an architect." (Holl, 1999)

However, it's worthwhile to remember that Abraham, Koolhaas and Holl are global starchitects who can enjoy the freedom to teach what and where they want without necessarily becoming entangled with the burdensome bureaucracy that has taken over and plagues much of the educator's life today. There is a common romantic belief that universities are unique places of freedom that stimulate and foster independence and promote and encourage pluralism. This is not necessarily the case. In the 21st century, unfortunately, the university system is running the risk of losing these inherent qualities it once possessed to become more like private corporations.

Through globalisation, the commodification of education is seen as a malaise that has eroded the ethos of universities around the world, and the difference between universities and corporate companies has been diminished. In fact, today we can find pretty much identical strategic plans at the different universities, with university leadership moving from one institution to another institution, implementing the same often-ineffective strategies. If this unfortunate trend continues and universities cannot get a handle on the development, they will soon stop attracting the brightest people to become educators, as these talented people will instead prefer to work for the large tech companies with their impressive R&D budgets. To succeed, it will be essential for universities and schools of architecture to keep and maintain their independence, freedom and attractiveness of teaching and researching, of being involved in optimistic and forward-looking actions that form the basis of all education and scholarship.

Criticism of the Educational System in the 21st Century
There is also plenty of criticism of the educational system in the Anglo-Saxon world, and the US system of higher education in particular. In "The Decline of Universities, where Students are Customers and Academics Itinerant Workers" (2020), Elizabeth Farrelly writes that time studying at university was meant to be an "immersive and life-changing few years. For some it became a lifetime, which was possible because it was free. These were teaching institutions, dedicated to cultivation of the mind." But with globalisation, all this appears to have changed, and management techniques are mistaken for wisdom. Farrelly blames the corporate values that universities have adopted and too much globalism. "With an estimated 80 percent of teaching now casualised, academics have become itinerant workers. Teachers report widespread pressure to pass low-grade students but cannot speak of it, fearing reprisal. This too is indicative, since the whole point of tenure was to guarantee free speech," she adds. Yet never have we needed independent universities more. Academia was the place where open discussion is expected to be fostered and protected. Farrelly adds that "hard-head countries such as

Germany still offer free university education. It is not altruism; it is political recognition of the huge economic, cultural and wellbeing benefits from nurturing otherwise undiscovered young minds." Germany's free universities regularly figure in the world's top 100, so there's no sacrifice of standards; entry is competitive, but on intellect not wealth. When we consider what's at stake, the decline of universities hurts us all. The education in the arts and architecture is important as these feed the mind and soul of society.

In current architecture education there is too much focus on objects and technology, and not on discourse. In a 2019 interview, Peter Eisenman argues another point when he notes that "today there is a crisis in the schools of architecture. Pedagogy has become too obsessed with technology and the digital. We have lost the relationship between history and theory in regard to digital composition. The culture in the schools is in a crisis. Yale, for example, is interested in the sciences and technology, and not in the culture of architecture. Computers and digital fabrication are popular, but these have little to do with architecture" (2019).

In *Empire of Illusion: The End of Literacy and the Triumph of Spectacle* (2009), Chris Hedges describes the erosion of culture and decline of the American education system. He notes that "a third of high-school graduates never read another book for the rest of their lives, and neither do 42 percent of college graduates. In 2007, over 80 percent of the families in the United States did not buy or read a book" (p. 44). Hedges lays blame for this cultural decline primarily on the shoulders of what he calls the "educated elites" who created and now exist to serve the corporations that are the real power in America. He shines a dazzlingly bright light at the American education system: "We've bought into the idea that education is about training and success, defined monetarily, rather than learning to think critically and to challenge. We should not forget that the true purpose of education is to make minds, not careers" (Hedges, 2009).

In both countries, Germany and the US, there is criticism of the changing role of the university and schools of architecture in the 21st-century. Several intellectuals have recently spoken out to challenge architectural education and the context in which future architects are "produced", making it impossible to continue the original ethos of the modern university (de Graaf, 2017). One of the most outspoken critics of today's architectural education is Dutch architect Reinier de Graaf, a declared European and partner at OMA. He is mostly a practicing architect, with global teaching engagements as visiting professor. In his book *Four Walls and a Roof: The Complex Nature of a Simple Profession* (2017), de Graaf candidly shares his observations, launches an attack on schools of architecture and speaks about the misplaced confidence of the architecture profession today. His self-declared aim is "to debunk the myths that are looming over the architecture profession and its educational models, ranging from the myth of authority, to the myth of individual inspiration, the myth of good causes, the myth of independence and the myth of progress." De Graaf writes, "What I was led to believe as an architecture student is in complete contrast with the banality of the everyday work of an architect." In criticism of US architecture schools, he notes about his recent experience at a prominent school and the clash between different worlds:

> "As the evening progresses, the event develops into an unpleasant x-ray
> of American academia—a strangely insular world that is governed by its

own autonomous codes and dominated by an antiquated pecking order and estranged value systems, with little hope of finding corrections from within. The Western architectural ivory tower has become a theatre of the absurd, self-obsessed, blind to its own decline, and largely oblivious to the real forces that determine the general state of the built environment today" (de Graaf, 2017, 42).

4. German-trained Educators Influencing Contemporary Architectural Education and Future Practice

As Parts I and II have illustrated, since the 1930s, architectural education has gone through a series of transitions, with different competing philosophies. The one thing that has remained consistent in architectural education throughout this time is the constant broadening of the field. Over time, more and more subject areas have been added to the architecture curriculum, all seen as essential to the knowledge base; for example, in 1990 computing and sustainability were added as additional subject areas. This led to a move away from more traditional hand-sketching or the teaching of architectural history and theory.

The recent changes in higher education are a global development that has given rise to numerous questions. Architecture journalist Oliver Wainwright provocatively asks if "architectural education is becoming outmoded, overpriced and increasingly irrelevant" (2020). Given the crisis of relevance that engulfed architectural practice over the last decade, he explores what could be new education models to ensure future impact and value for money in a consumer-oriented higher education sector.

The criticism against the established modes of architectural practice ranges from running an exploited labour force of overworked, underpaid, and precariously employed staff, to fuelling an industry devoid of the influence and decision-making power it once had. We now see new practice-based models of education emerging in the US, UK and Europe, where the role of the architect is expanded, for example, through establishing online platforms for new tools for affordable housing or crowdfunding of projects. The growing number of live projects, commonly called "design–build" in the US, and collaborative, interdisciplinary studios that engage with real development sites has also started to signal a change in schools of architecture worldwide. The Yale Building Project and Auburn University's Rural Studio are some of the most well-known of the design-build initiatives, and most schools bring studios to the public to engage in solving "real" problems for those in need. Since 2002, the US Department of Energy sponsors a biannual international design + built competition between schools of architecture, the Solar Decathlon, which awards a prize for the most energy-efficient solar house. In 2007 and 2009, the German teams of the TU Darmstadt, led by Professor Manfred Hegger, won these competitions with their energy-surplus houses.

The relationship between education and architectural practice is always interesting, as it is becoming increasingly ambiguous; some believe the relationship has deteriorated. A long-discussed question is whether the gap between architectural practice and academia has been widening, a claim that is many years old. Thus, is it true that the contemporary graduate is less practically trained or qualified than thirty or fifty years ago?

For centuries, practitioners have criticised schools of architecture for their inability to teach construction technology and prepare students for the real world of practice. A frequently heard argument is that the design studio system avoids the teaching of the hard realities of the profession. In the 1940s and 1950s, when Gropius and Mies were active as educators, architectural education was still closely tied to practice and the needs of the profession. In the late 1960s, this radically changed when architectural education became increasingly dominated by social sciences and sociology, and the gap between education and practice widened. In the architecture schools, writing became more important than making drawings or models, and the centuries-old, established relationship between master and apprentice— still enacted by Mies, Gropius, Lloyd Wright, Kahn and others—finally came to an end. This system relied for almost the entirety of its history on the transmission of knowledge through a master and pupil chain to reproduce itself (see Image 25).

Architectural pedagogy stands on the shoulders of theory, and there are numerous constructs and conceptual underpinnings available when it comes to educational models of architecture. In addition to their trans-Atlantic journeys, most of the educators profiled here have an unusual international background, a recognised research record and a dedication to innovative teaching methods. They have an appetite for seeking out interdisciplinary opportunities both within the university and externally, to transform the curriculum and pedagogy, and to increase their research impact. One particular concept familiar to German educators is the teaching–research nexus, which refers to the cross-fertilising node that can exist between teaching and research, with research themes such as sustainable urbanism being closely integrated into the teaching programme. Although this is an area of growing importance, it still appears to be underdeveloped in most North American universities and schools of architecture.

We are all a result of the education we received; hence, it is unavoidable that German-educated expatriate professors import their ideas of how architects should be educated based on their own experience. Historically, they always had highly transferable skills; thus, German immigrants import specific ways of thinking and pedagogical concepts. Generally respected for their diligence regarding technical details and practical knowledge, they are frequently praised for their expertise in sustainable building technologies, while others are prominently active in architectural history and theory (again, this is probably true for many people from different nations). Resistance in the recipient country to the import of educational innovations, such as the relevance of a research-driven interdisciplinary curriculum, is not uncommon.

There is also the German concept that modern and well-engineered glass buildings demonstrate an open, democratic and ultimately good society. While this reveals a naïve view of architecture, it is also a reason why German professors are frequently leaders in energy-efficient design: it is a serious problem to manage the resulting heat gain of these glass buildings. They teach and research how building performance is optimised so that less energy is used to build, operate and maintain structures as comfortable working and living environments. They require the students to engage with building users to conduct post-occupancy evaluations. Heine commented that she was "specially hired to bring the concept of sustainable design to the US." She went on to say, "I was trained in climate sensitive design since sustainability is not separately taught in Germany but expected as a holistic mind-set. I dedicated my research to affordable, energy-efficient housing design and teach it as an integrated element." Like the fhe famous advertisement slogan for German cars, "Vorsprung durch Technik" (Progress through Technology), there is still the subconscious believe that technology could fix any problem.

Klinkhammer noted that "following a period of theorising architecture in the 1990s, US architectural education today is heavily focused on design and computation/visualisation, and much less on technology, materials or construction" (2020; see interview transcript in Appendix III). Over the last decade, the area of integration of sustainable building design and urbanism has probably become the most recognised field of German expertise, with numerous professors actively contributing in these subject areas (e.g., Bechthold, Heine, Lehmann, Reinhart, Ruegemer and Schierle, among others). German-born architect Matthias Hollwich calls this phenomenon "the combination of German precision with American aspiration" (cited from Hollwich's website, hwkn.com).

Following the collapse of functionalism, new ideas for architectural curricula emerged, mostly around the integration of environmental design and the digital revolution. For twenty years, from 1990 to 2010, there was an intensive debate about the impact that the computer has had on the profession and on architectural education, but this seemed to have resolved itself. Peter Bosselmann states, "not long ago, the role of computation in design was much discussed. Today, our students no longer ask such questions. They design with computers" (2020). In a post-digital era, with the first digital transformation largely behind us, the search for processes to optimise building performance has changed: it has moved from form-making to informed form-finding through form-simulation, form-evaluation, and step-by-step form-refinement of prototypes or systems to perfect and optimise a building's performance. Numerous software packages can help in this process. What has emerged is a post-digital era in which we combine the best of both worlds: analogue and digital tools, whatever helps to deliver the best outcome.

Interdisciplinary Collaboration as Driver

Architecture is constantly looking outside the discipline for inspiration and answers. The seminal Boyer Report called this the "connected curriculum" that "would encourage the integration, application and discovery of knowledge within and outside the architecture discipline, while effectively making the connections between architectural knowledge and the changing needs of the profession, clients, communities and society as a whole" (Boyer Report, 1996). Interdisciplinarity—one of the key ideas and a cornerstone of the Bauhaus pedagogy—has since become even more relevant. In every profession, it seems that one can easily become a prisoner of the parameters and working methods of the particular profession, a reason why collaboration with other disciplines has become the "new basic". Koolhaas suggests that "if one is looking for new solutions, maybe one should not look at the solution that is defined by the architecture field, but outside of architecture" (2017).

Tomorrow's architects and engineers will be required to work collaboratively in complex, fast-changing environments. To allow for more collaboration and teamwork, the studio space will need to move from rows of individual desks to specifically designed collaboration spaces.

Interdisciplinarity is the Bauhaus idea that has entered every architecture school's strategic plan, and (after sixty years of failed experiments in inter- and transdisciplinary work) we have learned that we can only engage successfully in interdisciplinary work if, firstly, we are fully aware of the roots of our own expertise and embedded in our discipline and, secondly, if we have mastered our own discipline. Putting weak representatives of two disciplines together is unlikely to generate any strong interdisciplinary outcome.

> Most educators agree that there is a need to educate students to become effective team workers and that collaboration has become more important, as well as the capability to collaborate with others. Has the old-fashioned idea of the architect as "conductor" become less appropriate today? German architect and educator Thomas Herzog (2020) noted in a recent online lecture that "an architect deals with highly complex issues combining science, arts and technology; and there are many analogies for what the architect does. Architects are often compared to people who coordinate and control large complex activities, such as a captain on a ship, or a conductor with an orchestra. There is always only one captain on a ship, so it is not a democratic process. Same with the coordination of a concert: there may be some brilliant soloists, but you still need someone who can not only read the musical scores, but who also calls all musicians up in the right way, at the right time, for what the scores prescribe, and controls everybody towards perfection. Like in a highly complex project that consists of a multitude of subsystems, which all have to work for themselves and at the same time have to interact in a confidential manner. Complex projects are created in teams, in collaboration between the different disciplines. This means that the various forms of cooperation and the timing of cooperation is extremely important. It also includes the different qualifications of the individuals in the team, and that everyone is capable of dialogue." (Herzog, 2020)

Professional practice has been first to embrace the idea of interdisciplinary teams, and engineering consultancies such as Arup and Aecom have built their global success on it: we are told that the era of the sole master architect has passed and been replaced by today's globally interconnected professional practices. This has created the expectation of contemporary practice to embrace working in interdisciplinary teams with highly structured modes of operation and design processes. Accordingly, most schools emphasise the collaborative nature of design and foster collaboration and integration in the studio rather than supporting individual "innovation", providing more opportunities for teamwork.

Blurring the boundaries of different knowledge sectors is important to be able to look at the world in a new way and resolve complex issues of the built environment, in collaboration with other disciplines. While we will still need specialisations, most of the problems today require interdisciplinary teams to resolve them. To cross-refer between bodies of knowledge, e.g., science, fine arts, humanities, social sciences, IT and engineering, will allow to continuously evolve and enlarge the knowledge that is meaningful to society. Architecture by its nature has the unique opportunity to have bold ideas and make a real difference in the world. This means we should blend different knowledge sectors in teaching and research to best prepare our students for careers that maybe don't even exist yet.

Different disciplines bring different ways of working and problem solving, which is helpful, as future cities are increasingly complex and require diverse cultural, disciplinary and political perspectives to ensure optimal outcomes. The way teams of experts with different disciplinary and cultural background are working together is currently changing towards a much more collaborative and integrated approach, where the previously single disciplinary dominance has come to an end.

Architects are by their training in the unique situation to bring various disciplines together. They are important to society as they have different ways of thinking—and there are very few professions that can act as moderator of such a process. Using their competence in a convincing way during the design and building process, architects belong to the group of few people that are still with a capacity to think as generalists and able to synthesise different ways of thinking into one spatial solution. It is the architect's ability to brings experts together, synthesise different knowledge and visualise the future.

Strengthening the ties between academic and workplace training will be an important aspect of future education, where the role of practices in education is a key objective: practices will have an important and growing role to play in education. Indeed, students will need to learn during their studies to work with other disciplines and to be confronted with an educational framework that prepares them for the challenges they are likely to encounter in future practice. Rather than a linear, predefined path with predictable and likewise predefined results, these are interdisciplinary programmes structured more akin to a field of possibilities.

In the 1980s and '90s, US educational concepts were further shaped by the theory of the "reflective practitioner", as formulated by Donald Schoen in *The Reflective Practitioner* (1983), and by the already-mentioned Boyer Report (1996). Both documents provided a new framework for architectural education at the end of the 20th century. The full title of the Boyer Report is *Building Community: A New Future for Architecture Education and Practice*, with the name stemming from the report being dedicated to the memory of Ernest Boyer, a leading educational thinker who authored much of the text. The report is seen as a milestone and was jointly commissioned by the American Institute of Architects (AIA), American Institute of Architecture Students (AIAS), National Council of Architectural Registration Boards (NCARB), National Architectural Accrediting Board (NAAB), and Association of Collegiate Schools of Architecture (ACSA) as an independent study into the state of the education of architecture.

Over the last fifty years, the College of Environmental Design (CED) at the University of California, Berkeley has held a special place in US architectural education. Peter Bosselmann has been part of the evolution of design education at Berkeley (see his interview part). He recalls the evolution of Berkeley's influential pedagogy:

> "The CED was founded in 1959 by William Wurster, who was strongly influenced by the Bauhaus tradition. Wurster attracted several individuals with roots there to teach at UC Berkeley, including sculptor James Prestini, who had worked with

Mies and Moholy-Nagy in Chicago. Wurster, who had joined UC Berkeley in 1950 as dean of the then School of Architecture, imagined a college that strengthened each department through joint appointments and interdisciplinary courses, giving students the opportunity to combine studies in the different departments while also focusing on a chosen core area of study." (Bosselmann, 2020)

Today, it is almost natural that the disciplines of architecture, landscape architecture, and urban planning are housed together under one academic umbrella, with a focus on environmental design, but in the 1950s, no other university in the US had combined the three disciplines.

5. The Dilemma of Research and Scholarship in Architectural Education

Universities are a particular form of institution, different from any private company or corporation, foundation, local government or municipality. Part I mentioned the origin of the modern university concept based on the double strategy of teaching and research, and how the Humboldtian model of the research and teaching university was finally adopted by the US universities at the end of the 19th century. This model firmly put research and scholarship activities on the map as part of the regular activities expected from faculty besides teaching and other services.

The design studio continues as a major focus within the curriculum, usually comprising 40 to 50 percent of the overall programme. Consequently, the most impactful area to use research methods to inform students' learning is in the design studio, to implement what is called "research-based" or "research-informed" design. However, there are significant national differences in how research design studios are structured and delivered. I am in the unusual position to have worked as a tenured professor in various countries (Australia, the UK, and the US, with additional experience of the German and Chinese models of research integration), which allows me to compare the various degrees to which research and scholarship is embedded and seen as an essential activity within the different university contexts (see Images 26 and 27).

Image 25: The master—pupil (apprentice) relationship still enacted by Mies and Gropius, Wright and Kahn, which emerged out of the traditional system of pupillage, ended in the late 1960s. Image: Mies in the 1950s with students at the IIT

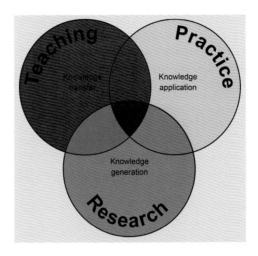

Image 26: Diagram of the intersecting and interrelated three domains of teaching, research, and practice

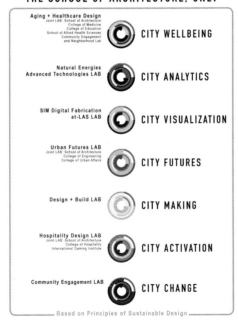

Image 27: Diagram of seven theme-based research concentrations dealing with the future of the American city in the age of global warming, with dedicated transdisciplinary research groups; model of restructured faculty research at the UNLV School of Architecture, introduced by the author (Lehmann, 2018).

Germany and its universities have undoubtedly made huge contributions in the field of design, architecture and arts education, and the quality of German architectural education has been very high. While Germany is frequently associated with civil engineering and environmental planning, German architecture graduates usually have access to excellent facilities and good job opportunities. Some architecture schools were founded in the early 19th century and are well known for their practice-related teaching methods and industry-funded institutes for new areas of research. Some of the strongest German schools of architecture today are part of the government's *Exzellenzinitiative* [Excellence Initiative]. The Excellence Initiative of the German Council of Science and Humanities (the Wissenschaftsrat, WR) and the German Research Foundation (the Deutsche Forschungsgemeinschaft, DFG) aims to promote cutting-edge research and to create outstanding conditions for young scholars at universities, to deepen cooperation between disciplines and institutions, to strengthen international cooperation of research, and to enhance the international appeal of excellent German universities. Since almost all German universities are public, there is no German Ivy League of private higher education institutions, like we find it in the US. However, the Excellence Initiative aims to strengthen some selected public universities more than others in order to raise their international visibility. The initiative includes the TU Munich, RWTH Aachen University, TU Dresden, Karlsruhe Institut of Technology, and TU Berlin, besides others.

Whether the Excellence Initiative has had a positive effect is currently still a matter of debate, as the effect has still to take place. A report by the Wissenschaftszentrum Berlin Social Science Centre (WZB) indicates that the programme "failed to create more diverse education options and produced little in the way of lasting change." (2014) Additionally, the Goethe-Institut claims that "competition up to now has focussed exclusively on the research rather than the teaching at universities," and that prevailing qualitative imbalances in East and West German education systems may potentially be perpetuated via the programme (by favoring more established Western universities over their younger Eastern counterparts), and, furthermore, that the funding may actually be insufficient to achieve the goal of creating "globally competitive universities." (2014)

With adapting the German model of the research university in the 19th century, US architecture schools firmly expect academics to produce research and scholarship as part of their core tasks. As German-trained educators are often trained in research methods, architectural research is an area that has allowed them to shine and make real contributions at US schools, as these educators share a passion for producing research that has value and real impact for the profession. Sustainable technologies and the interdisciplinary collaboration with industry and external partners is a field of strength for most German-trained educators; another field is the introduction of sustainable design principles. It is obvious that they do not shy away from collaborating with industry partners or government bodies if doing so advances their research agenda. This is likely another direct legacy of the Bauhaus model, as most of them were educated at German universities in the 1980s and 1990s, a time when architecture schools were still closely modelled on the strict Bauhaus doctrine.

Design studio teaching in architecture is particularly demanding in terms of time spent in the studio and in reviews, internaliy and externally, so there is usually limited time left to do any research. All this creates discipline-specific challenges and limits the visibility of much of the research endeavours in architecture. Members of architecture faculties produce a wide variety of research and scholarship, a result of many factors, including the diversity of research paradigms that operate within the discipline (e.g., historical, technical, cultural, artistic, professional and so on). The diversity of research output can include solo, collaborative, and participatory projects on a variety of scales, as well as competition entries and other speculative design work. Due to the wide range of diverse outputs, it is not always clear what contribution the research makes to the discipline or the profession (and this grey area has been cause for much tension when it comes to promotion and tenure). Each school of architecture needs to assess the research quality, and the following chapter attempts to offer some useful parameters used for evaluation internationally.

Universities set different research strategies and frameworks for their schools and faculty, depending on government policy and other factors. The UK government's focus in its recent Industrial Strategy (2017) is centred on four challenges: clean growth, mobility, healthy ageing and artificial intelligence. One key thematic focus of EU-funded research in architecture is on what is arguably today's key built environment challenge: the relationship of urbanisation to climate change. The European Commission traditionally frames its research and innovation policies in terms of grand challenges and missions that translate these challenges into concrete projects. The mission-oriented research and innovation policy of the European Union (2019) defines five main criteria for research missions; the research must

- be bold and inspire citizens,
- be ambitious and risky,
- have a clear target and deadline,
- be cross-disciplinary and cross-sectorial, and
- allow for experimentation and multiple attempts at a solution, rather than be micromanaged top-down by government or the university.

In a 2018 survey, the ACSA evaluated information on 186 research projects submitted by US architecture schools and found that 102 of the projects (55 percent) self-identified as "interdisciplinary in nature." Most of the projects were in the areas of sustainability and high-performance built environment, urban design and building systems. More than half of the projects were located in these three subject areas, whereas only three projects were in the classical research field of architectural history and theory (ACSA, 2018).

The recent *AIA Strategic Plan 2021-2025* lists a number of strategic priorities, including the following aims on research and education (AIA, 2020):

- Revolutionise research: leverage emerging technologies to accelerate architecture's progression to a knowledge-driven discipline and evidence-based, transformative solutions. Harness an intra/entrepreneurial start-up mentality to foster rapid innovation.
- Revolutionise architectural education: make architectural education more responsive to emerging trends, more inclusive of underserved audiences, and more oriented toward the future role of the architect.

Why a Clearer Definition of Architectural Research is Needed

Research has recently become more important in the education of architects. As educators, we have a mission to increase research in general and research on architectural education and practice in particular—research that creates and provides, or disseminates, new knowledge, data and evidence that is useful across the profession as a whole. Research in architecture is supposed to inform teaching, keep it up to date and add to the knowledge base of the profession and to better decision making. However, in the US, architecture academics typically do little research, as most of their time is spent on teaching. Few architecture schools produce scholarly works on the scale that would be considered normal for other university-based disciplines, such as engineering or the natural sciences.

Tenured professors often lack incentives to do more research, and some US schools can even display an "anti-research" attitude. Generally, my impression at the time of writing is that architecture schools in the UK and Australia are slightly more engaged in research activities than their US counterparts, simply because there are many more public funding opportunities available. Groák (1992) determined that fewer than half of British architectural academics were involved in research, and the proportion was even less for the United States, although research has started to slowly increase over the last two decades. Pressure on architecture schools has been growing to conform to university standards of scientific research and peer-reviewed publications, and to make an effort to win substantial external research funding, in line with other disciplines' promotion criteria and values.

Stevens (2014) notes that "if architecture were as research-oriented as the average university discipline, it would graduate almost ten times as many doctoral students each year as it actually does. Over the entire period 1920 to 1974, American universities graduated only 56 people with a doctorate in architecture, a minuscule figure." It almost sounds like an excuse when the Boyer Report (1996) states that "professional service and the application of knowledge together can constitute much of the scholarly output of architecture." Consequently, the low research activity is reflected in the small number of architectural academics with doctoral degrees. Perhaps less than only one quarter of US academics in architecture schools hold a Ph.D., a degree which in other fields is mandatory for even the lowest academic ranks.

In general, the profession and the universities agree on the need for research in the development of the knowledge triangle of education, research and innovation. The AIA calls it "vital to project success", while the Royal Institute of British Architects (RIBA) recognises "the intimate relationship between research and design innovation." Similarly, the stated mission of the Association of Collegiate Schools of Architecture (ACSA) "is to lead architectural education and research", and the European Association for Architectural Education (EAAE) "advocates stronger links between theoretical and practice-based research" (Buday, 2017). However, we need to define what exactly constitutes architectural research and scholarship in architecture and the creative industries.

Clearly, there is still a long way to go for artists, designers and architects to get the desired acknowledgment of their research activities and creative outputs. *The Vienna Declaration on Artistic Research* (2020) has recently been developed by a group of deans of fine arts colleges to get a better understanding and acknowledgment of their research activities as equivalent to scientific research. It's a policy document for funding bodies and research institutions that notes, "Artistic Research is practice-based, practice-led research in the arts which has developed rapidly in the last twenty years globally and is a key knowledge base for art education in Higher Arts Education Institutions." The declaration argues that "today there is a rapidly growing number of doctoral programmes all across Europe dedicated to Artistic Research, supported by an increasing number of international peer-reviewed scholarly journals." It points towards the specific features of artistic research: "Excellent Artistic Research is research through means of high level artistic practice and reflection; it is an epistemic inquiry, directed towards increasing knowledge, insight, understanding and skills. It is undertaken in all art practice disciplines—including architecture, design, film, photography, fine art, media and digital arts, music and the performing arts—and achieves its results both within those disciplines, as well as often in a transdisciplinary setting, combining artistic research methods with methods from other research traditions" (p. 1). The declaration asks for recognition of the full range of artistic research at national and international levels, and eligibility for formal quality assurance and career assessment procedures, validated through peer review; however, it remains vague about what exactly constitutes artistic research and where the boundaries are.

The quality and quantity of research output, usually evidenced as academic peer-reviewed publication, is one of the primary indicators of institutional quality for universities worldwide. In the US, scientific research related to the built environment is mostly done outside schools, in government research centres and private industry. The research that is conducted at schools is usually fragmented and takes place more within particular sub-disciplines, including, for instance, sustainability, behaviour studies, façade engineering, IT science and physics. The only area which has been unequivocally a legitimate subject for architectural research in the US is in architectural history and theory. It appears that in most US schools, there is still some way to go until research is acknowledged at the same level as teaching.

There are also new trends and positive developments. For example, the Philadelphia-based firm Kieran Timberlake Architects combines practice with research, publishing and teaching like few other practices do. The firm has a reputation for its strong commitment to research and innovation, and manages to treat the practice, publications and teaching of research studios as one "collective, interconnected holistic project." In a 2017 online interview, James Timberlake calls it "an attempt at the re-design of the profession as we currently know it, where projects become calculated steps in a systematic research program." They see the design and construction of each building as an opportunity to advance the agenda of architecture through research.

As in the UK and in Europe, US universities are increasingly looking at evidence for positive impact from taxpayer-funded research and scholarship conducted by their faculties. A comparison of several strategic plans of US universities reveals that teaching excellence is important, but in itself not sufficient. This comparison further highlights that all schools of architecture should aspire to deliver research-informed teaching, to activate the teaching–research nexus, and that all faculty members are expected to be active researchers.

The architecture discipline also has room for considering *built and creative works* that might be equivalent to peer-reviewed published articles. However, the assessment of creative and built works is not straightforward when they are equated to peer-reviewed research published in high-impact journals, as it depends on the measurable, quantifiable evidence of excellence, innovation and impact. The assessment of equivalence of creative activity is discipline specific, and it requires a close examination and a case-to-case assessment of the individual impact from the creative and built works.

Over the last years, the *Journal of Architectural Education* published several issues that focused on design as research, framing the type of investigations and projects that embody equivalence to published peer-reviewed research. A key question for such assessment is if the professional output of the architectural practice is creating any new knowledge. The usual architectural production for commercial clients is unlikely to qualify as research because it does not systematically create new knowledge. The criteria used by most universities and schools of architecture to assess if creative output constitutes an equivalence with evidence-based peer-reviewed research today includes the following five parameters:

- Influence. Is the work influential for national or international architectural culture?
- Innovation. Does the work go beyond a narrow definition of architectural practice?
- Evidence of impact. Is there evidence of a consistent critical discourse and rigor in method that looks at the wider context of the process applied to the creation of these works? For example, is it linked to design innovation, the creating of lasting positive impact and a wider influence on the profession, beyond its locality?
- High quality. Does the work create research of high standard (technologically or socially)? For example, does the building have an innovative façade system or use an emerging new material?
- Widely disseminated. Has the result been widely disseminated and communicated through peer-reviewed publications in established journals or reviewed exhibitions, or publicly presented at important conferences, and does it have clear impact and influence on future practice beyond its locality (is it influential nationally or internationally)?

Christopher Frayling (1993) explores the relationship between creative activity, the production of building designs and scholarly research, comparing the output of designers, architects, and artists, with the output by scientists. Building upon Herbert Read's framework—"Research *for* art, research *into* art, research *through* art"—Frayling points towards the need for methodological clarity and a hypothesis. He makes two arguments:

- "Research through architecture" needs to include evidence for the creation and generation of new knowledge and improvement of design practice (a view also shared by Selena Savic, 2014, and Kroes, 2002).
- "Research into architecture" has to contribute new knowledge to the discipline's knowledge base (similar to Jeremy Till, 2005, who sees the advancement of architecture as practice inextricably linked to the acquirement of new knowledge).

Most of the literature agrees that a comparable rigour in method or process applied is crucial for the assessment of architectural research. Raisbeck (2019) highlights innovative inquiry and points out that it is "not enough to simply develop ideas about speculative design projects or competitions, as this does not automatically present a valid form of research." He notes that most practices lack a formal systematic R&D procedure, which makes it difficult to ascertain which aspects might be a real contribution to new knowledge. He argues that the use of methodology is relevant because the logical progress from hypothesis to experiment, to observation and evaluation, and leading to logical conclusions and findings—the basis of the creation of any new scientific knowledge—must be recognisable. Raisbeck further notes that "managing design knowledge as a distributed ecosystem (namely a project network) rather than being project-centric (namely the notion that knowledge is solely embedded in one particular built object) will cede more significant results." He asks if the firm's research focus arises out of the firm's strategic planning, and questions whether there are any knowledge management systems in place to document, store and allow this knowledge to be retrieved and made available.

Interdisciplinary or multidisciplinary research is widespread today—it has even become the new normal in most fields. An interdisciplinary or multidisciplinary approach can therefore no longer be regarded as a value in itself; it is a value only if it leads to a fruitful examination of a disciplinary (or multidisciplinary) research question that will inspire further research along new lines. The types of research-driven practice are exemplified by interdisciplinary offices involved in teaching and knowledge creation, such as UN Studio, AMO, Shigeru Ban and Renzo Piano Building Workshop. These firms have a strong commitment to cultivating, shaping, and supporting a peer-reviewed research culture, with dedicated research groups leveraging methods from diverse fields, such as environmental design, urban ecology, computer science and materials science, and a managed process for data collection, analysis, modelling, and simulation; physical prototyping; and experimentation. All this goes far beyond the usual expectations of the paying client who just wants a building (Lehmann, 2015).

Faircloth (2019), head of research at Kieran Timberlake Architects, underscores the importance of the type of practice involved in teaching and research. He notes, "There are crucial questions one has to ask to assess if the practice is serious about research: Will the practice impart to its staff the agency to ask questions and provide the resources necessary, such as materials, tools, research partners and leadership, to answer these research questions? Will the architectural practice share the products of its research as open source externally even when it recognises that a perceived competitive edge is eclipsed by the greater need for transformation in the profession?"

6. An Impact-Driven and Research-Based Curriculum for 21st-Century Architectural Education?

Educational models greatly differ in the US and Europe, such as the larger class, master-student atelier European model versus the more intimate professor-student studio model in the US. The interviews with German-trained educators revealed the diversity of their pedagogical positions and the differences in their reflections on the discipline of architecture. The role of the architect-theorist-educator is to prepare young architects for new forms of architectural practice. Gropius was always interested in speculative approaches, in interdisciplinary collaboration and in exploring new methods, tools and technologies. He saw architecture as an intellectual practice, and the question that kept him occupied was how could teaching, research, and academic work be incorporated into an informed practice, and vice versa?

As shifting social, cultural, economic, technological and ecological paradigms redefine architecture, the contemporary educator speculates on how architects will practice in the future. The work in the studio can become a platform from which a new generation of academic architects will evolve. In this way, architects are re-establishing their relevance to society, and there are many good reasons why we want the profession to be relevant again. For instance, by pointing out the possible impact from improving the human condition: when we design schools that contribute to the learning process or when we design hospitals that support faster healing, this is when architecture transcends the built environment.

In the 1990s, the emergence of digital technologies transformed the way we teach, design, represent and produce architecture. Architecture is a very slow art form when compared to other forms of expression, and we need to constantly ensure not getting overwhelmed by the rapid speed of the digital landscape. Today, in the post-digital era, architectural educators are required to navigate a number of trends, pressures and challenges, with the ability to operate within an unpredictable sector in uncertain times while formulating robust conceptual tools for educating the next generation of architects. Social responsibility, ethics and rapid technological change are seen as important drivers of future curriculum development. Programmes need to balance fundamentals with emerging subject areas, using teaching approaches that embrace the new technologies (e.g., online teaching) while keeping students critically engaged in a meaningful discourse of architectural education appropriate to the 21st century.

Preparing students for a rapidly changing discipline and future practice
A student commencing their architecture studies today is likely to be entering a very different kind of profession in the late 2020s with an uncertain future. By this point, the pressure of climate change will have radically shifted the practice of architecture. So how should architecture schools respond to the climate crisis? What knowledge and skills do architecture students need to learn in order to bring sustainability in a different future and deliver true ecological design? This has much to do with communicating an ethical position and placing practice into a critical context. As outlined by the "Architecture 2030" initiative and the AIA, all new buildings will need to be carbon neutral by 2030 and embodied emissions will need to be at least halved. Buildings can be part of the low-carbon solution, or white elephants that are part of the problem. It is clear that this will require profound change to architecture education, it will not be sufficient to change the curriculum by small steps incrementally.

Flatman (2016) argues that "architectural education is too constrained in its ability to engage with the rapid changes taking place within creative and construction industries, the economy and how careers are built today. Reforming architectural education for the 21st century must be an ongoing project—constantly adapting and changing to meet the needs of the industry, researchers and students."

The 2020 coronavirus pandemic has led to changes in every part of society, including the educational system and, in particular, the future way we teach and learn architecture, and the way we travel. Globalisation will be very different in a post-pandemic future, and architecture education will be deeply affected by this. Thomas Friedman (2012) notes that "big break-throughs happen when what is suddenly possible meets what is desperately necessary." In early 2020 we found ourselves suddenly in a situation where we had to rethink everything to fight a global pandemic and, consequently, the entire educational system was forced to move to remote delivery and online teaching and learning within the short period of a few weeks. The move to online learning offered architecture schools the opportunity to redefine their learning experience. Great teaching can happen through any medium, digital or analogue, or a hybrid of both. The forced move to online learning is a real-world example of the future of work and lifelong learning in action, a process that was accelerated by the pandemic. It appears that the future of work is online, not only for educators but for the entire architectural design profession.

But much of the online learning material we currently produce is not meeting the students' expectations of the online experience. Clearly, we cannot continue to create the same ineffective online experiences we used to. What is often missing online is the interaction and spontaneity of in-person learning; here, asynchronous learning offers some advantages, as it allows students to learn at their own pace.

Looking Ahead

The next generation of architects will enter a rapidly changing workforce. They will have to grapple with more complexity and uncertainty than ever before, and universities should help students prepare for these challenges and respond to the shifts towards resiliency and diversity. Drivers of change include digital disruption, artificial intelligence, robotics, the need to tackle climate change and deal with significant shifts in society and demographics.

The beginning of the 3rd millennium created a condition of enormous change. The last time this happened, it triggered all kind of fundamental shifts and led to a new architecture. Most universities are going through a phase of significant reform, reassessment and budget cuts. This has an enormous impact on architectural education worldwide. Kirk McCormack (2015) recently argued that

> "the circumstance that makes us most need to drastically reconsider the delivery of architectural education is the advancement of technology in the last 15 years. The premise of an academy (the university) was founded on the principle of providing access to information, along with a sheltered learning environment. Until recently, this meant knowledge contained in printed media in libraries, or knowledge conveyed through expert instruction—that is, lecturing. The growing online data trove that now exists may mean this model is moving toward obsolescence, an idea highlighted by the news that Google has completed the digitisation of over a quarter of all books ever written. With this in mind, it becomes reasonable to suggest that the future of architectural education (and, in fact, of all education), is likely to be more dispersed, networked, and self-guided." (McCormack, 2015)

Every architect has a desire to be useful to society. In 2020, teaching architecture means also to find solutions that deal with the age of the Anthropocene, the human-made climatic period that poses an existential threat to the future of our species. Knowledge of climate change, the effect of fossil fuels upon the environment and the role of the built environment within this crisis has ushered in the sustainable design movement. Architecture schools have accepted their role and responsibility in training the next generation of architects that can develop and apply design solutions and prepare future designers to be leaders in the fight against climate change. Out of this, it appears that new evolutionary models of design education have evolved where guiding principles have replaced the concept as the primary driver of design projects, and in the studio, stakeholder-driven design charrettes at the start of projects are increasingly replacing arbitrary final juries.

It is a critical issue now to meet the challenge of climate change. Education and better monitoring of performance are critical, as well as reforming the building codes. Minimum standards for acceptable performance have to be lifted very significantly if we are going to get to a zero-carbon built environment. The construction industry cannot radically change in a short time, regrettably, but it can continuously improve its performance, and architects must be trained to lead this discussion and ask for better performance. In order to bring the building and construction codes up to the appropriate standards, we will need to commission research to develop the evidence, and use this evidence to advocate and lobby government for updated building codes. Architecture schools play obviously an important role in this.

Today, the time of the so-called "starchitects" belongs to the past, even if there are always going to be charismatic masterminds in architecture with a strong impact on the next generation. The upcoming generation of architects knows because of the continuously growing complexity of the built environment, architecture can only be approached successfully through interdisciplinary teamwork. In the end, architecture is not an autonomous discipline or art form. For instance, architecture is not capable of defining or giving laws to itself (the definition of "autonomy"). Architecture is a result of collaboration, a product of many actors, hands and forces. And, it's also true that architecture always thinks that it is in crisis, challenging itself. At any time in architectural history, one can find that architects felt their discipline was in crisis and at some point of rapture.

Being involved in teaching has always allowed young architects arriving in the US the freedom to further develop their own language through a connection with the academic world, which in return informed their practicing world. While teaching can be time consuming, young architects crossing the Atlantic can still benefit from teaching at a time when they do not have many projects, which allows them to extend their own interests and discovery while earning a stable salary and staying closely connected with the practicing profession. There can be a rich cross-fertilisation between the academic world and practice, back and forth until these young architects start getting their first larger projects.

The German-trained architects documented in this study spend the second halves of their careers as internationally influential educators while living and working in the US. The cities of New York, Chicago, Philadelphia, San Francisco and Los Angeles provided both context and content to inform their theories of designing for the American city and society.

German mid-20th-century immigrant architects were once involved in the richness of modernist practice and pedagogy in the US. However, the hagiography of Gropius and Mies as saints, icons or ecclesiastical leaders of modernism, and the presumption that the 1950s triumph of functionalism is still in the ascendancy, clearly does not apply. As this study shows, German-trained educators' positive contributions to and impacts on architecture schools in the US have been and continue to be significant. While the current German-born educators are well aware of the Bauhaus legacy, they made it clear that the functionalism and modernism of the 1930s immigrant architects plays little or no role in their educational strategies today. We can see an impact-driven, interdisciplinary and research-based curriculum for 21st century architectural education emerging. Thinking of new possibilities and being uncomfortable with outmoded ways of creating means challenging the accepted norms of architectural design, and this is where education can regain its strength. Hence, to stay relevant, future architecture education should explore these questions:

- How can architecture continue to challenge the status quo?
- What might be the new forms of emerging practice?

There are two concluding observations. Firstly, architectural education in the US is strong and seems to be in good hands, and German-trained educators continue to make significant contributions—especially in finding solutions for the age of the Anthropocene. Secondly, architectural education needs to radically change to focus on the challenge of climate change. Signs are again visible at US schools of new radical and meaningful pedagogies emerging.

Appendix Part III
The Interviews with Current Educators

In Conversation with the Author: Six German-Trained Educators

There are currently more than fifty German-speaking architecture professors teaching in the US, who are active in shaping architectural and design education and influencing and moulding thousands of students. The book features a directory with 39 biographies of current educators and six in-depth interviews with selected professors. The directory presents educators with a broad range of academic backgrounds, practice and research interests; they all grew up in Germany or Austria the 1970s and '80s during a period of extraordinary stability, advancement and progress.

The study aims to advance the knowledge of architectural education across the United States by illuminating the various educational strategies deployed by these professors at a range of architecture schools. The interviews serve to capture their unique approaches to educating architects, reflecting on pedagogy and curriculum. Some of the answers have been edited for clarity and brevity. The conversations are organised in alphabetical order and based on professors' responses to a set of twenty-five identical questions. The respondents could reject some questions if they did not want to answer them. In June 2020, I asked them to consider how two pivotal German educators—Walter Gropius and Ludwig Mies van der Rohe—influenced their own contemporary educational strategies. The interviews also addressed the various teaching programmes and the legacy of modernism in architectural education and thought today.

The Interviews: An Analysis of Key Messages
The pedagogical experiments of the Bauhaus, once imported by Gropius, Mies, and others to the US system, challenged traditional Beaux-Arts thinking and played a crucial role in shaping modern architectural education over eighty years. Their modes of teaching architecture and design had a long-lasting impact, but they have now been transformed again by German-born educators offering fresh perspectives.

The study concludes with the interviews with influential professors devoting their careers to architectural education. What has become clear is that each of them has the authenticity and dedication to make truly meaningful contributions that positively affect the lives of others. The interviews reveal a deeper insight into their pedagogical strategies, and the dynamics influencing why they prefer to teach at American universities when they could instead hold an appointment at a university in Germany.

The group is as diverse as the two countries and their cultural contexts. The countries share many values and challenges, and the interviewees shed light on their global interconnections while providing an overview of their unusual international careers. They are key player in the transfer of pedagogical models, the hybridisation between various pedagogical models, producing collective trajectories through the importation of methods and the translation of concepts, exporting their ideas to North America.

Most of the interviewees have indicated that they do not want their identity to be defined by one national category; some said that they feel "European". As tenured professionals living in the US, they admitted that they live as privileged "expats", and most of them have come to terms with the fact that they will remain outsiders in their adopted home. As immigrant, one does not share the history and the deep cultural understanding to truly fit in, even if one identifies with the American values. But when you live in a culture that fits your values, you can feel at home.

A key aspect that emerged from the conversations is that being a full-time academic today, involved with numerous responsibilities at the university, leaves little opportunity to develop an impactful body of practice or built work on the side. The reasons for this are multifold: first, the excessive burden of compliance and bureaucracy at US universities; secondly, the risk averseness, which makes any risk of doing experimental or innovative work impossible due to the often-excessive liabilities and unmanageable constraints; and finally, the lack of support structures for strong individual leadership at schools of architecture. Even deans, directors and chairs of schools of architecture are locked into hierarchical reporting structures and compliance systems that put ideas of shared governance and controlling above any individual excellence. Today, the contemporary university system would simply not allow for a Gropius or Mies to succeed and operate in the way it was possible seventy years ago.

I asked how the role and impact of German educators in the US has changed since the Bauhaus immigrants' era, and found it fascinating to examine if there are certain similarities among all of the immigrants. The interviews further explored the legacy of Gropius and Mies in their current educational strategies and thinking about the Bauhaus legacy. All the interviewed educators have spent more than a decade primarily involved in architectural education, making significant contributions to teaching programmes in the US and the wider Anglo-Saxon context. Interestingly, each of them interprets the Gropius/Mies legacy in a different way. Some commented that from a direct assessment, the educational legacy means little today, and the influence of the Bauhaus period on educators in the US is not as profound as it once was. However, indirectly, it is still more relevant than it might seem, having introduced important concepts such as interdisciplinarity, design and built programmes, and industry collaboration.

The interviews revealed the following key points about the German-trained architects interviewed:

- No matter what their nationality, they bring a solid education to the foundational building sciences, building technologies, and principles of sustainable design, with a good understanding of the construction process.
- Most do not practice architecture in the US; instead, their practice outlet is their academic research at the university.
- They consider themselves "global architects" with a thorough European identity.

The six architecture professors, interviewed by the author, are (in alphabetical order): Martin Bechthold, Cambridge, MA; Peter Bosselmann, Berkeley, CA; Ulrike Heine, Clemson, SC; Barbara Klinkhammer, Philadelphia, PA; Mark Mueckenheim, San Francisco, CA, and Antje Steinmuller, San Francisco, CA.

Interview 1

Conversation with Martin Bechthold,
Harvard University, Graduate School of Design, Cambridge, Massachusetts

Dr. Martin Bechthold is Director of the Doctor of Design Studies Program and the Master's in Design Engineering Program, and Kumagai Professor of Architectural Technology at the Graduate School of Design, Harvard University. Dr. Bechthold has served as professor of architectural technology at the GSD since 2008. His current research investigates material and fabrication technology as a catalyst of innovation for design practice. Bechthold studied architecture at the Rheinisch-Westfaelische Technische Hochschule (RWTH) in Aachen, Germany, and holds a Doctor of Design Degree from the Graduate School of Design at Harvard University.

Where did you grow up? Please tell us about your education. What year did you move to the US?
As a young child I lived in Essen, in Germany's industrial heartland, but during elementary school we moved to a small town called Heiligenhaus. In this small manufacturing town I attended a traditional high school, where my electives were primarily focused on physics, geography, mathematics and art. I graduated from high school in 1983 and started social service. I moved to the Boston area in 1998.

Where did you study? In hindsight, how was your education?
I studied architecture at the RWTH University in Aachen, while living across the border in the Netherlands. My education provided a solid foundation in building materials, building physics, construction and structures, a somewhat less solid training in history, and only a cursory exploration of theoretical topics. Design studio, over the first few years, involved a visit to the University every two weeks or so, where an assistant, not the professor, would look at my drawings and models and make some suggestions. Funded by a scholarship, I spent two trimesters studying in the UK, where I enjoyed a sophisticated theoretical and conceptual discourse – exactly what I had missed up to that point in Aachen. Only after my return had I finally meetings with my professors that helped me complete my formation as an architect. Professors Peter Kulka, Hadi Teherani and Wolfgang Döring were my outstanding teachers in my final years in Aachen.

Was there an architect who particularly inspired you?
Carlo Scarpa's attention to detail, his narrative approach to materiality and construction definitely struck a chord with me. I spent a fair amount of time studying his work and eventually interviewed Arrigo Rudi, Scarpa's collaborator, who drove up to Aachen from Italy in his British sports car.

What made you come to the US?
I moved to the US to pursue a doctoral degree at Harvard's Graduate School of Design.

Did you teach at a German university before you immigrated to the US?
No, I never taught in Germany.

Did you practice architecture in Germany? If yes, how long, and where?
I worked about three and a half years in Paris, and for another three and a half years in Hamburg.

Today, do you consider yourself a German or an American architect? Is national identity still relevant?
After my arrival in the US, I initially considered myself primarily European, not necessarily German. After all I had lived in four European countries up to that time. Over the years, I have come to consider myself more as someone in the middle between both countries, and national identity is irrelevant for me when it comes to questions of architecture.

After arriving in the US, how did you assimilate to your new context and home country?
Harvard and Cambridge are quite international, so assimilation to the new context came easy. I had visited the US before, and my in-laws lived in the Boston area as well, giving me extended family connections.

You are aware of the extensive discussion on issues of design and national identity. Would you say that there is something very specific about being German-born?
I have been very disconnected from this discussion. The question of national identify has never greatly mattered to me, most likely because I have experienced architecture and design culture in multiple countries. I am sure that my German upbringing and training has shaped me as an architect but working for over three years in France has equally affected my perspective. This is particularly true for the intense years working for Santiago Calatrava in Paris, where I learned to appreciate and tame complex architectural geometry before it became fashionable, translating his watercolours into 3D CAD and ultimately buildable form. Given my research interests into the material and technical aspects of architecture, I have paid more attention to the specifics of national construction cultures, which differ dramatically between Germany (and Europe) with its dominance of concrete and masonry construction versus the US with its light timber framing and steel skeletal structures.

Based on your familiarity with North American and German culture, how do you relate to US culture?
I consider myself very much a person in between both cultures and find this place both reassuring and unsettling at the same time. Reassuring, because my multi-cultural understanding makes me somewhat comfortable in both cultures; and unsettling, because I find myself slightly outside

each culture at the same time. With respect to my relationship to US culture, I believe my East-Coast, Boston and Harvard based experience is hardly representative of the country at large, so despite the time I have spent in the US, my view of the country's culture is flavoured by living in the very international, relatively affluent, and liberal context of Cambridge, MA.

What is your understanding of architectural education in North America over the last 50 years?
I have not done much historical research on the education of architects here, but if the past two decades are any indicator of the past fifty years, then the teaching objectives in the programs that I am familiar with have leaned heavily towards studio and design teaching, often coupled with a substantial dose of history and theory, built over a relatively thin layer of technical and scientific skills. This approach could be a recipe for disaster, was it not for the professional licensing system that completes the training of the architect in the US after graduation.

What do you think are the particular qualities and contribution that German architects bring to the education of architects in the US?
German-trained architects, no matter what their nationality is, bring a very solid education in the foundational building sciences and in building technologies to the US. This quality can nicely complement the more theoretical and conceptual attitudes towards teaching architectural design, provided both approaches are seen as complementary and not contradictory.

What does the legacy of Gropius and Mies van der Rohe mean to you today? What is their relevance to contemporary German-born educators in the US today?
The interest of the Bauhaus in industrial production, in materials, tectonics and construction definitely continues to resonate with me today, despite the pervasive presence of computational methods and digital culture today. The Bauhaus-related approach of integrating the realities of materials, construction and industrial production into architectural design remains highly relevant today – in particular in the US where building culture has been driven by appearance, not tectonics, as is evident in light-frame residential and commercial steel construction that are often carefully crafted to provide the suggestion of a different materiality. The introduction of the digital in design and construction has, however, added a new variable to the Bauhaus pedagogy. While the fundamental approach of the Bauhaus remains relevant, the definition of material and construction has been expanded through the new opportunities afforded by digital design, analysis and construction technologies.

Which concepts did you import from Germany that influenced your teaching and research?
I have continued to embrace the technical and performance-based aspects of buildings. I am teaching my students to look at these aspects as powerful ways to enhance and even drive their designs, and not consider them an afterthought in studio. Gravity or rain should be the architect's friend, they are not the death of architecture.

Is there a pedagogical or educational innovation you could introduce to your department or school, e.g. the way you conduct design studios or integrate research in your teaching?
Since I am mostly committed to leading and running non-architectural programs like the Doctor of Design program and the Master's of Design Engineering (MDE) program, my only teaching in my home department of architecture is the Structural Design II class. Here

I introduced, among other aspects, a design project whereby students work in groups to design a building structure and then do all needed analysis and structural engineering using somewhat simplified methods. In and by itself this is not innovative, of course, so one new aspect I introduced is the design lottery. After the design is complete, I run a lottery and projects are randomly assigned to a different group for the engineering part of the work. This helps students understand the need for good documentation of their designs, they take greater responsibility in producing designs that are feasible and can be engineered properly; all while letting them experience, firsthand, the sort of negotiations that take place between architect and engineer in practice.

There is much scholarship on the issues of design and national identity. Do you think that national attributes and identities, including the aim to preserving German cultural values of "efficiency and simplicity in design", are still relevant in a globally inter-connected society and profession?
Those values seem to work quite well for firms like van Gerkan, Marg & Partners and their extensive international operation, but I have generally found that German cultural values have softened and lost significance in this age of globally connected design cultures.

Please briefly describe your particular strategies or philosophy as an architecture educator.
My interest, when occasionally teaching design studio, is to empower students to leverage the technical and scientific aspects of our multidisciplinary profession in order to advance their designs. The reverse is true when teaching Structures – I teach it as a design class, which, while definitely including substantial amounts of quantitative work, is about understanding design from the lens of forces and moments, stresses and strains. I encourage my students to remain critical of the digital as well. I am trying to have my students see the beauty in thoughtful and innovative structural design!

How do you balance your time in teaching with research and practice? And how do these various pursuits make their way into your work and influence you as educator?
I don't practice architecture in the US, instead, my practice outlet has become my research operation at the GSD, the Material Processes and Systems (MaP+S) group. The balance simply happens through lots of really long days, as it often seems like having two jobs plus administration. I am looking at research and teaching as mutually beneficial settings that inform and inspire each other. I try (but don't always succeed) in teaching at least one course that allows for this to happen, for example in the area of robotics or material innovation, where students get access to some of the latest research developments while the researchers might be inspired by the ideas students develop. Often students then join our research team in some capacity after the course ends.

Do you collaborate with people outside architecture? If yes, which disciplines are of particular interest to you and your pedagogical concept?
In my research, I collaborate extensively with material scientists, chemists, a zoologist, and engineers. In academic leadership in the MDE program I also engage frequently with my instructors that have backgrounds in law, electrical engineering, physics, business, industrial design, to just name a few. Interdisciplinarity has become second nature, despite its

occasional challenges. Even when teaching architecture, I find it valuable to help students understand the problem they are framing from different viewpoints, much as is common in interdisciplinary teams.

Culture can manifest itself in many different forms. How strongly does your German cultural heritage inform your approach to teaching?
Mostly through my accent! Frankly, this is more a question for my students – but I have to admit that I use a lot of European and German example buildings when teaching Structures, so there is definitely a European "flavour" to that course, even though I strive to diversify the case studies I show to my students.

What do you think is the main contribution of German architecture educators in US schools today, to the American educational system?
The numbers of German architectural educators must be pretty insignificant in the US - I assume it is a single digit percentage? So realistically it is a minor influence on the systems level, but possibly a more pronounce influence in specific schools. If anything the more integrated, professionally grounded approach to architecture as a combination of design and its technical dimensions might be a contribution ... or is that just wishful thinking on my part?

What advice would you like to give young professors?
Always think about your teaching not just from your vantage point, but from the perspective and experience of the students as well.

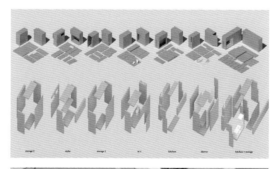

Images 28 and 29: Examples of student work from Professor Bechthold's teaching: urban housing, student work by David Ling (GSD, 2020)

Interview 2

Conversation with Peter Bosselmann,
University of California at Berkeley, California

Peter Bosselmann is a professor of the Graduate School in Architecture, City and Regional Planning, Landscape Architecture and Urban Design at the College of Environmental Design, University of California Berkeley. He graduated from Karlsruhe University in architecture in 1972, where he started his architecture education under Egon Eiermann and completed his diploma with Gunnar Martinsson. He came to the US in 1974 (DAAD supported) to study architecture with Bill Mitchell at UCLA, later with Christopher Alexander at Berkeley and in Mexico until 1976. His first job was with Donald Appleyard until 1982. He joined the UC Berkeley CED faculty in 1983 to teach Urban Design and moved through the ranks, became full professor and Chair of Landscape Architecture and Environmental Planning. In 1995, he was a founding member of the Master of Urban Design Program at UC Berkeley and chaired the program until 2016. His main interest is in urban architecture and the transformation of neighbourhoods and cities. Bosselmann published three books on design research methods: Representations of Places (1998), Urban Transformation (2008), and Adaptation of the Metropolitan Landscape (2018).

Where did you grow up? Please tell us about your education.
I grew up in the City of Hannover, learned English from playing with children of the British occupation forces prior to learning Latin and Greek at a classical high school.

What year did you move to the US?
With a two-year German Academic Exchange Service (DAAD) stipend, I arrived in Los Angeles in September 1974. For the first year, I enrolled in the master program at UCLA. I transferred to UC Berkeley for my second year.

Was there an architect who particularly inspired you?
My plan had been to learn about computation in architecture and to learn about the approach Christopher Alexander had taken with his prescriptive system theory in architecture and planning.

In Los Angeles I worked with William Mitchell (1944-2010), an Australian architect who was a pioneer in teaching computation to architects. Charles Moore was there and so was Oswald Mathias Ungers.

Ungers' rational architecture inspired me. We both had studied under Egon Eiermann (1904-1970) in Karlsruhe, where I graduated in 1972 (Ungers considerably earlier). At the University of California at Berkeley, I studied with Donald Appleyard, who had come from MIT in 1968 after having worked with Kevin Lynch. In the spring semester I moved to Mexico to work with Christopher Alexander on a self-help housing project.

What made you come to the US?
When the Swedish architect Carl Axel Acking came to Karlsruhe in 1971 as a guest professor, he gave me some advice that included the importance of learning about new trends in architectural education. He suggested I should try to work with Donald Appleyard and Christopher Alexander. I knew about Kevin Lynch's work at the time, but not about Appleyard. I had read the Architecture Press publication about the PREVI competition in Lima Peru. Alexander's contribution to the competition truly inspired me; a systematic approach with the goal of supporting people's lives in buildings and cities.

Did you teach at a German university before you immigrated to the US?
After graduation, the Swedish landscape architect Gunnar Martinsson hired me as an assistant. Martinsson was a member of the faculty at Karlsruhe. I had completed my diploma at his department.

Did you practice architecture in Germany? If yes, how long, and where?
In addition to working with Martinsson on a new university campus in Kaiserslautern. I worked in a conventional architecture firm in Karlsruhe for about one year.

Today, do you consider yourself a German or an American architect? Is national identity relevant?
National identities are not important for me.

You are aware of the extensive discussion on issues of design and national identity. Would you say that there is something very specific about being German-born?
Undeniably there is, but there is a difference between being born into a culture and being educated within various cultures. I still draw extensively from my education in Karlsruhe which was clearly Bauhaus inspired. That meant I learned how to create three-dimensional space and how to use materials. When I started to study with Gunnar Martinsson, who came from a related modernist tradition that was influenced by C.Th. Sørensen, Gunnar Asplund and probably Alvar Aalto, I learned how to apply myself to a larger context, both in physical design, but also to designing the world around us – the always changing social and natural environment.

Based on your familiarity with North American and German culture, how do you relate to U.S. culture?
At the time of this writing in the summer of 2020, I do not relate very well to the culture we live in. But that observation I have in common with many of my friends and professional colleagues here in California. I have tried to stay close to my roots in Europe. I have greatly

enjoyed serving as a guest professor for extended periods of time at the Art Academy in Copenhagen, the Polytechnic in Milan, the school at Versailles and the Technical University at Delft. In addition, I held positions in Japan and China that included both teaching as well as professional work. I am grateful to the University of California's educational system for giving me the freedom to pursue these interests. The result has been a continued education that I hope my students have benefitted from.

What is your understanding of architectural education in North America over the last 50 years?
When I arrived here in California in the mid-seventies, students were still rebellious. A purely form-based education was rejected, so was the laissez-faire economy that did not support greater equity in society, nor was there a meaningful response to the degradation of the environment. Students were hungry for an educational foundation with a more robust base in the sciences. At Berkeley, more so than at Los Angeles, schools of architecture and planning had to respond. This response brought new faculty to prominence, faculty who had training in natural and social sciences. The form-based education suffered, some would say, but students did not care. More important matters deserved greater attention. By the late 1980s, a reaction set in at Berkeley. Despite manifestos to keep the focus on the broader context of our work in society, students correctly insisted on learning skills that made them employable in the increasingly larger and more corporate architectural practices. The faculty had to adapt by teaching design skills, but also keeping a focus on professional ethics. I think Berkeley did reasonably well in this approach by establishing new joint programs whose aim was to integrate knowledge in design with policy. The results were dual degree programs between architecture and planning, architecture and landscape architecture and landscape architecture and planning. The College of Environmental Design (CED) was also uniquely qualified in establishing a post-professional degree program in urban design. The new program is staffed by faculty from all three departments. It was the first in the United States and is currently in its 23rd year.

What do you think are the particular qualities and contribution that German architects bring to the education of architects in the US?
Prior to writing the answers to this interview, I contacted six people, either former students or faculty, who came to Berkeley after receiving their education in Germany. Three returned to teach or practice in Germany or Europe (see comments in the *Foreword*). The six respondents agree upon their strong foundation in design skills; consensus however suggests a strong reversed influence from the US to Germany.

What does the legacy of Gropius and Mies van der Rohe (who were both refugees and in exile in the US, in leading schools of architecture and in reforming the curriculum) mean to you today?
It means little today. Mies, Gropius and others came when schools of architecture in the US were still steeped in the École des Beaux-Arts education. In the 1930s at Berkeley, students rebelled. The classical eclecticism was meaningless for them. Modern architecture held great promise to address the problems that had led to the world economic crisis. University presidents exercised their authority to make architecture education conform to the policies of the New Deal. The return to simplicity, affordability and good design for people of all incomes inspired young faculty and their students. The result in the 1940s was exemplary work in

farm worker housing and other social housing in California. But the total disregard for history, culture and context that found expression in urban renewal projects of the 1950s and '60s turned the tide against an unrelenting form-based focus. Those who immigrated learned to adapt.

Among the younger emigrates who were an influence, "Willo" von Moltke (1911-1987) comes to mind. He graduated from the Technische Hochschule Berlin-Charlottenburg as an architect, left Germany in 1937, the year his older brother was executed for his involvement with the resistance. The younger Moltke went to Philadelphia, worked with Louis Kahn and Alvar Aalto in New York, and then applied for a teaching position at Black Mountain College in North Carolina. The college attracted, in addition to Josef and Anni Albers, other Bauhaus refugees, but was modelled after the pedagogy of John Dewey. After completion of a Master's degree at Harvard, where Moltke studied with Martin Wagner and Walter Gropius in 1942, he returned to Philadelphia to work with Edmond Bacon at the planning commission. In 1964 he led the MIT/ Harvard Joint Center for Urban Studies to work on Ciudad Guyana in Venezuela. The project was not a success, but a lesson in a promising approach to urban design that involved future residents in the process.

Do you think there are any parallels between the very strong pedagogical education of the Modernists of Mid-Century with any movements and schools of thoughts today?
If today means literally today, like this day in the summer of 2020, when people are inflicted by a pandemic that has infected people's health and economic wellbeing in a manner more damaging to those less privileged, I can only imagine that it will also affect strongly the schools of thought in architecture and urban design. Not in an exclusive focus on the design of form, but today's events have the force to bring about reform, or renewal of an education that focusses on human values, a higher regard for each other, our cities and our natural resources.

How do you think have the early German-influenced pedagogies (Bauhaus, Gropius, Mies) changed or transitioned, and what is their relevance between contemporary German-born educators in the US today?
In my view, the influence of the 1919 to 1933 Bauhaus period on educators in the US is not as profound as it once was. As evidence for the waning influence I like to cite the history of the New Bauhaus at Ulm (HfG) which was characterised by the conflict among faculty over the role of design versus the role of science.

There is much scholarship on the issues of design and national identity, which was extensively debated after the fall of the Wall. Do you think that national attributes and identities, including the aim to preserving German cultural values of "efficiency and simplicity in design", are still relevant in a globally inter-connected society and profession?
Simplicity, yes, but efficiency can easily be hijacked by non-critical forces.

Please briefly describe your particular strategies or philosophy as an architecture educator.
Designing essentially means decision making. Critical thinking should be at the heart of architecture and urban design. Design remains paramount, criticality alone is insufficient in addressing how to create better life experiences. If there is a philosophy with German roots that I adhere to, it is the one of the Frankfurt school which has its foundation in Immanuel

Kant's 1781 writings about the limits of objectivity.

The emergence of the computer has transformed the way we teach, design, represent and produce architecture. How do you incorporate the digital and/or the analogue in your teaching?
Not long ago, the role of computation in design was much discussed. Our students no longer ask such a question. They design with computers. In this context I am more concerned about teaching direct observation and not relying solely on digital recordings that are fleeting and capture only certain easily measured aspects.

Do you collaborate with people outside architecture? If yes, which disciplines are of particular interest to you/your pedagogical concept?
Important for me has been cooperation with colleagues in environmental psychology, and - at a different level- with those who understand natural processes such as water, climate and vegetation.

What advice would you like to give young professors?
To concentrate more on learning than on teaching.

Images 30 and 31: Examples of student work from Professor Bosselmann's teaching: Student presentations at UC Berkeley, Urban Design Studio of Prof. Peter Bosselmann (Photos by Steffen Lehmann, 2012)

Interview 3

Conversation with Ulrike Heine,
Clemson University, Clemson South Carolina

Ulrike Heine is an associate professor and assistant director of the School of Architecture at Clemson University in South Carolina. Since 2007 in the US, her approach to architecture in teaching and research are based on sustainability, in the way of applying simple natural laws in reaction to climatic conditions. She teaches architectural design as a process of integration. She graduated from the Brandenburg Technical University in Cottbus in 1999 and worked with Hascher Jehle Architekten in Berlin. Prior to coming to Clemson University, she spent three years teaching Design, Construction and Energy Responsible Planning at the Technical University Berlin. Professor Heine argues that architecture is a science, not an art form.

Where did you grow up? Please tell us about your education. What year did you move to the US?
I was born and raised in Bonn, Germany. I attended a traditional high school, with special focus on math and languages (English, Latin, French and Spanish). I immigrated to the US in the fall of 2007.

Where did you study/go to college? In hindsight, how was your education?
I attended architecture school at Brandenburg Technical University in Cottbus and studied at ETSAB in Barcelona, Spain, to learn other approaches in design. Overall, my German architectural education was technology oriented and was similar to a double major in civil engineering and architecture.

Was there an architect who particularly inspired you?
Guenther Behnisch, Peter Zumthor and Renzo Piano – all for very different reasons.

What made you come to the US?
Initially, I was ready for a new challenge and influence in my life. I wanted to get to know a different culture and I was intrigued by the concept of new teaching approaches. After visiting for my interview, I was impressed by the resources, the collegiality, and work atmosphere at

Clemson University – incomparable to my German experience in academia.

Did you teach at a German university before you immigrated to the US?
I taught as a lecturer at the Technical University in Berlin in the field of "Construction and Climatic Design" with Professor Rainer Hascher.

Did you practice architecture in Germany? If yes, how long, and where?
I started working for the young, international, and innovative office Clarke und Kuhn Architekten in Berlin. I was trained as a practitioner in their office and quickly gained responsibility in every field. After that, I transitioned to the larger firm Hascher Jehle Architekten in Berlin. Hascher and Jehle at this time were leading architects in climate adaptable design. They were award winning and built landmark architecture all over Germany. This is where I was introduced to the concept of environmentally responsive design in architecture.

Today, do you consider yourself a German or an American architect? Is national identity relevant?
I consider myself a global architect with thorough European training. While national identity was relevant in former times, today in a digital inter-connected society, it is not as relevant anymore.

After arriving in the US, how did you assimilate to your new context and home country?
Professionally I had to readjust – construction in Europe is driven by durability and longevity, whereas the US market is ruled by costs. I switched gears from concrete and masonry assemblies to timber and steel frame, while also considering the climatic requirements in the US, specifically in the South. Arriving in the rural South, compared to downtown Berlin, where I lived before, may sound like a challenge, but the Southern US is known for its unprecedented hospitality and therefore the transition was very easy.

You are aware of the extensive discussion on issues of design and national identity. Would you say that there is something very specific about being German-born?
I would say two characteristics: rationality and efficiency.

Based on your familiarity with North American and German culture, how do you relate to U.S. culture?
I enjoy the cultural diversity, and admire the positivity and ease of living in the American culture.

What is your understanding of architectural education in North America over the last fifty years?
Architectural education has shifted enormously during the last fifty years, not just in North America. While a lot of time used to be invested into skills like hand drawing and calculating structures, today an architect is more of a 'problem solver' with great resources.

What do you think are the particular qualities and contribution that German architects bring to the education of architects in the US?
Efficiency and simplicity.

What does the legacy of Gropius and Mies van der Rohe (who were both refugees and in exile in the US, in leading schools of architecture and in reforming the curriculum) mean to you today?
Gropius and Mies van der Rohe were some of the first global architects; they were the pioneers of modern architecture and introduced simplicity, economy, and aesthetic beauty as design concepts. Today we are faced with different challenges, especially environmentally, than in the early last century. But I would argue that all of their ideas are still the foundation and benchmark of a good design process.

Taking a long-time view of 50 years, has architectural education in the US become more relevant or less relevant to the profession?
If architects do not embrace smart building design and accept that our discipline is a science, influenced by various parameters, they soon will be obsolete in the construction business. Luckily, the discipline of architecture is still highly respected in the US, most definitely more than in Germany and most European countries.

Do you think that the relationship between architectural practice and education is widening or narrowing?
That depends where you are. In Clemson (South Carolina), we have a mission to educate future leaders in architecture with a local and global understanding. We prepare students to address the challenges of the time like health care, resilience and an increasingly digital society, through innovative, interdisciplinary research, practice and scholarship.

Which concepts did you import from Germany that influenced your teaching and research?
I was hired to bring the concept of sustainable design to the US. I was trained in climate sensitive design since sustainability is not separately taught in Germany but expected as a holistic mindset. I dedicated my research to affordable energy-efficient housing design and teach it as an integrated element, rather than an afterthought.

Is there a pedagogical or educational innovation you could introduce to your department or school, e.g. the way you conduct design studios or integrate research in your teaching?
A teaching concept I brought to our school was co-teaching – exposing students for the full semester to multiple professors with different expertise and opinions, similar to the practicing office environment. While this is more work, it is a more inspiring environment for both students and professors, leading to truly sustainable project design.

There is much scholarship on the issues of design and national identity. Do you think that national attributes and identities, including the aim to preserving German cultural values of "efficiency and simplicity in design", are still relevant in a globally inter-connected society and profession?
I don't think it is as relevant and still architecture in the US looks much different than in Europe. Affordable building materials and construction methods and affordable energy sources allow less efficiency, not always benefitting the building design.

Please briefly describe your particular strategies or philosophy as an architecture educator.
As an architect it is imperative to anticipate how the world will develop in the future. On a faster-moving, more densely populated planet, new problems are constantly emerging that need to be addressed. Three critical developments impacting human living space are population explosion, pollution, and depletion of natural resources. This expands planning complexity and makes it no longer possible to discuss architectural concepts without considering sustainability.

Sustainability is not exclusively a matter of massive, unalterable construction, just like ecology is not a matter of technically expensive solutions. Rather, it is about systems that adapt to local and climatic conditions and utilise the specific potential of a location. This is always different, because there is never a single correct solution. These systems are based more on passive, reactive, and self-regulating natural processes than active, technically supported systems. What remains after an intensive planning period is the constructed environment, providing living forms for people who spend their lives there. Architects should pursue the quality of these living spaces in their work. It is the objective to merge the socio-cultural, ecological and economic aspects to the greatest extent possible, integrating form and function, construction and aesthetic, architecture and nature to a complex collective.

How do you balance your time in teaching with research and practice? And how do these various pursuits make their way into your work and influence you as educator?
Currently I apply my research in the design studios I teach, one is participating in the environmentally driven ACSA and AIA COTE Top Ten Competitions, the last couple years brought great success. I am not licensed in the US and not practicing at this time.

The emergence of the computer has transformed the way we teach, design, represent and produce architecture. How do you incorporate the digital and/or the analogue in your teaching?
While the computer is a great tool to support the production and representation of a project – I still believe good design is derived from thorough analysis and a lot of sketching, drawing, and model-making.

Do you collaborate with people outside architecture? If yes, which disciplines are of particular interest to you/your pedagogical concept?
Sustainable design is impossible without communication between multiple disciplines. I collaborate often with other architects; landscape architects; civil, mechanical, and electrical engineers; and material sciences professionals.

Culture can manifest itself in many different forms. How strongly does your German cultural heritage inform your approach to teaching?
Given that I grew up in a country with no or few natural energy resources, my teaching is highly influenced by the need to make the built environment more resourceful and less dependent on energy supply. While this is not the case in the US, I feel it is mandatory to include these strategies in the buildings of our future.

What do you think is the main contribution of German architecture educators in US schools today, to the American educational system?
Cultural diversity and different, innovative thinking.

What advice would you like to give young professors?
Stay curious and flexible and keep learning. Get to know other cultures and let them influence you and your work.

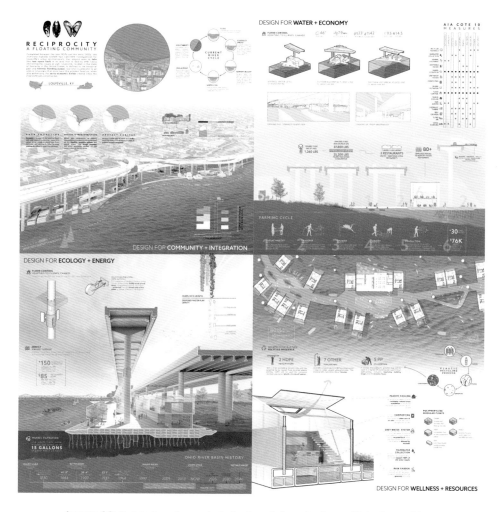

Image 32: Examples of recent student work from Professor Heine's teaching:
Bremerton Project: Students: Cameron Foster and Philipp Riazzi;
Faculty: U. Heine, D. Franco and D. Harding. Louisville RECIPROCITY Project:
Students: Lindsey Sinisi and Marissa Cutry; Faculty: U. Heine, D. Franco and G. Schafer;
Louisville Reclaim Resiliency project: Students: Joseph Scherer and Ryan Bing;
Faculty: U. Heine, D. Franco and G. Schafer

Interview 4

Conversation with Barbara Klinkhammer,
Jefferson University, Philadelphia

Barbara Klinkhammer is Dean of the College of Architecture and the Built Environment and Professor at Thomas Jefferson University (Philadelphia University + Thomas Jefferson University) in Philadelphia. Klinkhammer immigrated in 1999 with architect husband Edgar Stach to the US to start an academic career at the University of Tennessee. Klinkhammer studied at RWTH University in Aachen. She brings a deep understanding of the contemporary professional design world and a timely vision of the future of design education to her leadership role.

Where did you grow up? Please tell us about your education. What year did you move to the US?
I was born in Sankt Tönis near Krefeld and grew up in Germany. After two short visiting lecturer- and professorships, I moved permanently to the US in July 1999.

Where did you study? In hindsight, how was your education?
After completing the Abitur in 1984, I studied architecture at the Rheinisch-Westfälische Technische Hochschule Aachen (RWTH Aachen) following in the footsteps of my father Werner Klinkhammer who graduated from the same institution in 1966. Together with my close friend Eva von der Stein, I enrolled parallel as a part-time student from 1986 to 1989 at the Staatliche Kunstakademie Düsseldorf as a student of Professor Ernst Althoff. I spent my fourth year in architecture at the Ecole d'Architecture de Paris La Villette, UP 6 in the studios of Pierre Boffi and Fernando Montes. Graduating with a Diplom-Ingenieur degree in Architecture in 1992, I was the selected as the University's recipient of the Friedrich Wilhelm Prize for outstanding academic accomplishments.
Compared to the American education, the German architecture education was at the time more focused on an understanding of technology, detailing and knowledge of materials. It exposed students to a broader field of the architecture professions. Unlike accredited programs in the US, my education included required classes, studios and exams in art history, sculpture, landscape architecture, interior design and urban design.

Was there an architect who particularly inspired you?
During my studies and afterwards, I was very inspired by the Ticino architects Mario Botta and Luigi Snozzi, and travelled several times to the region to see and sketch the buildings. Later on Peter Zumthor had a similar effect on me as an architect and so did Le Corbusier, who is the object of my scholarship.

What made you come to the US? Did you teach at a German university before you immigrated to the US?
While I was teaching full-time as a lecturer (Wissenschaftliche Mitarbeiterin at the chair of Interior Architecture, Professor Dr. Egon Schirmbeck) at the Bauhaus-University in Weimar from 1994 to 1999, I taught for six weeks as a visiting lecturer in 1996, and in 1997 as a visiting assistant professor for one semester at the University of Tennessee College of Architecture and Design. I returned to Germany and, following an international search, I was offered a tenure-track position as an assistant professor. I moved with my young family to the US to join the faculty at the University of Tennessee in the summer of 1999.

Did you practice architecture in Germany? If yes, how long, and where?
I worked for several internships during my studies with local architects Harald Willen and Ohrem & Scheidt-Pegels in Aachen. I then worked with Dt8, Professor Coersmeier in Cologne and Werner Klinkhammer in Krefeld, before establishing Klinkhammer & Stach in Weimar and Cologne.

Today, do you consider yourself a German or an American architect? Is national identity relevant?
I still consider myself a German architect. I am a registered architect since 1994 in North Rhine- Westphalia and was registered in Thuringia from 1995 to 2010. My identity as an architect is heavily impacted by my upbringing in historic cities and the value of urban density and regional cultural differences.

After arriving in the US, how did you assimilate to your new context and home country?
As a woman, I found my new home country very easy to adapt to and very welcoming. As somebody who chose academia as the career path, the US offers so many more opportunities. Until today, the percentage of women in professorial positions in architecture are very low and it would have been impossible at this time, or at least very difficult, to achieve in Germany what I have achieved in the US.

You are aware of the extensive discussion on issues of design and national identity. Would you say that there is something very specific about being German-born?
The history of Germany is always part of my own national identity, including the understanding that buildings and cities can be easily transformed for political purposes and are expressions of their own time reflecting political powers and systems. This is particularly true after spending five years in Weimar which served as one of the Gau-centres during Nazi Germany. The Janus-faced history of this city as a Nazi domain and cultural center during the Weimar Republic and Bauhaus time, has always fascinated me, as buildings and the layout of the city are built expressions of each of these times and serve as witnesses of cultural identity.

Based on your familiarity with North American and German culture, how do you relate to US culture?
I became naturalised as citizen of the United States in 2016, which not only was an act of realizing permanency of my life in the US, but also an act of acceptance — while still forming — of American culture as my main identity.

What is your understanding of architectural education in North America over the last 50 years?
Post-war American architecture education was originally heavily grounded in the teaching and pedagogies developed under Walter Gropius, Hannes Meyer and Ludwig Mies van der Rohe at the Staatliches Bauhaus in Weimar, and later in Dessau and Berlin. With schools such as Harvard's GSD (Gropius), IIT's Institute of Design (Moholy-Nagy) and IIT School of Architecture (Mies), Black Mountain College and later Yale's Design Department (Joseph and Anni Albers) falling in the 1930 and 40s under the leadership of the Bauhaus refugees and exiled architects who fled Nazi Germany, German Modernism and its interpretations in the US as a style and German pedagogies were absorbed into the US architecture education and started to spread across the country. A second, smaller wave of German born architects and educators continued to influence US architectural education in the 1970s and 80s, such as Werner Seligmann, dean and professor at Syracuse University School of Architecture, educated at the TU Braunschweig and trained as an educator at the ETH Zurich. Following a period of theorizing architecture in the 1990s, US architectural education today is heavily focused on design and computation / visualization, and much less on technology, materials or construction. In fact, many schools see the architectural experience (internship) as a period where students learn the ropes of the architectural profession and construction.

What do you think are the particular qualities and contribution that German architects bring to the education of architects in the US?
As a German educated architect and teacher, I see the biggest difference in the deep understanding of German architects of the design and building process, which is an integral part of German architectural education. Young graduates in Germany take on more responsibility in architecture offices upon starting their professional careers than in the US.

What does the legacy of Gropius and Mies van der Rohe mean to you today?
As an architect educated during postmodernism, and an educator who taught for five years at the Bauhaus-University Weimar, the legacy of Walter Gropius and Ludwig Mies van der Rohe had a fundamental impact on me. As one of the successors of the Staatliches Bauhaus Weimar, the 1996 renamed Bauhaus-University Weimar continues to occupy the same buildings which were once the academic home of Gropius, Klee, Kandinsky, Arndt, Itten and Schlemmer. The understanding of *Art and Technology - a New Unity*, which once served as the guiding principle for the early Bauhaus envisioned by Gropius, lives on in the idea of the Gesamtkunstwerk. For me as an educator this unity still lives on and has become a principle in my own teachings. Both, Gropius and Mies brought a pedagogical model to the US routed in abstraction, industrialisation and the integration of the different building arts. Their work until today serves as precedents in the education of many students and continues to live on.

Which concepts did you import from Germany that influenced your teaching and research?
German universities are built on a hierarchical system of assistants (lecturers and senior lecturers) and professors, with professors giving the general direction of the pedagogy and assistants delivering the actual teaching in the classrooms. As a young architect, I taught at the Bauhaus-University in Weimar with Professor Egon Schirmbeck who chaired the interior architecture section. His pedagogy was built upon Franz Oswald's famous "Lehrgerüst: über die Erziehung zum Architekten" (*Educational Framework: About the Education of Architects*, 1984, developed at his chair at the ETH Zurich). Educated in this very rigorous and analytical approach to teaching students to become architects, I am still using the same methodology in an adapted form to educate beginning architecture students.

Please briefly describe your particular strategies or philosophy as an architecture educator.
As an educator, I believe that the most significant aspect of architectural education is to foster critical and synthetic thinking, enabling the students to master the different and diverse design parameters to create a meaningful and responsible design. Critical analysis and design thinking are the two pillars of architectural education that enable students to develop the capacity to make conscientious decisions, insightful connections and informed propositions.

How do you balance your time in teaching with research and practice? And how do these various pursuits make their way into your work and influence you as educator?
As dean, my time in the studio or class is limited and my work today focuses primarily on leading the College of Architecture and the Built Environment at Thomas Jefferson University. Together with my husband, we continue to participate in architectural design competitions and we are able to maintain a small practice based in Germany. With regards to my own practice, my cultural identity and upbringing in Germany is evident in the simplicity and efficiency of my design projects. Additionally, my scholarship on Le Corbusier's *Polychromie Architecturale* and my deep understanding of his work and use of color have certainly influenced me as an educator, and has found its way into a variety of different courses including studio teaching and a color theory course which I have taught for many years.

Culture can manifest itself in many different forms. How strongly do you think does your German cultural heritage inform your approach to teaching?
Comparing the two educational systems, I think that the German architecture education is broadly speaking driven by place and culture and a performance-based understanding of materials and technology; whereas the American architectural education is heavily focused on form and space, enabled by a much earlier adoption of computational design. In my own teaching, I have brought a rigorous approach to the design process by understanding the integration of the fundamental elements of architecture such as place and cultural context, materials and technology, form and order as the drivers of great and lasting architecture.

What do you think is the main contribution of German architecture educators in US schools today, to the American educational system?
In a world threatened by climate change, sustainable design and a deep understanding of the impact of buildings and construction on the future of our planet are key in the education of young design professionals. This important topic found its way into the American architectural

education relatively late, while it was already central to the German education in the 1980s and 1990s. Sustainability in Germany was not understood as an add-on, but as an integral part of the design process and has found its way into the building code and professional architectural practice early on. Besides the dominant "less is more" thinking in German architecture, the fundamental understanding of sustainable approaches in the design process is maybe the most important contribution of current German architects to the American education.

What are your plans for the future?
Personally, I have always been fascinated by other cultures. With more time at hand, I would start traveling more to remote places in the world to explore and learn from the different forms of human culture and habitation. Professionally, I believe that architectural education needs to radically change and focus on the new paradigm: climate change. We have entered an age where we cannot ignore anymore the impact of our profession on global emissions. It is time to reconceptualise curricula in the architecture fields, requiring all students to have upon graduation a deep knowledge of the design of net-zero and carbon neutral buildings and spaces. I intend to lead this effort at Thomas Jefferson University and whatever institution may follow in the future.

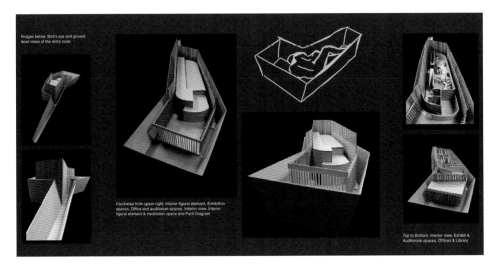

Image 33: Examples of recent student work from Professor Klinkhammer's teaching: Holocaust Documentation Centre at former concentration camp site (Student: J. Robertson)

Interview 5

Conversation with Mark Mueckenheim,
Academy of Art University, San Francisco

Mark Mueckenheim is a licensed architect in Germany and founding principal of MCKNHM Architects. Before establishing his own architecture practice in 2001, he worked and collaborated with different architecture firms in Germany, USA and England. He received his Master of Architecture from Parsons School of Design, New York, and his Graduate Diploma in Architecture at the Bartlett School of Architecture, University College London. Before moving to the US, he taught for six years at the RWTH University in Aachen and as visiting professor at the TU Munich from 2009 to 2012. Since 2013, he is appointed as Graduate Director of the School of Architecture at the Academy of Art University in San Francisco.

Where did you grow up? Please tell us about your education. In what year did you move to the US?
I was born in Aachen, a small but old city close to the Dutch and Belgian border. I am convinced that the famous Aachen Cathedral from the 8th Century had some influence on Ludwig Mies van der Rohe, who was also born there. Later on, I grew up in the Rhineland, in a small town between Aachen, Cologne and Duesseldorf. Since my early childhood, I remember being exposed to diverse urban environments and cultural activities in the surrounding cities. I moved to the US twice, the first time to New York as a student in 1997; and the second time in 2013, to take on the Director's position at the Academy in San Francisco.

Where did you go to college? In hindsight, how was your education?
My education began at the Peter Behrens School of Architecture in Duesseldorf, which I left to continue my studies at Parsons School of Design in New York on a Fulbright Scholarship. I completed my Master of Architecture there and went on to work in Los Angeles for about two years. While in LA, I met Sir Peter Cook, at the time the Chair of the Bartlett School of Architecture at the University College London. The connection was pivotal to me, as I didn't feel that my education was complete. I continued my studies at the Bartlett, aided by a DAAD scholarship, and obtained a Dipl.Arch. I received a comprehensive and diverse education: a strong technical and design foundation in Germany, digital skills and architecture theory

knowledge from my time in New York, and a critical approach and necessary design rigour that I attribute to the Bartlett. I value all three experiences equally, and I feel very fortunate to have been exposed to such diverse influences.

What made you come to the US?
While I was growing up, America was a role model and a strong cultural influence. Art, pop-culture, and music were all coming from the US. After I was finally able to visit America at the beginning of my studies, my desire to live in the US was sparked, and later fulfilled. After my studies in the US, I always considered coming back, an opportunity that presented itself in 2013.

Did you teach at a German university before you immigrated to the US?
I taught at the RWTH in Aachen from 2002 to 2008, and I was a Guest Professor and acting Department Chair for Architectural Design and Methodology at the Technical University in Munich from 2009 to 2012.

Did you practice architecture in Germany? If yes, how long, and where?
I opened my office in 2001 in Duesseldorf, right after my return from London to Germany.

Today, do you consider yourself a German or an American architect? Is national identity relevant?
I do not consider national identity significant to me at all. Being born near the border of three countries and growing up in Europe's border-free Schengen Area, I see myself more as a European now living in the US. However, I would say that there is definitely a Central European cultural imprint that is influencing how I approach architecture, teaching and research.

After arriving in the US, how did you assimilate to your new context and home country?
Professionally, I didn't try to assimilate but rather incorporated my European lens into the already diverse educational fabric of the University. I always strive to support this cultural diversity. Since I began my tenure at the Academy, we hired people from all over the world — from Europe, Asia and South America. The faculty now reflects the diversity of our international student body.

You are aware of the extensive discussion on issues of design and national identity. Would you say that there is something very specific about being German-born?
While there is nothing specific about German-born, there is something particular about being German-raised, at least in my generation and from my point of view. Through that, I have a strong aversion to nationalistic tendencies due to our country's history. If one deals decisively with the topic of globalisation and design, it becomes very apparent that there is a longing for a more distinct or regional cultural identity even in Germany. This desire is also quite evident in the shift towards a neo-historic architectural language taking place in Germany and other European countries in the last decades. I am concerned about this trend to recycle historical or national design attributes in an attempt to create what I consider a false value. This "retro-symbolism" is a dangerous development, especially as more and more societies seem to move into a post-factual era. I discuss this very briefly in my first book, published in 2012, where I speak about the cultural significance that good design needs to inherit. In architecture, the technical benefits of a local vernacular and the specific expression that comes with it

can play a significant role in the design of a building. However, it is in my mind an erroneous belief that a return to national identities is the answer in design, as it is similarly not an answer in politics. As a designer, I would rather see regional or geographical specificity as one of many parameters driving the design process. These distinct influences might then, in turn, lead to a modern or contemporary vernacular with a tangible benefit.

Based on your familiarity with North American and German culture, how do you relate to US culture?
If I am allowed to stereotype a bit in explaining cultural differences, my impression is that Germans have what you can call an "engineering mind" when approaching a design question: they identify "problems" as an equation they need to solve. Americans, on the other hand, tend towards more of an "entrepreneurial mind" in that they see "opportunities" to move things forward. In this unique way, I think that Germans and Americans may complement each other perfectly. *(laughs)*

What is your understanding of architectural education in North America over the last 50 years?
There are a lot of good things to say about the way architects are educated in the US, from the strong studio culture to the way innovations are quickly incorporated in curricula. On the other hand, there seems to be disconnect between education and practice, which has further grown over the last decades. Design studios can sometimes be overwhelmed with many particular aspects of design that they forego the question of design itself. The danger is that design education may become an academic means in its end and not necessarily concerned with teaching the ability to actually design good and meaningful buildings.

What do you think are the particular qualities and contributions that German architects bring to the education of architects in the US?
I think that in the German-speaking countries of Europe, there is a solid tie between academic theoretical ideas and the actual act of building, including craftsmanship and engineering. Buildings and architecture are seen as a cultural reflection of society.

What does the legacy of Gropius and Mies van der Rohe (who were both refugees and in exile in the US, in leading schools of architecture and in reforming the curriculum) mean to you today?
I have the impression that in the US, modernism is often seen as merely a style that took place some-time in the mid-20th century. But when viewed as a reflection and reaction to industrialisation in the 19th century, modernist ideas still resonate in how the profession approaches the practice of building today. While there is a lot of research that has taken place to overcome the modernist paradigm, we still have not moved past it, at least not on a larger scale. In this sense, modernism is not a style but rather an epoch, and Gropius and Mies were two of the most central figures in shaping its beginning.

Which concepts did you import from Germany that influenced your teaching and research?
I don't know if this is particularly German, but I maintain a profoundly practical and down-to-earth no-nonsense approach. The graduate programs that I lead are extremely process-driven, and physical models, as well as two-dimensional abstractions, are a large part of this process.

There is much scholarship on the issues of design and national identity. Do you think that national attributes and identities, including the aim to preserving German cultural values of "efficiency and simplicity in design", are still relevant in a globally interconnected society and profession?
In my mind, it is always about the value one brings to the table within a larger mosaic of design contributors, and it shouldn't matter if the value has something to do with where it originated. I do not think that Germans have a patent on efficiency and simplicity — many other cultures in the world appreciate these things. It is my hope that our global culture will continue to evolve without the advocacy of national ownership.

Please briefly describe your particular strategies or philosophy as an architecture educator.
I am interested in the core values and the inherent power of architecture to evolve how we live together and utilise buildings and cities for the progression of our culture. In this regard, I see architectural design not only as an academic reflection of culture, but also as an active agent in its development. The correlation of architecture with other fields, such as sociological, political, environmental, or economic, affords the possibility of actively influencing our world positively, while simultaneously defining a profound relevance for what we do as architects. The work of my students often reflects this core interest. My design and thesis studios discuss and encourage engagement into practical and technological, as well as philosophical, societal, or political aspects of a design proposal. This engagement is then gauged to positively influence the culture of a specific place or to address relevant contemporary issues.

How do you balance your time in teaching with research and practice? And how do these various pursuits make their way into your work and influence you as educator?
Like many German professors, I maintain an active architectural practice with the goal to build. Research, teaching, and practice all enrich each other. Dedicating enough time to the office besides my family with two small children and my obligations as a department chair is a constant struggle.

Do you collaborate with people outside architecture? If yes, which disciplines are of particular interest to you or your pedagogical concept?
In the curricula I oversee, we instituted Technical Advisors in all studio courses from the first semester on. These advisors are comprised of structural engineers, building technology and sustainability experts, landscape architects, and others who come into the studio when needed. Through this, we can ensure a thorough understanding and resolution for all studios and projects, right from the start. This collaborative approach is very critical to me; my practice also had a collaborative approach from the beginning.

What do you think is the main contribution of German architecture educators in US schools today, to the American educational system?
Interestingly, almost every architecture school in the US that I visit seems to have a German educator somewhere. The relationship between the academic and more tangible aspects of architecture, which sees design and the act of building equally connected with intellectual, poetic, and philosophical considerations, seems to be a common trait I frequently observe, their work usually resonates with me on this level.

What are your plans for the future? What advice would you like to give young professors?
I have a few book ideas I might want to dedicate more time to. I am also building my own house, which is the scariest and hardest thing to do. I am not sure if I am in the position to dispense advice, but if I am pressed, I would say to young educators not to follow trends and things other people find interesting, but instead to figure out what you are uniquely interested in. Be authentic in anything you do. Also, embrace your role as a mentor and forget your ego. Many students I taught in the past twenty years have entered very successful careers and surpassed what I was able to do. They are a group of peers and in many cases also friends, who are now part of a vibrant and diverse network, and I am happy to be still in touch with many of them.

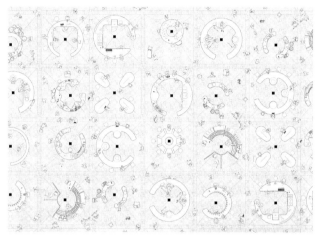

Images 34 and 35: Examples of recent student work from Professor Mueckenheim's teaching: a speculative proposal for an underground market and open public plaza that establishes a new active street culture for the San Francisco civic centre area. Project: Political Bazaar - Architecture as a Political Agent – Urban Market. Student: Nojan Adami

Interview 6

Conversation with Antje Steinmuller,
California College of the Arts, San Francisco

Antje Steinmuller is an architectural designer and educator whose research explores the agency of design (and designers) at the intersection of citizen-led and city-regulated processes. Her work investigates tools for citizen engagement in the formation of urban space, new forms of collective living, and the agency of architecture vis-a-vis the current housing crisis. Antje is an Associate Professor at California College of the Arts where she chairs the Bachelor of Architecture program and co-directs the Urban Works Agency research lab. She is also a co-founder of ideal X, a design consultancy focused on the potentials of public spaces in transition. She holds a Master of Architecture from University of California, Berkeley (2002), where she was a John K. Branner Fellow, an undergraduate degree in Architecture from the Technische Universitaet of Berlin (1998), and a professional degree in Interior Architecture from Hochschule fuer Technik Stuttgart.

Where did you grow up? Please tell us about your education. What year did you move to the US?
I grew up in Stuttgart where I attended Porsche Gymnasium (high-school). I moved to the US in 1998, right after completing my studies at the TU Berlin.

Where did you study/go to college? In hindsight, how was your education?
I graduated from Hochschule fuer Technik Stuttgart with a degree in Interior Architecture, taught by faculty who were either Bauhaus scholars, or had studied with graduates of the Bauhaus. An Erasmus Fellowship brought me to Paris, where I spent a semester studying exhibition design at Ecole Nationale Supérieure du Création Industrielle. An architecture internship in the U.S. led me towards a second degree in Architecture at Technische Universitaet of Berlin. The direct engagement of architectural education –shaped by faculty from the U.S., London, and the Netherlands– with the city in the aftermath of the opening of the Berlin Wall was formative to my career, exposing me to questions of citizen agency and the role of architects in the transformation of urban space. I also completed a Master of Architecture degree at University of California, Berkeley where I was offered an opportunity to contribute

to the International Laboratory of Architecture and Urbanism (ILAUD) in Venice, Italy, and also benefitted from a year of global research travel through the John K. Branner Fellowship. The strong peer-to-peer learning environment at UC Berkeley, the graduate student instructor position I was offered there, as well as the overall exposure to diverse teaching cultures were important stepping stones in my trajectory to become an educator.

Was there an architect who particularly inspired you?
Of the German architects I was exposed to during my education, Guenther Behnisch's ability to engage in cities through architecture was the most formative.

What made you come to the US?
While German architecture pedagogy to this day offers greater synthesis between architecture and urbanism than U.S. education, the degree offerings are characterised by the schism between the technically focused and the political-artistic –as manifested by the Technical University versus Kunsthochschule (Arts Academy) models. I was looking for a discourse about the formal spatial qualities and social performance of architecture and saw this take place more at US schools.

Did you practice architecture in Germany? If yes, how long, and where?
I practiced part-time in Berlin for three years, working on housing and the Berlin Parliamentary Offices.

Today, do you consider yourself a German or an American architect? Is national identity relevant?
I am a German citizen, but the vast majority of my practice has taken place in the US. I consider it an integral part of my identity to have been shaped by more than one education systems and culture.

After arriving in the US, how did you assimilate to your new context and home country?
The ethnically and culturally diverse context of the San Francisco Bay Area appealed to me for the lack of need to assimilate and conform – a pressure I had strongly felt growing up. Assimilation mostly took the form of improving my command of the English language.

You are aware of the extensive discussion on issues of design and national identity. Would you say that there is something very specific about being German-born?
Charles Correa described identity as always evolving, based on cultural, social, economic, or political change. Wary of stereotypes, I consider national attributes and identities as continuously in flux. The German identity of Bauhaus educators – shaped by a world war and industrialization – is not the German identity of today. The awareness of German history and politics that permeated the education of my generation has perhaps shaped a sense of responsibility towards society that may manifest itself in the stereotypical emphasis on the functional and practical.

Based on your familiarity with North American and German culture, how do you relate to U.S. culture?
The diversity of urban culture in the US has always appealed to me, promoting individual

freedom of expression and the space to pursue one's goals.

What do you think are the particular qualities and contribution that German architects bring to the education of architects in the US?
Architecture schools in Germany approach architecture and urbanism as integrated and co-dependent. The experience of European cities produces an understanding that giving form to buildings is inextricably linked to the performance of cities, and the perception (and actions) of their citizens.

Do you think there are any parallels between the very strong pedagogical education of the Modernists of Mid-Century with any movements and schools of thoughts today?
The original pedagogies of the Bauhaus combined both social and aesthetic concerns in its exploration of new construction methods. This past decade has been characterised by pedagogies that treat new technologies as foundational to design considerations. The social agency of architecture remains also present in architecture education, but as a separate school of thought.

How do you think have the early German-influenced pedagogies (Bauhaus, Gropius, Mies) changed or transitioned, and what is their relevance between contemporary German-born educators in the US today?
Bauhaus pedagogy shifted over time from exploring the transformational potentials of mass production to the styling of consumer goods. Correspondingly, perception of such pedagogies shifted with changing contexts from symbolising democracy and representing radical progress to signifying conformity. In today's context, Hannes Meyer's Bauhaus leadership in its awareness of social and economic conditions as a catalyst for design resonates more than the legacy of Gropius and Mies.

Which concepts did you import from Germany that influenced your teaching and research?
In Berlin, I saw architects exerting agency through instigating public events, catalysing discussion in and on public space and designing artefacts and interventions that produced spontaneous spatial change and community with long-term and far-reaching effects. These experiences shaped what I think of as an architectural skill-set today, and how it can be applied in the world.

There is much scholarship on the issues of design and national identity. Do you think that national attributes and identities, including the aim to preserving German cultural values of "efficiency and simplicity in design", are still relevant in a globally inter-connected society and profession?
Architects work increasingly globally today and were exposed to other cultures early on through travel and education, bridging more than one culture. In this context, it becomes more pressing to consider how architecture retains locally specific identity through considerations of culturally rooted use patterns, local climate response, and materials and labour considerations. That said, Oskar Schlemmer's statement (1922) that "in the face of economic plight, it is our task to become pioneers of simplicity" feels just as relevant today amidst wide-spread inequality.

Please briefly describe your particular strategies or philosophy as an architecture educator.
Foundational to my teaching is the desire to empower students to find their place within the discipline of architecture, and to challenge conventional notions of how architectural expertise plays out in the world. I am committed to introducing students to their agency as architects and critical thinkers vis-a-vis contemporary urban conditions that, on the surface, appear to be driven by factors outside of architecture. My approach stresses the development of clear positions on a studio thesis and considers each design project as a catalyst for collective discussion within the studio and beyond. I emphasise the link between critical thinking, ideas, and representation as a key learning outcome as students frame conversations with the audience of their work at CCA, and in their professional careers.

The emergence of the computer has transformed the way we teach, design, represent and produce architecture. How do you incorporate the digital and/or the analogue in your teaching?
Linking design to the means of production, be they analogue or digital, is as much an economic (and ecological) responsibility today as it was at the time of the Bauhaus. Each new tool inevitably shapes new ways of seeing, representing, and constructing the world. Yet, I don't believe that tools should become the subject of architectural production and use a synthetic approach that is guided by the larger questions of the studio.

Do you collaborate with people outside architecture? If yes, which disciplines are of particular interest to you/your pedagogical concept?
Architecture touches many other fields, making collaboration critical in both practice and education. In my own work, I collaborate with policy makers, activists, planners, artists, and citizens.

Culture can manifest itself in many different forms. How strongly does your German cultural heritage inform your approach to teaching?
My German education was characterised by an outdated top-down model that I strongly reject. Yet, I do believe in the value of tight pedagogical frameworks that narrow students' decision-making scope in favour of enabling greater depth of exploration and focus on the most critical aspects of the studio.

Is the relationship between architectural practice and education widening or narrowing?
Confronted with a world in crisis, the architects of the future will need to work increasingly across disciplinary boundaries in dialog with a broader range of stakeholders and experts. If we understand architectural education as training the thinkers of tomorrow, we have to acknowledge that this widens the scope of what students need to be exposed to while in school, taking attention away from the practical concerns of assembling a building.

Taking a long-time view of 50 years, has architectural education in the US become more relevant or less relevant to the profession?
It is clear that architectural education has expanded beyond the technical and formal focus of Gropius's pedagogy at Harvard. The increased awareness and mounting urgency of global crises have changed what architects are confronting in their professional lives. Architectural education is tasked with becoming more relevant to the world, even if that means becoming less relevant to conventional notions of architecture as a profession.

What are your plans for the future?

The breadth of perspectives I was exposed to in my education across cultures has been formative to my own development as a thinker, designer and urbanist. As chair of a Bachelor program, I work to expose each student to work from range of cultures.

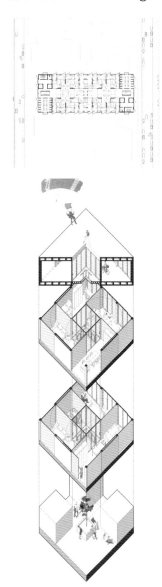

Images 36 and 37: Examples of recent student work from Professor Steinmuller's teaching: The images illustrate pedagogy from Steinmuller's studio on the agency of architecture in the current housing crisis, exploring typologies for alternative living at a time when the nuclear family is no longer the norm. Student work by Duy Nguyen.

References

Adams, George (1968). "Memories of a Bauhaus student", Architectural Review Sep. 1968, London.

Anderson, R.D. (2004). "European Universities from the Enlightenment to 1914", Oxford University Press, New York.

Alofsin, Anthony (1993). "Frank Lloyd Wright—The Lost Years, 1910-1922: A Study of Influence", University of Chicago Press, Chicago.

Appleyard, Donald (1976). "Planning a Pluralistic City, Conflicting Realities in Ciudad Guayana", MIT Press, Cambridge, MA.

Bannister, Turpin C. (Ed.) (1953). "Pioneering in Architectural Education: Recalling the First Collegiate Graduate in Architecture in the USA: Nathan Clifford Ricker", *Journal of the American Institute of Architects* 20 (July–August 1953): 3–8, pp 76–81; based on the report by Bannister, T.C. and F.R. Bellamyal (1954).

Bannister, T.C. and F.R. Bellamyal (1954). "The Architect at Mid-Century. Report of the Commission for the Survey of Education and Registration of the American Institute of Architects", Vol. One, Reinhold Publishing Corporation, New York.

Barber, Benjamin (12013). "If Mayors Ruled the World. Dysfunctional Nations, Rising Cities", Yale University Press, New Haven and London.

Baur, Joe (2020). "What makes Germans so orderly?" online article BBC.com, June 1, 2020, BBC, London.

Beam, Alex (2020). "Broken Glass: Mies van der Rohe, Edith Farnsworth, and the Fight over a Modernist Masterpiece", Penguin Random House, New York.

Bennhold, Katrin (2019). "Germany Has Been Unified for 30 Years. Its Identity Still Is Not", The New York Times, 8 Nov. 2019, New York; available online: https://www.nytimes.com/2019/11/08/world/europe/germany-identity.htm

Blundell Jones, Peter (1999). "Hugo Häring: The Organic versus Geometric", Ed. Axel Menges, Stuttgart.

Bosworth FH. Jr, and Jones, Roy Childs (1932). "A Study of Architectural Schools for the Association of Collegiate Schools of Architecture", New York.

Boyer, Ernest (1996). *Building Community: A New Future for Architecture Education and Practice*, commonly called "The Boyer Report", a report jointly commissioned by the organizations AIA, AIAS, NCARB, NAAB, and ACSI as an independent study; Washington, D.C.

Buday, Richard (2017). The Confused and Impoverished State of Architectural Research, Common Edge, available online.

Burchard, Charles (1959). "Gropius at Harvard" in *Journal of Architectural Education*, Volume 14 No 2 (1959): 24

Buerklin, Thorsten and Reichardt, Juergen (2019). "Albert Kahn's Industrial Architecture. Form Follows Performance", Birkhäuser Verlag, Berlin.

Caragonne, Alexander (1993). "The Texas Rangers: Notes from the Architectural Underground", MIT Press, Cambridge, MA.

Crinson, Mark & Lubbock, Jules (1994). "Architecture: Art or Profession? Three hundred years of architectural education in Britain", Manchester University Press, Manchester.

Curtis, S.J. (1977, fifth ed.). *A Short History of Educational Ideas*, University Tutorial Press, Slough, UK.

de Graaf, Reinier (2017). "Four Walls and a Roof. The complex nature of a simple profession", Harvard University Press, Cambridge, MA.

de Quincy, Quatremère (1803). De l'architecture égyptienne: considérée dans son origine, ses principes et son goût, et comparée sous les mêmes rapports à l'architecture grecque, Paris..

Dickens, Charles (1844). "The Life and Adventures of Martin Chuzzlewit", originally serialised between 1842 and 1844, London.

Drexler, Arthur (1977). *The Architecture of the Ecole des Beaux-Arts*, Secker & Warburg, London / New York.

Durand, Jean-Nicholas-Louis (1802). Précis des leçons d'architecture données à l'École polytechnique, Paris.

Durth, Werner and Wolfgang Penth (2019). "Bauhaus 100: Sites of Modernism", Hatje Cantz, Stuttgart.

Eisenschmidt, Alexander (2018). Chicagoism. A History of Chicago in Ten Architectures, available online: https://www.aeisenschmidt.com/talk-_-chicagoism-a-citys-visionary-architectural-dreams-and-nightmares

Faircloth, Billie (2019). Searching and searching again. Research in practice, article online, *ArchitectureAU*.

Farrelly, Elizabeth (2020). *"The decline of universities, where students are customers and academics itinerant workers", article in Sydney Morning Herald*, May 30, 2020, SMH, Sydney, Australia.

Fiedler, Jeannine and Feierabend, Peter (eds) (2000). "Bauhaus", Konemann Verlag, Berlin.

Flatman, Ben (2016). "Reforming architectural education for the 21st century is taking an awfully long time", BD Online, Dec. 2016. London.

Foster, Hal (1983). *The Anti-Aesthetic: Essays on Postmodern Culture*, Bay Press.

Frayling, Christopher (1993). Research in art and design, London: Royal College of Art.

Froehlich, Martin (1974). *Gottfried Semper als Entwerfer und Entwurfslehrer*, ETH Zurich, Switzerland.

Gimeno-Martinez, Javier (2016). "Design and National Identity", Bloomsbury Academic, London.

Ginoulhiac, Marco (2013). "Design Education through Toy Design. Old and New Paradigms in Architectural Toys Design", proceedings: *Crafting the Future 10th European Academy of Design Conference,* April 17-19, 2013, Gothenburg, Sweden.

Goddard, Jacqueline E. (2019). "Best of Intentions", Ph.D. Thesis, University of Sidney, Australia.

Goldberger, Paul (1984). The Cranbrook Vision, *The New York Times Magazine*, April 8, 1984, p. 48, New York.

Groák, S. (1992). The Idea of Building: Thought and Action in the Design and Production of Buildings, E&FN Spon, London.

Gropius, Walter (1937). Education toward Creative Design", *American Architect and Architecture* (2657), pp 27-30, USA. Quoted after: Walter Gropius: "Scope of Total Architecture", "My Conception of the Bauhaus Idea" pp 19-29 (1943/1962). Collier Books, New York.

Gropius, Walter (1937). 'Architecture at Harvard University' in *The Architectural Record*, May (1937), Washington D.C.: 8-11

Gropius, Walter (1950). "Blueprint for an Architects Education" in *L' Architecture d' Aujourd'hui*, No 28 February (1950), Paris, pp 68-74

Gropius, Walter (1962). "Scope of Total Architecture", Collier Books, New York.

Habermas, Jürgen (1982). "Modern and Post-Modern Architecture," trans. H. Tsoskounglou, *Critique 416 and 9H Publications No 4*: pp. 9-14.

Harrington, Kevin (1986). "Order, Space, and Proportion – Mies's Curriculum at IIT", in: *Mies van der Rohe: Architect as Educator*, Illinois Institute of Technology, University of Chicago Press, Chicago, p.56.

Hatherley, Owen (2019). "Bauhaus just wasn't British", online article at www.dezeen.com

Heathcote, Edwin (2019). "Foreign Exchange: Bauhaus in Britain", in *Architectural Review*, Dec. 2019, London.

Hedges, Chris (2009). *Empire of Illusion: The End of Literacy and the Triumph of Spectacle*, Perseus Books Group.

Heidegger, Martin (1951). "Building, Dwelling, Thinking," in *Poetry, Language, Thought*, trans. A. Hofstadter, Harper and Row, New York, pp. 145-161.

Hejduk, John (1971). *Education of an Architect: A Point of View*, The Cooper Union for the Advancement of Science and Art, New York.

Herdeg, Klaus (1983). "The Decorated Diagram: Harvard Architecture and the Failure of the Bauhaus Legacy", MIT Press, Cambridge, MA.

Hitchcock, Henry Russell and Johnson, Philip (1932). "The International Style", MoMA; WW Norton, 1966; reprinted 1995, New York.

Hochman, Elaine S. (1989). "Architects of Fortune: Mies van der Rohe and the Third Reich", Weidenfeld & Nicolson, London.

Hoge, Jack (2007). "O.M. Ungers' time at Cornell in 1970s was transformative -- both for CU and for the architect, panel asserts", Cornell University web site, Ithaca.

Huyssen, Andreas (1984). "Mapping the Postmodern" in the *New German Critique* special issue "Modernity and Postmodernity", Duke University Press, pp 5-52.

Jansen, J. et al. (1989). Architektur lehren, Institut gta, ETH, Zürich, Switzerland.

Jencks, Charles (1977). *The Language of Postmodern Architecture*, Rizzoli, New York.

Kamin, Blair (1998). "Shunned here, Helmut Jahn is out to prove he's more than flashy", Chicago Tribune, Chicago, Jan 25, 1998, available online.

Kentgens-Craig, Margret (2018). "Nowhere did the heritage of the Bauhaus find ground as fertile as in America", online article at www.dezeen.com

Kentgens-Craig, Margret (2018). "The Bauhaus in America: the modernist émigrés and their influence on American architecture, interiors and design, 1920-1940", MIT Press, Cambridge, MA

Kentgens-Craig, Margret (2001). "The Bauhaus and America: first contacts, 1919-1936", MIT Press, Cambridge, MA

Kimball, Roger (1989). "Is modernism the enemy? The case of Mies van der Rohe" in *The New Criterion*, Vl. 7, No 9, p. 67-70.

Kostof, Spiro (Ed.) (1977/2000). "The Architect: Chapters in the History of the Profession", Oxford University Press, Oxford.

Kroes, Peter (2002). "Design methodology and the nature of technical artefacts", *Design Studies*, 23(3), pp. 287-302.

Kruty, Paul (1997). "A New Look at the Beginnings of the Illinois Architects Licensing Law." *Illinois Historical Journal* 90 (autumn 1997): pp 154–72.

Kruty, Paul (2004). "No Boundaries", University of Illinois Press, Chicago. Online: http://www.arch.uiuc.edu/about/history/ricker/

Laing, Alan K. (1973). "Nathan Clifford Ricker, 1843–1924: Pioneer in American Architectural Education", Urbana Champaign, Illinois: Building Research Council, 1973.

Lalami, Laila (2017). "What does it take to 'assimilate' in America?", The New York Times Magazine (Aug. 1, 2017), available online.

Lambert, Phyllis (Ed.) (2001). "Mies in America", Exhibition catalogue CCA, Toronto, Canada.

Layton, Elizabeth (1962). "The Practical Training of Architects", RIBA, London.

Lehmann, Steffen (2015). "Low Carbon Cities. Transforming Urban Systems", Routledge, London and New York.

Lerner, Fern (2005). "Foundations for Design Education: Continuing the Bauhaus Vorkurs Vision", *Studies in Art Education*, 2005, 46(3), pp 211-226.

Lewis, Michael J. (2012). "The Battle between Polytechnic and Beaux-Arts in the American University", in *Architecture School: Three Centuries of Educating Architects in North America*, edited by Joan Ockman, MIT Press, Cambridge, MA.

Loos, Adolf (1910). "Ornament und Verbrechen", essay from lecture published in 1930, Innsbruck/reprint Vienna.

Lyotard, Francois (1984). *The Postmodern Condition. A Report on Knowledge*, University of Minnesota Press.

MacCarthy, Fiona (2019). "The Life of Walter Gropius: Visionary Founder of the Bauhaus", Faber & Faber, London. Republished: MacCarthy, Fiona (2019). "Gropius: The Man who Built the Bauhaus", Harvard University Press, Cambridge, MA.

MacCormac, R.C. (1974). "Froebel's Kindergarten Gifts and the Early Work of Frank Lloyd Wright", Environment and Planning Vol. 1,1 (June 1974), pp 29-50, Sage, UK.

McCormack, Kirk (2015). "There is another way: 21st century architectural pupilage already exists", *RIBA Journal*, Oct 2015, London.

Mertins, Detlef (2014). "Mies. Larger than Life", Phaidon Press, London and Munich.

Middleton, Robin (1982). *The Beaux-Arts and Nineteenth-Century French Architecture*, Thames and Hudson, London.

Mitscherlih, Alexander (1965). *Die Unwirtlichkeit unserer Staedte. Thesen zur Stadt der Zukunft* ("The Inhospitality of Our Cities. Theses on the City of the Future"), Suhrkamp, Frankfurt a.M.

Mulke, Wolfgang (2018). "Bauhaus at Universities. A Global Legacy", article online, Goethe-Institut; available online: https://www.goethe.de/ins/jp/en/kul/sup/boe/21633067.html

Neumann, Matthias (2012). "Made in USA: -German Architects in New York" exhibition March 1-23, 2012, German House, Consulate General of the Federal Republic of Germany, available online: http://normaldesign.com/consulate/made_in_USA.html

Ockert, Darren (2020). "What Coronavirus can teach Architecture Schools about Virtual Learning", *ArchDaily* online (May 9, 2020).

Ockman, Joan, and Williamson, Rebecca (eds) (2012). "Architecture School: Three Centuries of Educating Architects in North America", MIT Press, Washington D.C.

Oswald, Franz (1984). "Lehrgerüst: über die Erziehung zum Architekten" (*Educational framework: about the education of architects*), Institut für Geschichte und Theorie der Architektur, gta, Verlag ETH Zürich, Switzerland.

Otero-Pailos, Jorge (2010). Architecture's Historical Turn: Phenomenology and the Rise of the Postmodern, University of Minnesota Press.

Pearlman, Jill (2007). "Inventing American Modernism: Joseph Hudnut, Walter Gropius, and the Bauhaus Legacy at Harvard", University of Virginia Press, Charlottesville.

Posener, Julius (1972). "From Schinkel to the Bauhaus", Lund Humphries, London.

Powers, Alan (2019). *Bauhaus goes West: Modern Art and Design in Britain and America*, Thames & Hudson, London.

Raisbeck, Peter (2019). Arrested Development, article online, *ArchitectureAU*, Melbourne, Australia.

RIBA (1962). Report: "The Architect and His Office: A Survey of Organisation, Staffing, Quality of Service and Productivity Presented to the Council of the Royal Institute", RIBA, London.

Rossi, Aldo (1966). The Architecture of the City. Typological Questions, Oppositions Books and MIT Press (English Edition: Ed. Peter Eisenman), New York.

Rowe, Colin (1996). "Comments of Harwell Hamilton Harris to the Faculty" (written by Rowe with Bernard Hoesli) in: *As I Was Saying: Recollections and Miscellaneous Essays*, (Cambridge, Ma: The MIT Press, three volumes edited by Alexander Caragonne, 1996, pp 25-40.

Rubin, Jeanne S. (1989). "The Froebel-Wright Kindergarten Connection: a new Perspective", *Journal of the Society of Architectural Historians* Vol. 48, No. 1 (March 1989), pp 24-37, University of California Press, USA.

Schulze, Franz and Windhorst, Edward (1985). *Mies van der Rohe: A Critical Biography*, University of Chicago Press, Chicago and London; especially Chapter 7, "Architect and Educator: 1938-49", pp 189-217.

Soletta, Federica (2010). Radical Pedagogies - *The Texas Rangers*; online, The University of Texas at Austin, USA.

Stevens, Garry (2014). History of Architectural Education in the West, online, Sydney, Australia.

Swenson, Alfred and Chang, Pao-Chi (1980). "Architectural Education at IIT 1938-1978"; Chicago: Illinois Institute of Technology, p. 19-28.

Taylor, W. and Levine, M. (2010). "Philosophy of Architecture", Australia, online article: https://www.iep.utm.edu/architec/

Till, Jeremy (2005). "Three myths of architectural research", in: *Architectural research futures*, Edinburgh: RIBA.

Tschanz, Martin (2015). Die Bauschule am Eigenössischen *Polytechnikum in Zürich: Architekturlehre zur Zeit von Gottfried Semper* (1855-1871), Zurich, gta, ETH Zurich, Switzerland.

Ungers, O.M., Koolhaas, Rem, et al (1977). The City in the City. Berlin: A Green Archipelago, Cornell University, Ithaca, New York; Lotus International No. 19, June 1978 (republished as *Die Stadt in der Stadt—Berlin das grüne Stadtarchipel*, by Lars Mueller, 2014).

Varnelis, Kazys (1996). The Language of Space: The Unwritten Politics of the Theory and Criticism of Architecture, Proceedings, 84th ACSA Annual Meeting, ACSA, Washington, D.C. pp 258-262.

Von Osten, Marion and Watson, Grant (eds) (2019). "Bauhaus Imaginista: A School in the World", exhibition catalogue, Thames & Hudson, London.

Weatherhead, Artur Clason (1941). Doctoral thesis: "The History of Collegiate Education in Architecture in the United States", Ph.D. Thesis, Columbia University/Avery, New York.

Wetzel, Catherine (2008). "An Integrated and Collaborative Approach", Proceedings, the 24th National Conference on the Beginning Design Student was held in Atlanta, Georgia, USA, March 13-16, 2008; available online.
Wick, Rainer (1982). "Bauhaus-Pädagogik". Du Mont Verlag, Köln (4th revised edition, Köln 1994).

Wolfe, Tom (1981). "From Bauhaus to our House", Picador/Farrar, Strauss and Giroux, New York

Woods, Mary N. (1999). *From Craft to Profession: The Practice of Architecture in Nineteenth-Century America*, University of California Press, Los Angeles.

Zucker, Paul (1942). "Architectural Education in Nineteenth Century Germany", *Journal of the American Society of Architectural Historians*, Vol. 2, No. 3 (April 1942), pp 6-13.

Notes

[1] The number of German-Americans has remained constant. From 1850 to 1970, German was the most widely used language in the United States after English. In the 1990 US census, 58 million Americans claimed sole German or partial German descent, demonstrating the persistence of the German heritage in the United States. German architects settled in various locations, depending on when they arrived and where the best locations for economic opportunity were situated. The primary port of arrival for early immigrants was Philadelphia and many Germans chose to settle in Pennsylvania. With regard to specific states, Americans reporting German ancestry are the most numerous in California, followed by Pennsylvania, Ohio, Illinois and Texas. In terms of absolute numbers, the Germans have always been at their largest in New York City. (...) At the beginning of the 20th century, German schools in the US drifted into oblivion when World War I broke out: the German element was so discredited in the United States that within six months of Congress declaring war in April 1917, legal action was brought not only to dampen considerably German cultural activities but also to eliminate the German language from American schools (source: https://www.everyculture.com/multi/Du-Ha/German-Americans.html).

[2] The first school in the United Kingdom to offer a structured program of architectural instruction was the Architectural Association (AA) School of Architecture, founded in 1847, and as more schools were founded the system of articled pupillage declined. From the 1920s on, the RIBA established visiting boards to monitor the quality of education at the schools.

[3] Gottfried Semper had travelled across Europe as a student and teacher and therefore knew well the various types of pedagogies of the mid-19th century. His exile had forced him to accept the position of director of the architecture school at the Zurich Polytechnicum in 1855; however, he had always regretted not having the freedom to design the curriculum according to his own views. He thought that studies should last longer and that students should be encouraged to carry out actual architectural projects; instead, the Zurich programme comprised a multiplicity of courses and exercises.

[4] The idea of "learning through doing," familiar to us since our first encounter with it in kindergarten, is a product of discourse on education that goes back to Jean-Jacques Rousseau, who proposed to teach children by exposing them to appropriate stimuli that would generate lasting life experiences. Swiss educator and reformer Johann Pestalozzi (1746-1827) took up Rousseau's ideas of pedagogy and began experimenting with ways of teaching students how to perceive through visual experiences. Rather than forcing students into disciplinary exercises, Pestalozzi devised coherent nurturing activities in the form of observations of objects for children to engage in. In order to learn to draw, Pestalozzi believed that the child needed to understand what he called "the simple elements of the laws of form," an alphabet of geometric forms, such as lines, shapes, and angles in order to learn to observe and represent abstractions. Pestalozzi's work was extended and popularised in the 19th century by Friedrich Froebel (1782-1852), the German educator who developed a series of didactic exercises in which children would learn by playing. The most widely known of these were his *Gifts and Occupations*, and the *Froebel Blocks*, intended to teach a visual language of geometric solids to the child. Froebel had a pervasive influence in late 19th and early 20th century education and many artists and architects, among them Frank Lloyd Wright, Le Corbusier and Kandinsky were students of his system. In the United States, the Froebelian kindergarten movement met with some success after being introduced as simultaneously a place for upper-class children to learn the principles of art and as a proper foundation for an industrial education.

[5] In 1950, the French journal *L' Architecture d' Aujourd'hui* published the interview in English and French as part of an exploration of Gropius's main ideas and methods and the consequences for architectural education at Harvard and for American architecture at large. The international influence of the "Blueprint for an Architect's Training" was now assured. Goddard (2019) notes that "the spread of Gropius's approach was also encouraged by the CIAM Education Commission first developed by Sigfried Giedion, Jane Drew and Jaromir Krejcar in 1947. The Commission took Gropius's manifesto as the reference with the title "In search of a better architectural education". The CIAM Education Commission encouraged an international network of like-minded architectural educators with Ernesto Nathan Rogers, Cornelius van Estereen, Serge Chermayeff and Jaqueline Tyrwhitt joining the Commission at CIAM VII in 1949 to attempt a Charter of Education. The reflection on education was consolidated at later CIAM congresses with a debate in 1953 in Aix-en-Provence on "'What to teach?' and 'How to teach?'"

[6] Andrea Palladio's four books of architecture are probably more important to the world than the buildings he ever did. "I quattro libri dell'architettura" are a treatise on architecture written in Italian and first published in four volumes in 1570 (translated into English in 1663, with the title "The Four Books of Architecture"); the books are illustrated with woodcuts after the author's own drawings. The first book discusses building materials and techniques, and the second book covers the designs of private urban townhouses and country villas; while the third book addresses matters of city planning, and the fourth book discusses the design of temples. *The Quattro Libri* are still alive today.

Supporting Institutions

The author would like to express his gratitude to the following institutions. Thanks to:

- Association of Collegiate Schools of Architecture (ACSA)
  Washington, DC
  www.acsa-arch.org

- BAUHAUS-Archive:
  BAUHAUS-Archiv Berlin and Open Archive Walter Gropius
  BAUHAUS-Archiv Dessau, Germany
  www.bauhaus.de

- Canadian Centre for Architecture (CCA)
  Montreal, Quebec
  www.cca.qc.ca

- Museum of Modern Art – MoMA Study Center
  Mies van der Rohe Archive and
  The Lily Auchincloss Study Center for Architecture and Design
  New York City
  www.moma.org

- Mies van der Rohe Society
  Chicago, IL
  www.iit.edu

- Goethe-Institut USA
  Washington, DC
  www.goethe.de

- Harvard Art Museums Archives
  The Bauhaus Archives and Walter Gropius Papers
  Harvard University, Cambridge, MA
  www.harvardartmuseums.org

- Graham Foundation for Advanced Studies in the Fine Arts
  2021 Grants to Individuals Program
  Chicago, IL
  www.grahamfoundation.org

- University of Nevada, Las Vegas
  Urban Futures Lab
  w ww.city-leadership.com

About the Author

Photo by Cida de Aragon

Dr. Steffen Lehmann is a professor of architecture and immediate-past director of the School of Architecture at the University of Nevada Las Vegas. He is founding director of the interdisciplinary Urban Futures Lab and of the Future Cities Leadership Institute. Previously, Steffen has led three architecture schools, as head of school and director, in Las Vegas, Perth and Brisbane (Australia).

He has taught and practiced architecture for thirty years, and defines both as one activity. Over the last twenty years, Steffen has been a tenured chair professor at four research-intensive universities on three continents (in the US, the UK and Australia), leading and transforming schools of architecture, establishing new highly successful research institutes, and managing more than $15 million in research grants. This unique experience has provided him with a deep insight into different cultural contexts and models of architectural education. Since 1991, he has taught urban and architectural design studios and research methods and developed effective design teaching for which he received the Award for Teaching Excellence at the University of Newcastle, and the Top 100 Global Leaders in Education award (2020).

In 2019, he became a member of the American Institute of Architects and joined the AIA Board of Directors of the Las Vegas Chapter. In 2016 he was appointed to the UK's Academy of Urbanism and became a member of the RIBA. In 2003 he joined the Royal Australian Institute of Architects (RAIA). In 1995, he was appointed *Freier Architekt BDA* in Berlin.

An ambassador of sustainable design principles, Steffen has been called a "global academic nomad" who is always interested in new challenges, enjoying working in different cultural contexts to experience a variety of cities and cultures. In 2018, he was invited to join UNLV in Las Vegas to reform its school and curriculum through principles of sustainable design. His thinking is deeply influenced by, first, studying at the Architectural Association in London in the 1980s; second, by British and Japanese modernism and the years he spent working as a young architect with James Stirling in London and Arata Isozaki in Tokyo; and third, the privilege to have been able to make significant urban and architectural contributions to the city of Berlin after the fall of the Wall, during the 1990s.

In recognition of the international significance of his work, Steffen was appointed in 2008 as UNESCO Chair for Sustainable Urban Development in the Asia-Pacific. Since 1991, he regularly travelled to China and witnessed the enormous urban transformation of Asian cities.

He was invited as visiting professor to prominent universities worldwide to lead Global Studios, including at the University of California, Berkeley; TU Munich (as DAAD professor); TU Berlin; NUS Singapore; Tongji University Shanghai; Tianjin University; Iberoamericana Mexico City; Anant University Ahmedabad; University of Portsmouth, and Xi'an Jiaotong University as a distinguished visiting professor. In the last thirty years, he has presented more than 500 times at public events, conferences and symposia in 40 countries, including more than a hundred invited keynote addresses. His main research focus is in the field of 20th century urbanism, urban resilience, sustainable architectural, and high-performance urban design. His work has received funding from the NSF, ESRC, Innovate UK, AHRC, Belmont Forum, British Council, and other prestigious funding bodies.

Born in Stuttgart, Germany, Steffen graduated from the Architectural Association School of Architecture in London in 1991 after securing a two-year DAAD scholarship. In 2003, he completed a Ph.D. in Architecture and Urbanism at the Technical University in Berlin. Before establishing his own practice, *Steffen Lehmann Architekten + Stadtplaner GmbH*, in 1993 in Berlin, he worked with Pritzker Prize–winners James Stirling in London and Arata Isozaki in Tokyo. He became a licensed architect in 1993 in Berlin to pursue a more ethical practice.

He has a deep understanding of architectural practice, having been lead architect of large public and private buildings. Between 1993 and 2003, he built as lead architect more than $1bn in construction budget with his practice in Berlin. This architectural work was generated during an exceptional period of constant change. Most of Steffen's built work is the result of winning design competitions for historically significant places, including large mixed-use complexes at Potsdamer Platz and the Quarter at the Museumsinsel in Berlin. His buildings and project designs have been published extensively, and the firm has been the subject of two monographs. His work was the subject of various group and solo exhibitions throughout the world, including a solo exhibition at the Bauhaus in Dessau, at AEDES Gallery in Berlin, at Plan '99 in Cologne and QUT in Brisbane.

Steffen is best known for his pioneering work in and holistic view of urbanisation and for actively promoting sustainability. He always maintained the activity of writing as an architectural researcher, writer and critic; over the last thirty years, he has published twenty-one books with prestigious publishers, and more than 400 articles and papers on architecture and sustainable urban development. In the 1990s, he coined the concept of *Green Urbanism*; since then, he developed large urban designs exploring the concepts of *Density without High-rise* and *The City of Short Distances*.

He was founding director of three successful research centres at the University of South Australia and the University of Portsmouth, and principal investigator of several large multidisciplinary research grants. Since 2002, Steffen has successfully advised numerous Ph.D. students and postdoctoral research fellows as primary supervisor. He has advised more than a dozen cities on sustainable urban development, including Berlin, Stuttgart, Hamburg, Dresden, Shanghai, Singapore, Sydney, Melbourne, Adelaide, Brisbane, Abu Dhabi, Ho-Chi-Minh City, Oslo, Helsinki, Brighton, Southend-on-Sea, Las Vegas, Reno and Honolulu.

For more information, please visit www.city-leadership.com

Index of Names

List of persons mentioned in the study, in alphabetical order, with the page number when the name is mentioned the first time.